THE MUTILATION OF MARK'S GOSPEL

—⁂—

N. CLAYTON CROY

Abingdon Press
Nashville

THE MUTILATION OF MARK'S GOSPEL

This book is printed on recycled, acid-free, and elemental-chlorine-free paper.

Library of Congress Cataloging-in-Publication Data

Croy, N. Clayton.
    The mutilation of Mark's Gospel / N. Clayton Croy.
       p. cm.
    Includes bibliographical references.
    ISBN 0-687-05293-9 (pbk.: alk. paper)
    1. Bible. N.T. Mark—Criticism, Textual.   I. Title.

BS2585.52.C76   2003
226.3'0486—dc21

2002154916

All scripture quotations unless noted otherwise are taken from the *New Revised Standard Version of the Bible,* copyright © 1989, Division of Christian Education of the National Council of the Churches of Christ in the United States of America. Used by permission. All rights reserved.

Scripture quotations marked KJV are from the King James or Authorized Version of the Bible.

Excerpts from "The Promise and the Failure: Mark 16:7, 8" by Andrew T. Lincoln. Copyright © 1989 Society of Biblical Literature. Used by permission of Society of Biblical Literature.

Excerpts from "Sensing Endings" by Frank Kermode and "Exigencies of Composition and Publication: *Billy Bud, Sailor* and *Pudd'nhead Wilson*" by Hershel Parker and Henry Binder. From *Nineteenth-Century Fiction* 33. Copyright © 1978 by The Regents of the University of California.

Chapter 6 appeared in *Novum Testamentum* 43 as "Where the Gospel Text Begins: A Non-theological Interpretation of Mark 1:1" by N. Clayton Croy. It appears here courtesy of Brill Academic Publishers, copyright © 2001.

Vernon Bartlet, "Mark the 'Curt-fingered' Evangelist," *Journal of Theological Studies,* 1904–1905, volume 6, pages 121-124. Used by permission of Oxford University Press.

J. David Hester, "Dramatic Inconclusion: Irony and Narrative Rhetoric of the Endings of Mark," *Journal for the Study of the New Testament* 57 (1995) 61-86. Used by permission of Sheffield Academic Press.

Excerpts from *Sense and Absence: Structure and Suspension in the Ending of Mark's Gospel* by J. Lee Magness. Copyright © 1986, Scholars Press. Used by permission of Society of Biblical Literature.

Norman R. Peterson, "When Is the End not the End? Literary Reflections on the Ending of Mark's Narrative," *Interpretation* 34 (April 1980) 151-166. Used by permission of *Interpretation.*

Kurt Aland, "Der Schluß des Markusevangeliums." From *L'Évangile selon Marc: Tradition et Rédaction* by M. Sabbe, ed. Copyright © 1988, Leuven University Press. Used by permission.

Thomas E. Boomershine, "Mark 16:8 and the Apostolic Commission," *Journal of Biblical Literature* 100 (1981) 255-239. Used by permission of the author.

03 04 05 06 07 08 09 10 11 12—10 9 8 7 6 5 4 3 2 1

MANUFACTURED IN THE UNITED STATES OF AMERICA

TO

C. F. D. MOULE

ACKNOWLEDGMENTS

I would like to acknowledge the inspiration and encouragement of two special persons. The possibility that Mark's Gospel might lack not only its ending but its beginning as well was introduced to me by Robert W. Lyon in an exegesis class at Asbury Theological Seminary in 1980. Dr. Lyon dutifully credited his colleague, C. F. D. Moule, as the immediate source of this insight. When I began in earnest to research and write this book a few years ago, I initiated a correspondence with Professor Moule, now in his 90s, and he responded swiftly and enthusiastically to a series of letters, as if I had been a lifelong friend. In addition to being a scholar of significant stature, Professor Moule is one of the most gracious and self-effacing persons you will meet. (I had such an opportunity in the early 1980s when he gave a special lecture at Asbury.) Moule's correspondence has been of immense encouragement and pleasure to me. He also read an early draft of the book and offered many suggestions. For providing the initial seed as well as continual nurture, I dedicate this book to him.

Many other persons have provided assistance along the way. Space permits little more than a listing of their names. Several librarians have performed valuable service in locating resources, especially Ida Boers of Pitts Theological Library (Emory University) and Kathy Nodo of Hamma Library (Trinity Lutheran Seminary). Robert Lyon and Robert H. Gundry both read the manuscript and offered helpful criticism. Finally, I thank my wife, Marty, who has provided emotional and material support and has listened patiently to endless arcane musings about codices and quires over the last few years. To all of these persons, I say thank you. May the end result of this book, undeniably imperfect, contain sufficient merit to be worthy of your assistance.

CONTENTS

ABBREVIATIONS

AB	Anchor Bible
ABD	*Anchor Bible Dictionary.* Edited by D. N. Freedman. 6 vols. New York, 1992
ABR	*Australian Biblical Review*
ABRL	Anchor Bible Reference Library
ACNT	Augsburg Commentaries on the New Testament
ACTA	Adult Catechetical Teaching Aids
AGSU	Arbeiten zur Geschichte des Spätjudentums und Urchristentums
AJT	*American Journal of Theology*
AnBib	Analecta biblica
ANRW	*Aufstieg und Niedergang der römischen Welt: Geschichte und Kultur Roms im Spiegel der neueren Forschung.* Edited by H. Temporini and W. Haase. Berlin, 1972–
ASP	*American Studies in Papyrology*
AT	Author's Translation

ATR	*Australian Theological Review*
BA	*Biblical Archaeologist*
BBR	*Bulletin for Biblical Research*
BDAG	Bauer, Walter. *A Greek-English Lexicon of the New Testament and Other Early Christian Literature.* 3d ed. Edited and revised by Frederick William Danker. Chicago: University of Chicago Press, 2000.
BETL	Bibliotheca ephemeridum theologicarum lovaniensium
Bib	*Biblica*
BibInt	*Biblical Interpretation*
BJRL	*Bulletin of the John Rylands University Library of Manchester*
BN	*Biblische Notizen*
BR	*Biblical Research*
BRev	*Bible Review*
BT	*The Bible Translator*
BZ	*Biblische Zeitschrift*
CBQ	*Catholic Biblical Quarterly*
CGTC	Cambridge Greek Testament Commentary
ChrCent	*Christian Century*
CQR	*Church Quarterly Review*
CTM	*Concordia Theological Monthly*
CurTM	*Currents in Theology and Mission*
EKKNT	Evangelisch-katholischer Kommentar zum Neuen Testament
EstBib	*Estudios bíblicos*
ET	English Translation
ETL	*Ephemerides theologicae lovanienses*
EvQ	*Evangelical Quarterly*
EvT	*Evangelische Theologie*
ExpTim	*Expository Times*
FRLANT	Forschungen zur Religion und Literatur des Alten und Neuen Testaments
GBS	Guides to Biblical Scholarship
Greg	*Gregorianum*
HeyJ	*Heythrop Journal*
HNT	Handbuch zum Neuen Testament
HTR	*Harvard Theological Review*

ICC	International Critical Commentary
IDB	*The Interpreter's Dictionary of the Bible*. Edited by G. A. Buttrick. 4 vols. Nashville, 1962
Int	*Interpretation*
JBL	*Journal of Biblical Literature*
JETS	*Journal of the Evangelical Theological Society*
JR	*Journal of Religion*
JRH	*Journal of Religious History*
JSNT	*Journal for the Study of the New Testament*
JSNTSup	Journal for the Study of the New Testament: Supplement Series
JSOT	*Journal for the Study of the Old Testament*
JSOTSup	Journal for the Study of the Old Testament: Supplement Series
JTS	*Journal of Theological Studies*
JTSA	*Journal of Theology for Southern Africa*
KEK	Kritisch-exegetischer Kommentar über das Neue Testament (Meyer-Kommentar)
LB	*Linguistica Biblica*
LCL	Loeb Classical Library
LEC	Library of Early Christianity
LQ	*Lutheran Quarterly*
NAC	New American Commentary
Neot	*Neotestamentica*
NIGTC	New International Greek Testament Commentary
NovT	*Novum Testamentum*
NovTSup	Novum Testamentum Supplements
NRTh	*La nouvelle revue théologique*
NTD	Das Neue Testament Deutsch
NTG	New Testament Guides
NTS	*New Testament Studies*
OCD	*Oxford Classical Dictionary*. Edited by S. Hornblower and A. Spawforth. Oxford, 1996
ÖTK	Ökumenischer Taschenbuch-Kommentar
Poet.	*Poetica* by Aristotle
PTMS	Pittsburgh Theological Monograph Series
QD	Quaestiones disputatae
RB	*Review biblique*
ResQ	*Restoration Quarterly*

RevExp	*Review and Expositor*
RivB	*Rivista biblica italiana*
RTR	*Reformed Theological Review*
RUO	*Revue de l'université d'Ottawa*
SANT	Studien zum Alten und Neuen Testaments
SBLMS	Society of Biblical Literature Monograph Series
SBS	Stuttgarter Bibelstudien
SemeiaSt	Semeia Studies
SJT	*Scottish Journal of Theology*
SNTSMS	Society for New Testament Studies Monograph Series
SP	Sacra pagina
SR	*Studies in Religion*
ST	*Studia theologica*
STRev	*Sewanee Theological Review*
TBl	*Theologische Blätter*
TBT	*The Bible Today*
TD	*Theology Digest*
TDNT	*Theological Dictionary of the New Testament*. Edited by G. Kittel and G. Friedrich. Translated by G. W. Bromiley. 10 vols. Grand Rapids, 1964–1976
THKNT	Theologischer Handkommentar zum Neuen Testament
Thuc.	*De Thucydide* by Dionysius of Halicarnassus
TJ	*Trinity Journal*
TLZ	*Theologische Literaturzeitung*
TQ	*Theologische Quartalschrift*
TRu	*Theologische Rundschau*
TSK	*Theologische Studien und Kritiken*
TU	Texte und Untersuchungen
TynBul	*Tyndale Bulletin*
TZ	*Theologische Zeitschrift*
WBC	Word Biblical Commentary
WUNT	Wissenschaftliche Untersuchungen zum Neuen Testament
ZKG	*Zeitschrift für Kirchengeschichte*
ZNW	*Zeitschrift für die neutestamentliche Wissenschaft und die Kunde der älteren Kirche*
ZPE	*Zeitschrift für Papyrologie und Epigraphik*
ZTK	*Zeitschrift für Theologie und Kirche*

ONE

INTRODUCTION

"The greatest literary problem in the New Testament is: What is the matter with the Gospel of Mark? Something happened to the end of it."

"Far too much, you might think, has been said and written about the abrupt ending of St Mark's Gospel. And yet the matter has not been settled to the general satisfaction of the learned."

"But is there any need to take up the question of the ending of Mark again, after so much has been written on the subject in the last fifty years? That the Gospel is complete cannot be regarded as one of the generally accepted results of biblical criticism."[1]

In high school I had a nearly complete collection of *Conan the Barbarian* comic books. A close friend, my partner in pulp fantasy, was an avid collector of Spiderman. We would frequently meet after school to show off our latest acquisitions, whether from the local drugstore or the occasional treasure from a mail-order house. We soon developed an eye for appraising what most people regarded as attic debris. At one point our enterprising search for back issues of our favorite titles led us to place an ad in a local paper expressing an interest in purchasing old comics. The most intriguing call came from an elderly woman in the foothills of northern California, a short drive from our town. She had several boxes of comic books, left behind by her son, who had long since grown up and left home.

My friend and I made the drive, price lists and catalogues in hand, and were permitted to sort through several boxes of material stowed—where else?—in the woman's attic. There were a few discoveries of modest value, twenty-year-old issues of certain titles worth several times more than their face value. But the crowning discovery made us tremble: a copy, in seemingly good condition, of an early issue of *Detective Comics*. It was the debut, or nearly so, of the character Batman, prior even to the comic book that bore that hero's name as its title. Our catalogues showed its value to be well over $100. (It would be worth several times more than that today.) It was the equivalent of an original Van Gogh to our teenaged minds. But we had not progressed far in negotiating an opening bid to our elderly hostess, when we made a heartbreaking discovery. We had *only the cover* of the comic! Inside was another comic, minus its own cover, from about the same era but of a nondescript title such that its value was nil. We had a curious but worthless artifact. Through normal use or some mishandling, the interior of our presumptive treasure was, in fact, a twentieth-century pulp codex that had lost its outer leaves.

The thesis of this book is that something similar has happened to the Gospel of Mark. I believe that through some mishap, the Second Gospel lost its original beginning and ending not too many years after its composition. In some respects this thesis is unoriginal; indeed, it could be dubbed retro. For over a century New Testament scholars have thought that the beginning and ending of Mark are odd.[2] The ending in particular has often been seen as abrupt in terms of style and unsatisfactory in terms of narration. Mark 16:8 draws the Gospel to a close without narrating resurrection appearance stories and with a conclusion that has struck some readers as cut off in midsentence: "So they went out and fled from the tomb, for terror and amazement had seized them; and they said nothing to anyone, for they were afraid." The beginning of Mark's Gospel has generated far less controversy in scholarly discussions, but it too is terse, "The beginning of the Gospel of Jesus Christ, the Son of God" (AT), and it connects awkwardly with an abrupt quotation of two Old Testament texts. It is not clear whether Mark 1:1 is a superscription, a title, the main clause on which verse 2 depends, or a purely functional manuscript marker inserted by a scribe faced with a document beginning with "As it is written in the prophet Isaiah."

Despite the peculiarities of Mark's beginning and ending, the thesis of a truncated gospel will strike many readers as unusual and some as preposterous. Such reactions are not surprising given the last few decades of Markan scholarship. During that time the view that Mark's Gospel has literary integrity has achieved a strong majority status. Nowadays, scholars who regard Mark as incomplete are in the minority, and their views are sometimes dismissed summarily. As early as 1963 Etienne Trocmé rejected theories of accidental mutilation or an unfinished gospel as "imaginative suppositions in the naïve mode."[3] A few years later Robert Meye insisted that "the history of Marcan and gospel studies has provided us with ample evidence *to compel* the conclusion that Mark 16:8 was indeed the original and intended ending of the Gospel. It is important *to stop asking the wrong questions*, and to integrate into a meaningful whole insights already available" (1969, 33). More recently Ched Myers wrote that "such speculation [about a lost ending] can now be considered obsolete."[4] But are such resolute judgments truly based on compelling evidence, or do other factors account for the current majority view?

Initial resistance to the thesis of Markan mutilation is, in a way, a reasonable reaction. In the late nineteenth century and the first several decades of the twentieth, scholars sometimes ran amok with elaborate fragmentation theories and reconstructions of supposedly truncated or rearranged New Testament writings.[5] Wiser now as a result of those excesses, biblical scholars usually approach theories of textual fragmentation with some skepticism. A minimum threshold of evidence is required for such ideas to receive a hearing.

On the other hand, the strongly skeptical and dismissive reactions sometimes met by the thesis of Markan mutilation betray the short memory of contemporary scholarship. A generation ago the idea that Mark had lost its original ending was nearly as strong a contender as the view that 16:8 was the author's intended conclusion. Two generations ago the thesis of a mutilated Mark (at least in regard to its conclusion) was the *majority* view. And prior to about 1940, the view that the Second Gospel lacked the ending written or planned by its author was *overwhelmingly* popular. So how did we reach the point today that the mutilation theory is so easily dismissed?

Before I address that question, let me offer two clarifications of the book's thesis. First, I am *not* resurrecting the textual question of the authenticity of Mark 16:9-20, the so-called Longer Ending of Mark. The textual question and the literary question are two separate issues, although on occasion they have been confused.[6] The textual question concerns the authenticity or authorship of these verses. Did the evangelist write 16:9-20 as part of the original Gospel, or did a later author compose these verses? It is hardly necessary here to rehearse the arguments against authenticity. The secondary nature of these verses has been established to the satisfaction of virtually all scholars.[7] On the basis of both extrinsic evidence (the oldest, most reliable manuscripts) and intrinsic evidence (vocabulary, style, narrative coherence, and so forth), 16:9-20 is clearly a non-Markan pastiche of early traditions about the resurrection appearances.[8] These verses may be a window into some quarter of early second-century Christianity, but they do not offer any clues to Mark's theology or literary strategy.[9] I am, therefore, in wholehearted agreement with the scholarly consensus that affirms that Mark 16:8 is the last extant verse from the hand of the evangelist. However, one may readily grant this and still be convinced that the evangelist intended to write more or, in fact, did write more, but that this ending was lost. This is a literary question quite independent of the text-critical question.

As a second clarification, and as I hinted above, the two halves of the thesis—the loss of the ending and the loss of the beginning—clearly have different histories. Textual, syntactical, and interpretive problems bedevil both ends of the Second Gospel, but the debate surrounding the conclusion is much better known and has generated far more literature. When I point out that the consensus of scholarly opinion about Mark's integrity has shifted over the last two generations, I am referring to the debate about its ending. The interpretation of "the beginning of the gospel" (1:1, AT) has been overshadowed by this debate, but the problems of Mark's beginning are by no means insignificant. Those scholars who have suspected some disruption or loss at the beginning of Mark have been far fewer than those who regard its ending with suspicion, but both cases have merit, and the cumulative force of the arguments supporting both views deserves a full and fair hearing.

The question of Mark's integrity is not just academic, a matter of interest to no one but a few paleographers and literary historians. It clearly has bearing on the interpretation of the gospel. The ending of a work, in particular, often enables the reader to make sense of the whole.

> Part of what readers want from an ending seems to be the opportunity to look back over what has come before and interpret it, to engage in what Barbara Herrnstein Smith calls "retrospective patterning." Only when the work has come to an end can we be confident that the patterns are as we see them and will not change. Our ability to read a work of literature is then end-dependent in a manner analogous to our ability to judge a human life; we can call no human being happy until death.[10]

This generic observation about literary endings certainly applies to the Second Gospel. As one scholar wrote, "the nature of the unresolved general question of the Marcan ending is of critical importance. *The whole meaning* of Mark is in some measure, perhaps quite intimately, associated with the answer to this question."[11] One need only to read some of the more provocative interpretations that assume Markan integrity to imagine how they go astray, if that assumption is mistaken. One recent commentator has asserted that "the only manifestation of the resurrected Jesus with any significance for Mark is that of his return when 'they will see "the Son of Man coming in clouds" with great power and glory.' " Another avows that "Mark wants nothing about risen apparitions here below and nothing about confessions of faith generated by them." Another interpreter, pondering Mark's "open" ending, muses, "This new way must be traveled in the absence of Jesus. The reader's faith must be that of the centurion and of Joseph, faith in the absence of God with only the text as guide."[12] Such interpretations might be called into question even on the basis of *the extant form* of Mark's Gospel, but they would certainly be overturned if Mark, in fact, had a resurrection appearance as the climax of his story. The assumption of Markan integrity might also lead one to believe that there was never a reunion of the disciples—neither men nor women—no reconciliation with their Lord, and no sure vindication of Jesus. If Mark intended to end at 16:8, his Gospel certainly has a different tone and may make a different point altogether. How the evangelist intended to conclude the story is, therefore, vitally important for both literary and theological reasons. Endings often function as explanations, such that if Mark's ending is missing and we wrongly construe his penultimate scene as that ending, then our interpretation of his narrative will either be thwarted or led astray. Interpreting Mark would then become a bit like attempting a postgame wrap-up of a baseball game in the middle of the eighth inning.

But to return to the question at hand: How did we reach this new consensus, one nearly as unanimous and strong as the previous consensus that was 180 degrees opposed to it? What new evidence has been introduced? Has some astonishing textual discovery, an advance in linguistics, or a flash of interpretive genius overturned a view that was rarely challenged prior to 1940 and was the majority view until about 1970?

In the next chapter I will chronicle the shift, showing how confident claims that something was amiss at the end of Mark dwindled in the latter half of the twentieth century and ultimately gave way to affirmations of the Gospel's integrity. In chapter 3 I will offer some explanations as to why this sea change of scholarly opinion came about.

NOTES

1. Respectively, Edmunds (1917, 161), Farrer (1954, 144), and John Fenton (1994, 1).

2. Sometimes the two are seen as related to each other. See, e.g., Camery-Hoggatt (1992, 176), "The story ends as abruptly as it began"; Gould (1907, 304): "the brevity of this ending [at Mark 16:8] is quite parallel to the beginning of the Gospel"; and Stamm (1944, 309): "But . . . 'for they were afraid' is no more abrupt than Mark's beginning in v 2 of the first chapter with the particle *kathos*, 'even as'." See also Lightfoot (1945, 223-34), Grimme (1946), and Magness (1986, 89).

3. Trocmé (1975, 64). The original French work was published in 1963.

4. Myers (1988, 399). Blount (1998, 179 n. 4) quotes Myers approvingly and not only dismisses the mutilation theory out of hand but also dispenses with the need to argue for Markan integrity: "I am so persuaded by the evidence that has been amassed regarding the ending of Mark's narrative at 16:8 that I no longer feel pressed to offer argumentation on behalf of the point. Indeed, most recent commentaries follow suit."

5. Examples of watershed works that were, nevertheless, characterized by this defect are R. H. Charles's commentary on Revelation (1920) and Rudolf Bultmann's commentary on the Gospel of John (1941).

6. For example, Meye (1969, 34) claims that "the textual evidence strongly supports Mark 16:8 as the original conclusion of the Marcan Gospel." But one should clarify that the textual evidence supports 16:8 *as the earliest recoverable* conclusion. Strictly speaking, this is the aim of textual criticism. If primitive textual damage has occurred, all the text-critical evidence in the world may not be able to restore the original. In that case, whether or not we have the original conclusion of a document becomes a literary question. Similar confusion of the text-critical and literary questions seems to occur in Hendrickx (1994, 3) and, to a lesser extent, Spivey and Smith (1995, 93).

7. There have been, of course, several attempts to prove the authenticity of Mark 16:9-20. The classic statement in favor of authenticity was that of Burgon (1871). Most noteworthy among more recent scholars was Farmer (1974). For a list of the literature defending these verses as authentic, see Kelhoffer (2000, 17-20 nn. 63-69).

8. Treatments of the textual question can be found in most critical commentaries. See also Danove (1993, 120-25), Metzger (1994, 102-6), and especially D. C. Parker (1997, 124-27). For a graphic presentation of the various endings, see Appendix B. An excellent popular discussion of the textual problem can be found in Michael Holmes (2001).

9. On the theology of Mark 16:9-20, its literary relationships to the canonical gospels, and history-of-religions parallels to handling snakes and drinking poison, see the thorough treatment by Kelhoffer (2000).

10. Roberts (1997, 254). See also Juel (1994, 107): "No point in a story is as significant for appreciation and interpretation as its ending."

11. Meye (1969, 33), my emphasis. See also D. C. Parker (1997, 143): "The effect that the various endings have had on the understanding of Mark's Gospel can hardly be overestimated. For it almost goes without saying that a small alteration at the very end may have a momentous effect on the whole shape of a story."

12. Respectively, Cunningham (1995, 156), Crossan (1995, 200), and Tate (1994, 141).

Two

A Sea Change in Scholarly Opinion

"The rival arguments that Mark may have so ended [his gospel] in this way intentionally, and that he cannot possibly have intended to do so, may still be heard clashing in the corridors of scholarship."[1]

Once upon a time there was a lively debate over whether Mark intended to end his Gospel at 16:8. The above quote, published in 1972, reflects that era. But persons steeped only in New Testament scholarship of the last two decades might wonder just what corridors were the site of the swordplay described. The clashing has grown quieter as the contenders on one side have dwindled and those on the other side increasingly regard the skirmish as moot.[2] But the majority view that developed in the late twentieth century and continues to this day stands in contrast both to the lively debate of the 1960s and 1970s and to the opposite consensus that existed prior to that era. This chapter will survey this remarkable shift in scholarly opinion.

1. THE VERDICT OF TEXTUAL CRITICISM AND THE EMERGENCE OF THE FIRST CONSENSUS

In the first few centuries of the church's existence there was some awareness of the textual problem of Mark's ending. The writing known as *Quaestiones ad Marinum*, attributed to Eusebius of Caesarea (ca. 260–340), and a letter of Jerome (ca. 345–420) written to a certain Hedibia contain evidence of early church scholars wrestling with discrepancies in the manuscript tradition of Mark. Both of these writers attest that the Long Ending (16:9-20) was absent from almost all Greek manuscripts known to them. These testimonies are, however, *isolated* voices in the history of the early church. Once the Long Ending became attached to Mark's Gospel in about 120–140 C.E., it seems, so far as we can tell from discussions of it, to have been regarded almost universally as an authentic part of that gospel.[3]

Acceptance of the genuineness of the Long Ending prevailed for centuries. As long as this conviction held sway, there was obviously no reason to discuss the propriety of 16:8 as the ending. The authentic ending of Mark was thought to be 16:20.[4] Thus, it was necessary for textual critics to reach a negative verdict about Mark 16:9-20 before the literary debate about 16:8 could begin.[5] The majority textual tradition, embodied in the so-called *Textus Receptus* or "Received Text," included the Long Ending of Mark. It had attained an almost sacred status, especially as the Greek text that lay behind the immensely popular King James Version. Textual critic Bruce Metzger (1992, 106) remarks, "So superstitious has been the reverence accorded the Textus Receptus that in some cases attempts to criticize or emend it have been regarded as akin to sacrilege. Yet its textual basis is essentially a handful of late and haphazardly collected minuscule manuscripts."

It was a rather long and arduous process by which the pioneers of modern textual criticism (Griesbach, Lachmann, Tischendorf, Tregelles, Westcott, and Hort) accumulated manuscript evidence and formulated arguments so as eventually to overthrow the *Textus Receptus*.[6] Once those pioneers succeeded in persuading most scholars that the Long Ending of Mark was a secondary addition to the gospel, the way was cleared for a new debate: Could the abrupt ending at 16:8, so unsatisfying to most readers at that time, be Mark's intended conclusion?

The early textual critics were nearly unanimous on this issue. A strong majority regarded Mark as truncated, lacking the ending that the author either intended to write or actually wrote. J. J. Griesbach (1745–1812), a towering figure in New Testament textual criticism, mused that "No one . . . can imagine that Mark cut short the thread of his narrative so ineptly" (1775, 197). Later Griesbach elaborated, "[I]t is very unlikely indeed that Mark ended his book at verse 8 with 'for they were afraid'. It is therefore reasonable to conjecture that the real ending of the Gospel (one that undoubtedly mentioned the journey into Galilee) was accidentally lost."[7] Karl Lachmann (1793–1851), a celebrated classical philologist who was the first to break totally with the *Textus Receptus*, rejected the Long Ending as inauthentic and regarded it as credible that Mark "may have been unfinished and improperly expanded at its end" (1830, 841). Henry Alford (1810–1871), Dean of Canterbury and a strident critic of the *Textus Receptus*, wrote in his edition of the Greek New Testament, "The most probable supposition [to explain the incompleteness of Mark] is, that *the last leaf of the original Gospel* was *torn away*."[8] August Klostermann (1837–1915), a professor of the Hebrew Bible whose work frequently involved New Testament texts as well, devoted a short excursus in his book on Mark to the problem of Mark's conclusion. Klostermann was confident that 16:8 was not Mark's intended ending, but he inclined toward the view that the gospel had been left unfinished rather than that it had suffered mutilation.

> [T]here can be no doubt that the gospel originally reached only to 16:8, and that it therefore either remained incomplete or lost its ending early on. For 16:1-8 is unquestionably, as we saw, simple preparation for a narrative already anticipated long beforehand (14:28), and presents itself so plainly as the first member of several preparations for this [narrative] that the claim of *Schenkel* . . . that it is an unproven assumption that the ending to the second gospel is lacking when it concludes with ἐφοβοῦντο γάρ ["for they were afraid"] will itself qualify as an unproven assumption until he has proved that it must end in this way and that every continuation of the story beyond this end would contradict the plan and flow of the

book. . . . We must therefore assume that Mark in some way was hindered from bringing his work to the intended conclusion. (1867, 299-300, 309)

Other lesser known witnesses could be adduced in support of the growing consensus, but pride of place goes to two Cambridge professors, B. F. Westcott (1825–1901) and F. J. A. Hort (1828–1892). In 1881 Westcott and Hort published "the most noteworthy critical edition of the Greek Testament ever produced by British scholarship," an epoch-making event (Metzger 1992, 129). They produced the oldest and most reliable Greek text possible in their day and formulated principles of textual criticism whose general validity is still acknowledged today. In the companion volume to their Greek New Testament, written chiefly by Hort, we find the following remarks.

It is incredible that the evangelist deliberately concluded either a paragraph with ἐφοβοῦντο γάρ, or the Gospel with a petty detail of a secondary event, leaving his narrative hanging in the air . . . either the Gospel may never have been finished, or it may have lost its last leaf before it was multiplied by transcription . . . it becomes incredible not merely that St. Mark should have closed a paragraph with a γάρ, but that his one detailed account . . . should end upon a note of unassuaged terror. . . . There is . . . no difficulty in supposing . . . (1) that the true intended continuation of vv. 1-8 either was very early lost by the detachment of a leaf or was never written down; and (2) that a scribe or editor, unwilling to change the words of the text before him or to add words of his own, was willing to furnish the Gospel with what seemed a worthy conclusion by incorporating with it unchanged a narrative of Christ's appearances after the Resurrection which he found in some secondary record then surviving from a preceding generation. If these suppositions are made, the whole tenour of the evidence becomes clear and harmonious. Every other view is, we believe, untenable.[9]

The work of Westcott and Hort constituted a watershed. Some scholars argued thereafter in favor of the authenticity of the Long Ending, but they did so with diminishing credibility.[10] In addition, the theory of mutilation (or an unfinished gospel) was given a further boost by the Cambridge duo. For the next few decades one would be hard-pressed to name more than half a dozen scholars who thought that Mark intended to end his Gospel at 16:8. For reasons of style, grammar, theology, or literary conventions, the overwhelming majority of biblical scholars judged Mark to be either truncated or unfinished.

This verdict was held not just widely but fervently. In 1909 Benjamin Wisner Bacon declared the Gospel of Mark "a mere torso" (1909, xvii). With an extravagance immoderate even in his day Bacon asserted that "it is as certain as anything in the field of critical conjecture can be, that our evangelist's story once went on to relate the substance of the early narrative of Acts, and may even have wound up, as Acts does, with the planting of the gospel in Rome" (1909, xix). Although few would have made so expansive a conjecture, nearly all of Bacon's contemporaries would have affirmed that something was missing from Mark. Writing nearly two decades later, A. H. McNeile declared that the verdict of mutilation was "one of the most certain results of textual criticism. . . . [16:8] is an impossible ending to a Gospel."[11] About a decade after McNeile, E. F. Scott declared it impossible that the gospel could end with the conjunction *gar* (Gr. "for") and lamented the loss of Mark's ending, judging that ". . . the breaking off of Mark in the very middle of one of the cardinal passages is perhaps the worst disaster that has befallen the New Testament" (1936, 60-61). By the late thirties those scholars who accepted Mark 16:8 as intentional were dismissed by Floyd V. Filson with the words, ". . . it is impossible to believe with a few noteworthy scholars that [Mark] originally ended at 16.8" (1938, 158). Indeed, they were few at that time. R. H. Lightfoot, writing more than fifty years after Westcott and Hort, noted that the Cambridge scholars who had laid to rest the textual question in 1882, also rejected 16:8 as the intended ending, a verdict that had been "almost undisputed in [Great Britain]" to Lightfoot's day (1938, 4).

This view was by no means a British idiosyncrasy; continental scholars were often in agreement. H. A. W. Meyer, perhaps the most prominent New Testament commentator of his day, asserted that "[Mark 16:7 and 8] decisively show that Mark did not intend to conclude his treatise with these words" (1884, 197). Theodor Zahn, the prodigious Lutheran confessionalist, declared the ending of Mark at 16:8 "manifestly incomplete."[12] Similar opinions were held by Adolf Jülicher, Casper Rene Gregory, Friedrich Spitta, Maurice Goguel, and Rudolf Bultmann.[13]

2. Voices in the Wilderness

Although this first consensus about Mark 16:8 was strong, it was not without exception. The earliest contrary voice I have found is that of Samuel Prideaux Tregelles (1813–1875).[14] Tregelles devoted much of his life to the collation of manuscripts and the preparation of a critical text of the Greek New Testament. In his *Account of the Printed Text of the Greek New Testament* Tregelles writes,

> It has been asked, as an argument that [16:9-20] was actually written by St. Mark, whether it is credible that he could have ended his Gospel with . . . ἐφοβοῦντο γάρ. Now, however improbable, such a difficulty must not be taken as sufficient, *per se*, to invalidate testimony to a fact as such. We often do not know what may have caused the abrupt conclusion of many works. The last book of Thucydides has no proper termination at all; and in the Scripture some books conclude with extraordinary abruptness: Ezra and *Jonah* are instances of this. Perhaps we do not know enough of the circumstances of St. Mark when he wrote his Gospel to say whether he did or did not leave it with a complete termination. (1854, 257)

While this quote does not make Tregelles's position perfectly clear, he is at least open to the possibility of 16:8 being the intended ending of the gospel, especially as an alternative to regarding 16:9-20 as authentic. (Note that what he disputes is the harsh abruptness of 16:8 *as an argument* for Markan authorship of 16:9-20.) Later Tregelles even concedes that the Long Ending "might have been written by St. Mark *at a later period*."[15] Although Tregelles's comments are neither unambiguous nor emphatic, in the context of the nineteenth century he stands out as perhaps the first person even to suggest that 16:8 might be Mark's deliberate conclusion.

Less ambiguous openness to Mark 16:8 is found in the works of four German scholars writing in the latter half of the nineteenth and the early years of the twentieth centuries. Daniel Schenkel, professor of theology at the University of Heidelberg, is dismissive of the mutilation theory: "Of an actual appearance of Jesus, [Mark] affords no information. The idea that the last part of this document is missing is a mere conjecture." Later he adds, "[W]e have to recognize the appropriateness with which Mark concluded his gospel without relating the appearances of the Risen One as outward facts" (1869, 315, 329). Bernhard Weiss, a prolific author of both commentaries and critical editions of the New Testament, was similarly disdainful: "That the Gospel had originally a different conclusion . . . or remained incomplete, are entirely groundless assumptions." Elsewhere he writes that the loss of an original ending is "very unlikely," and all attempts to reconstruct such an ending are "pure hypotheses."[16] Julius Wellhausen, the independently minded professor of Semitic languages best known for his source critical work on the Pentateuch, also accepted 16:8 as the gospel's ending. In his commentary on Mark, Wellhausen wrote, "The Gospel of Mark ends with 16:8. Most expositors are not satisfied with this and assume that the author was hindered from completing his writing or that originally still more followed which later for whatever reasons fell victim to the censor. They have not understood 16:4. Nothing is lacking; it would be a shame if anything further came after this" (1909, 137). Wellhausen's reasoning is that Mark 16:4 implies that the Risen Christ moved the stone aside as he broke free from the tomb. The evangelist chooses to proclaim the resurrection through the visible result of the stone rather than through the resurrection itself, which was seen by no one. Finally, Johannes Weiss, son of Bernhard, wrestled with the peculiarity of Mark 16:8, particularly the failure of the evangelist to recount the rehabilitation of the apostle Peter through a resurrection appearance. Ultimately he concludes that "the truncation of the genuine Markan ending [which some have postulated] . . . remains a puzzle not yet sufficiently explained. . . . We are at this point obliged to reckon with the possibility that Mark actually concluded his work with 16:8" (1903, 342-43). The temperate quality of this remark should not obscure the fact that in its day such a statement was avant-garde.

3. GROWTH IN THE "GAR DEN"

Much of the early debate about Mark's conclusion at 16:8 centered on the stylistic awkwardness of an entire narrative ending with the words "for they were afraid." As is often pointed out, this ending is even more awkward in Greek since the conjunction "for" *(gar)* is in final position. *Gar* is a postpositive particle, meaning that it cannot stand first in its clause. Its normal position is second, so it is far more common for words to follow *gar* than for it to end a sentence.[17] The fact that *gar* was the very last word in the Gospel of Mark raised suspicion that something was amiss. Could a book end with *gar*? Scholars have called it "no proper conclusion," "impossibly abrupt," and "a shocking ending."[18]

In the 1920s and 1930s there was a flurry of articles and notes on the end of Mark's Gospel, several of them adducing grammatical parallels for 16:8.[19] These writings weakened the stylistic argument against 16:8 as Mark's intended ending. With every additional parallel of a sentence, paragraph, or book division concluding with *gar*, it seemed more and more possible that Mark could have ended his Gospel in this manner. But in fact, the stylistic argument based on *gar* has never been the major argument in favor of mutilation or an unfinished gospel. When the argument was posed in absolutist terms by its advocates, however, there was a kind of poetic justice in its gradual diminution through these comparative texts. In chapter 4 we will see that the stylistic argument has not been deprived of its entire force, but at this point in the century, the discovery of "final *gar*" parallels was instrumental in strengthening the case for accepting Mark 16:8 as the intended ending.

4. The Scale Tips: The Emergence of the Second Consensus

The shift in scholarly opinion that was barely perceptible in the 1920s and 1930s picked up speed by midcentury. In the English-speaking world the most influential voice favoring Markan integrity at this time was that of R. H. Lightfoot.[20] Lightfoot doubted that any continuation was even possible after Mark 16:8, a verse that brought the narrative to a screeching halt and seemingly forbade anything further. He also questioned why a truncated document would not have been restored, either by the author or the author's community. Finally, from both literary and theological perspectives, Lightfoot insisted that Mark be analyzed on its own terms, not, as he suspected that some interpreters did, by way of constant comparison with Matthew and Luke. These arguments by Lightfoot were persuasive to a number of interpreters.

At some point in the 1960s the number of persons who accepted 16:8 as the intended ending approached that of the other camp. Along with growth in numbers came a growth in confidence. In 1960 Philip Carrington wrote, "It has been argued, of course, that [Mark] cannot have intended to end his Gospel so abruptly. Either he was interrupted by death, or he wrote more, and the end is lost. These melodramatic hypotheses are very difficult" (1960, 335). In 1962 F. W. Beare flatly rejected the mutilation thesis:

> It must be emphasized that there is no basis for postulating a "lost ending", except in the feeling of some scholars that this is no way to end a gospel; it is far from certain that Mark shared this feeling. If the ending was lost, the loss must have occurred before a copy of the manuscript came into the hands of Matthew or Luke, for they make use of no common source from this point on. This really involves the assumption that the original manuscript was mutilated before it could be copied; that the author was dead and could not restore the lacuna; and that no one else in the Church, until the third century or later, ventured to complete the gap. All this I find totally inconceivable.[21]

In the decades of the 1950s, 1960s, and 1970s other heavyweights such as Raymond Brown, William Lane, Paul Achtemeier, James D. G. Dunn, Leonhard Goppelt, and Norman Perrin eventually lined up on the side of Markan integrity.[22] By the late 1980s Ched Myers's description of the lost ending theory as "obsolete" was beginning to appear accurate (1988, 399).

The chronology of the shift is intriguingly captured in the work of a single scholar: James L. Price. In the first edition of his textbook, *Interpreting the New Testament*, Price wrote, "The majority of scholars have concluded . . . that Mark's Gospel did not end upon such an awkward and unsatisfactory note. . . . Accidental mutilation seems more probable [than an unfinished gospel]" (1961, 187). Ten years later, in the second edition of his book, he added a new paragraph which acknowledged that scholars "have increas-

ingly sought to demonstrate the congruence and suitability of
16:1-8 as an ending for this Gospel." The earlier statement that
"The majority of scholars have concluded . . . that Mark's Gospel did
not end upon such an awkward and unsatisfactory note" was
changed to *"For many scholars* it is not credible that Mark's Gospel
should have ended with 16:8."[23] The remainder of the paragraph
was unaltered. Price, thus, still seemed inclined toward accidental
mutilation in 1971. But by 1987 when he published a new book,
The New Testament: Its History and Theology, Price had changed his
mind: "The present writer *now* agrees with those who hold that
[Mark's] 'conclusion' [at 16:8] is the original one."[24]

The point here is not, of course, to criticize Professor Price, nor
to suggest that he is being whimsical.[25] His evolving view reflects
precisely the shift of the scholarly consensus, both in the details of
the argument and in the chronology. In the early 1960s the view
that Mark was unfinished or truncated was still the majority view.
This had weakened by the early 1970s and been overturned by the
late 1980s. There were still significant challengers, but the scale
had tipped.

5. THE NEW CONSENSUS AND THE DOGGED MINORITY

In the last decade or so, more supporters have flocked to the
new consensus. During that time published opinions have
appeared from such Markan experts as Morna D. Hooker, Pheme
Perkins, Mary Ann Tolbert, Paul L. Danove, Joanna Dewey,
Vernon K. Robbins, Eugene LaVerdiere, and Joel Marcus.[26]
Frequently these interpreters have seen Mark's abrupt ending as
designed to spur readers to action, to continue the story in their
own lives. Making a virtue out of necessity, they found portentous
irony and a stroke of genius in a conclusion that earlier scholars
had seen as a clumsy, accidental formation. LaVerdiere expressed
the sentiments of many when he wrote in his recent commentary,
"Could it be that Mark completed the Gospel but the ending was
somehow lost? Today, such speculation smacks of scholarly desperation" (1999, 2:328).

There apparently are, however, several "desperate" scholars in
the guild of New Testament studies, for a persistent minority

continues to embrace the theory of mutilation. Among those whose opinions have been published in the last twenty years are Craig A. Evans, R. T. France, Robert Gundry, I. Howard Marshall, C. F. D. Moule, Stanley E. Porter, Walter Schmithals, Udo Schnelle, Georg Strecker, Ben Witherington, and N. T. Wright.[27] What is perhaps most notable about this stubborn minority is a modified tone. Unlike their extravagant and self-assured predecessors, lost ending theorists are now more likely to be tentative and cautious. I. Howard Marshall exemplifies this tone when he writes, "I confess to an intuitive feeling that Mark 16:8 is not the original, intended end of the Gospel, and that it is not beyond the bounds of probability that the Gospel proceeded further or that Mark intended some kind of sequel" (1991, 276). N. T. Wright acknowledges the new statistical reality when he says, "I am among the *minority* who think that the opening and closing of the original are lost."[28] Elsewhere Wright even admits to a failed attempt to join the "dark" side:

> I tried for some years to believe that Mark was really a postmodernist who would deliberately leave his gospel with a dark and puzzling ending, but I have for some time now given up the attempt. Grammatically, the gospel could have ended with "for they were afraid" (*ephobounto gar*); structurally, it could not have ended without the story of the risen, vindicated Jesus. (1998, 136)

The triumphalism is gone. As the party out of power, scholars who do not accept Mark 16:8 as the evangelist's intended ending find themselves on the defensive, regrouping, marshalling their arguments anew, and presenting their case to an often skeptical audience.[29]

Twentieth-century Markan scholarship thus began and ended with a firm consensus about the ending of the gospel, a consensus, however, which flipped 180 degrees in the latter half of the century. The change was gradual, but in retrospect, remarkable—so much so that persons trained in the last two decades who have not deliberately ventured into the terrain of pre–1970 Markan scholarship might be unaware of the monolithic support once enjoyed by what is now a minority position.

Persons unfamiliar with this history might be surprised to know the quality and the diversity of scholars who have been suspicious of Mark 16:8. As for quality, the list would include dozens of respected scholars from leading institutions, many of them well published, and some of them recognized leaders in their particular fields. As for diversity, the list includes scholars from Great Britain, France, Germany, and the United States. They come from a variety of Christian denominations and run the gamut from liberal to conservative.[30] On one side is Rudolf Bultmann, whom some would deem a radical German skeptic; on the other side is F. F. Bruce, an evangelical British scholar. A theory that finds Bruce and Bultmann as bedfellows deserves a second look. The list of scholars who think something is amiss with the ending of Mark is, thus, both deep and wide. In embracing what is currently a minority viewpoint, you could find yourself in worse company than this.[31]

But, of course, a legion of supporters does not decide the issue. An equally impressive list could be assembled for the opposing view. The purpose of listing names is twofold. First, it justifies bringing the issue to the table again. The impressive roster of persons sympathetic to the thesis should work to remove the thesis from everyone else's list of idiosyncratic or obsolete ideas. Scholarly viewpoints might be dubbed idiosyncratic when their popularity is limited to a particular era or group. They can be dubbed obsolete when new discoveries have shown them to be untenable. But neither of these scenarios pertains to the lost ending of Mark. Support for this hypothesis was chronologically, geographically, and theologically widespread. Contemporary biblical scholars should be careful not to dismiss an interpretive option that enjoyed virtually unanimous support until the beginning of the twentieth century, persuaded the majority of interpreters throughout its first several decades, and retains a significant minority group to this day. This alone justifies reconsideration of the issue by those who have adopted what is now the majority view.

Second, the above survey should raise the question, why? Why did scholarly opinion on this issue shift so dramatically, even if gradually? What new evidence was introduced? What new arguments won the day? I will argue in chapter 3 that the shift in opinion was not primarily related to the discovery of new evidence. There was no manuscript discovery that demanded a reappraisal of

Mark, no archaeological find or theoretical breakthrough that compelled a reinterpretation. The development of new interpretive methods gave rise to new readings of Mark's apparent conclusion, but these methods did not refute the old historical-critical arguments for an incomplete gospel. Fair-minded scholars with a broad view of the history of interpretation should recognize the overconfident rhetoric displayed by persons *on both sides* of this issue. The possibility of Mark's Gospel being truncated is by no means "as certain as anything in the field of critical conjecture can be," but the theory is far from "inconceivable" or "obsolete."

NOTES

1. Leaney (1972, 219).
2. C. Clifton Black wrote in 1994: "Whether the Gospel was unfinished or its original ending was lost or Mark intended such a provocatively open finale remains an issue of considerable debate" (1994, 16 n. 13). The vitality of the debate depends somewhat on the person who is describing it.
3. For references to editions of the primary texts of Eusebius and Jerome, see Kelhoffer (2000, 6 and n. 19). For a thorough discussion of the date of the Long Ending, see Kelhoffer (2000, 169-77).
4. See, for example, Bleek (1869, 312), F. Cook (1878, 295 and 301-8), and Morison (1873, 467-70 and 484-92), who wrote just prior to the watershed text-critical work of Westcott and Hort (1882) and still argued for the authenticity of 16:9-20.
5. For a survey of this early period, see Kelhoffer (2000, 5-20).
6. The rise and fall of the *Textus Receptus* is told in some detail in Metzger (1992, 95-146). I am indebted to his account at several points.
7. Orchard and Longstaff (1978, 127).
8. Alford (1863, 1:431); original emphasis.
9. Westcott and Hort (1882, 46, 47, 51). The full discussion of Mark 16:9-20 comprises pp. 28-51 of the appendix.
10. Writing more than two decades after Westcott and Hort, Michael Seilenberger (1905, 277) insisted that 16:9-20 should be recognized as authentic, in part because "It is in the highest degree improbable that Mark would have concluded his Gospel with the words ἐφοβοῦντο γάρ." In my opinion, Seilenberger made an accurate observation, but a faulty inference. See also Whitney (1892, 253-60), who is either unaware of or unswayed by the work of Westcott and Hort.
11. McNeile (1927, 57). While I am sympathetic to McNeile's conclusion, I would argue that it is not necessarily within the realm of textual criticism to determine when a text has been mutilated.
12. Zahn (1977, 2:477). German original: 1897–1899.
13. Jülicher (1904, 329), Gregory (1907, 512), Spitta (1907, 3.2.111-38),

Goguel (1909, 301), and Bultmann (1963, 285 n. 2). Note: Casper Rene Gregory was a native Philadelphian but became a professor at the University of Leipzig.

14. It has been claimed that Julius Wellhausen was the first to suggest that Mark intended to end his Gospel at 16:8. See Hooker (1991a, 391). Wellhausen was among the earliest to hold this view, but at least three persons did so before him: Tregelles, Schenkel, and B. Weiss.

15. Tregelles (1854, 258); original emphasis.

16. B. Weiss (1889, 2:256) and (1892, 265) respectively.

17. On the position of *gar*, see Denniston (1934, 95-98), Bird (1953, 171-87), and Thrall (1962, 41-50).

18. Respectively, Boring (1990, 68), Barclay (1975, 146), and van Iersel (1988b, 208). Even scholars who accept 16:8 as Mark's intended ending recognize the harshness of the expression. Collins (1993, 122), for example, calls it "a stupefyingly abrupt ending to the Gospel." Perrin (1977, 17) calls it "grammatically barbarous."

19. See Kraeling (1925), Probyn (1925), Kevin (1926), Moncrieff (1926), Ottley (1926), Nicklin (1926–1927), Cadbury (1927), Enslin (1927), Rist (1932), and W. K. L. Clarke (1934). Of these, only Kevin and Moncrieff argue for a lost ending, although Nicklin assumes it, and Ottley seems open to the possibility.

20. See especially his works of 1938 (1-48, 73-77) and 1950 (80-97, 106-16). An abbreviated version of Lightfoot's argument can be found in his review of Ned B. Stonehouse's *The Witness of Matthew and Mark to Christ* (1945, 221-24). On Lightfoot's influence, see Neill (1976, 77 and n. 5) and France (2002, 670 n. 1).

21. Beare (1962, 240-41). Beare's first and second assumptions are by no means inconceivable, and the third, namely, that no one in the Church attempted to repair Mark's Gospel "until the third century or later," is factually mistaken since the Long Ending (16:9-20) is to be dated in the first half of the second century. (See note 3 above.) Moreover, as soon as Matthew and Luke appeared, the impetus to repair Mark would have been substantially reduced.

22. Brown (1973, 123), Lane (1974, 591-92), Achtemeier (1975, 91), Dunn (1975, 389 n. 85), Goppelt (1981, 1:239), and Perrin (1977, 18-19).

23. Price (1971, 199); my emphasis in both cases.

24. Price (1987, 123); my emphasis.

25. A more sudden change of heart seems to have occurred for Barnett, who favored Markan integrity in 1957 (ix) but mutilation in 1958 (142). Similarly, see Guy (1957, 153-63; 1968, 186-87).

26. Robbins (1984, 192), Hooker (1991a, 391-94), Perkins (1992, 36), Tolbert (1992, 274), Danove (1993, 126-31), Dewey (1994, 156), LaVerdiere (1999, 328), and Marcus (2000a, 860).

27. References can be found in appendix A.

28. Wright (1992a, 390 n. 67); my emphasis. In favoring both a lost ending and a lost beginning, Wright is decidedly in the minority.

29. Although many present-day lost ending theorists acknowledge their views in passing remarks and footnotes, at least five recent commentators have argued at some length for the position. See Gundry (1993), Craig Evans (2001), Witherington (2001), Edwards (2002), and France (2002).

30. Among recent lost ending theorists are several prominent evangelical commentators (see n. 29). There is by no means unanimity in this group, however, since one finds William Lane, David Garland, D. A. Carson, James D. G. Dunn, and Murray J. Harris inclined to accept 16:8 as the intended ending.

31. A fuller list of scholars may be found in appendix A.

THREE

THE REASONS FOR THE SHIFT

"The change in scholarly opinion [about the ending of Mark] came from the development of new methodologies."[1]

In chapter 2, I chronicled the remarkable shift of scholarly opinion about Mark's ending, from a confident and near unanimous judgment of incompleteness to the current consensus (somewhat less unanimous), affirming the integrity of the gospel and the intentionality of 16:8. The earlier consensus was seen to comprise British, French, German, and American scholars. Supporters of the thesis were found in every decade from the 1860s to the present, across denominational divisions, and across the spectrum from conservative to liberal.[2] None of these factors can account for the shift.[3] Perhaps the only significant trend that emerged was a notable concentration of paleographers and textual critics in favor of the first consensus. The sea change, thus, does not fall along precritical versus postcritical lines, Catholic versus Protestant, European versus American, British versus German, or liberal versus conservative. It was, with several notable exceptions, largely chronological: pre-1970s versus post-1970s, with the decade of the 1970s itself being the period of greatest flux.

What occurred during the decades between 1950 and 1980 that might account for the change in the scholarly consensus about the end of Mark's Gospel? I propose that the cause of the shift was the advent of "New Criticism" in the guild of biblical studies and other developments in academia and society in general during those decades. A corollary to this proposal is that the shift was not caused *primarily* by the introduction of new evidence. There was a small amount of evidence adduced in the form of final *gar* clauses as parallels to 16:8 and various observations (some more significant than others) about Markan style and motifs. This evidence had some effect on the debate, but much more important was, as LaVerdiere observes in the above quote, "the development of new methodologies." It should be noted, however, that the development of new methodologies, unlike the production of better evidence and argumentation, normally leads to interpretations that complement past scholarship rather than ones that supersede it.[4]

1. THE INFLUENCE OF NEW CRITICISM

The beginning of the shift in scholarly opinion about the ending of Mark was approximately contemporaneous with the emergence of New Criticism, also known as formalism. The guiding principles of New Criticism were summed up in seminal essays by W. K. Wimsatt and M. C. Beardsley.[5] First, in accord with the "intentional fallacy," such critics questioned whether the examination of an author's intentions and life circumstances was necessary for the interpretation of that author's writings. On the contrary, New Criticism affirmed that

> the meaning and intentionality of a text can be found through a close analysis of the text itself, without extensive research into questions of social, historical, and literary contexts. For example, one need not have knowledge of the psychological state or social circumstance of a poet . . . in order to understand a poem.[6]

Thus New Criticism had relatively little interest in background questions about the history *of* the text and the history *behind* the text. The second principle was the "affective fallacy." This tenet asserted that the meaning of a text was quite independent of its effect on readers. A text's meaning was internal to the text. In simplified terms, the result of the intentional fallacy was to liberate the meaning of a text from its historical author; the result of the affective fallacy was to liberate the meaning of a text from its impact on the reader.

Although it took some years for the impact of New Criticism to be felt in biblical studies, it eventually changed the landscape by shifting the focus of inquiry from textual backgrounds to the text itself. By the late 1970s the heyday of historical-critical methods (form, source, tradition, and redaction criticism) was past. The focus of scholarly attention shifted to the text, viewed not so much as an intentional production of a particular human being whose psychology and historical circumstances would illumine the text's meaning, but as an autonomous, self-contained entity beyond which one need not investigate. The "final form" of the text was supreme.[7]

It was thus important to New Critics to have a well-established text. Peter Shillingsburg has pointed out that this predisposition of New Critics led to an unlikely alliance between them and textual critics.

> [The] central premise [of New Criticism] was that literary works were "organisms" exhibiting "artistic integrity," "internal coherence," and "wholeness." The critic's job was to reveal the integrity of the work of art. Since "corrupted texts" make that job a difficult one, the task of the textual critic was to insure that the text was free of corruption. (1997, 27)

Since the aim of New Critics was to interpret a text as an organic whole, they either had to be provided with a text whose integrity had been guaranteed or they simply had to bracket the question and proceed on the assumption of textual integrity.

The effect of New Criticism on the interpretation of Mark's ending is clear. Since textual critics had proved beyond any reasonable doubt that both the shorter ending (beyond v. 8) and 16:9-20 were secondary, the text to interpret was Mark 1:1 to 16:8. New Criticism was intent on making sense out of the ending at 16:8. To pose the question whether Mark intended to end with that verse was to commit the intentional fallacy. New Criticism was concerned to discover the meaning of the text as it stood.

2. THE DECLINE OF THE AUTHOR / THE RISE OF THE READER

New Criticism's intentional fallacy had shifted the locus of meaning, and hence the focus of investigation, from the author's environment to the text itself. On the other hand, the affective fallacy tended to devalue the reader's contribution to meaning. Further developments in literary criticism, however, shifted the focus once again. In the 1980s and 1990s rhetorical, narrative, and reader-response criticism began to challenge the autonomy of the text. The meaning of texts came to be seen as the product of interaction between texts and readers. Indeed, more radical practitioners of reader-response criticism would locate meaning almost exclusively in the reading community.[8]

As readers and their communities make a larger and larger contribution to meaning, the contribution of the text, to say nothing of authorial intent, tends to diminish. Thus, it becomes largely irrelevant whether or not the evangelist had certain intentions that may have been obscured by textual damage. The meaning that we derive as readers *is* the meaning of the text. As one person put it bluntly, "Texts, like dead men and women, have no rights, no aims, no interests. They can be used in whatever way readers or interpreters choose."[9] This sort of Machiavellian view of reading ("My *might* as a reader makes my interpretation *right*.") is true as a de facto description of how the Bible is often read, both among reader-response critics and simple persons of faith. Such people often read texts asking little more than, "What meaning can *I* derive from this text?" or "What does this text mean *to me*?" The question, "What did *the historical author* mean by this?" is either deliberately set aside or is simply not the meaning that is sought.

Such an approach to textual interpretation is highly subjective, potentially harmful, but, one would have to add, potentially edifying too. Indeed, texts sometimes gain transformative power that they otherwise lacked. Potential harm only enters the picture when active, contributory readers cease to be conscious of their contributory role and begin to attribute their individualistic meanings to the historical author. If readers set aside any concern about authorial intent, they must remember that they have done so! If not, a working assumption (for example, the physical integrity of the text's extant form) may become an unquestioned ideology.

Every critical method comes with a cost/benefit package. Narrative critics, among others, generally assume the unity and integrity of the texts they read. They "read the Bible as literature and, unlike source or redactional critics, assume that the texts are unified rather than discontinuous."[10] In a way this makes narrative criticism more efficient since one need not pause to explain the prehistory of every inconsistency and seam in the text. The cost of this assumption, however, may be a reduced ability to detect sources, discrepancies, and gaps.[11] In short, the narrative critic, acting *as* narrative critic, cannot be expected to do historical criticism!

3. THE ASSUMPTIONS OF MODERNITY

One of the assumptions of modernity is the progress of reason. David Hall has called this the "Dogma of Evolutionism." "Evolutionism is not the scientific theory of Evolution, but the philosophical theory that human thought is continually progressing so that the ideas of today are necessarily an improvement on the ideas of yesterday" (Hall 1990, 3). Human beings are continually amassing knowledge, sharpening skills, and gaining more insight into all facets of existence. This is perhaps most evident in technology and science.[12] Few are content with modes of transportation used a century ago. No physician would perform a delicate surgery employing technology and knowledge in vogue 50 years ago. Computer technology becomes obsolete in a few years and is discarded by anyone who wants to remain competitive. "Upgraded," "on-line," "wireless"—these are the watchwords of all who want to remain technologically viable. But science and technology are not alone in the assumption of progress. The humanities likewise generally assume that recent is better.

This is seen in the discipline of biblical studies in the preference for newer methods and recent research. It is commonplace in biblical studies nowadays to speak of a new paradigm, historical criticism having given way to literary, rhetorical, and reader-oriented criticisms. There are still plenty of historical critics among biblical scholars, but the vanguards of the discipline lie elsewhere. Indeed, historical criticism has been pronounced bankrupt, obsolete, moribund, or simply dead.[13] With the alleged demise of historical criticism, new methodologies that should have been alternative approaches slowly become exclusive approaches. *New* becomes synonymous with *better*; *recent* is equated with *superior*. Eventually, supplementary methods that entered and forever changed the hermeneutical court as peers decide that the (rightly) dethroned, former monarch is no longer needed in a democratic society even as a partner. Likewise, interpreters of the Bible employing the latest methods sometimes show disdain for pre-1970 research. This phenomenon is described by A. K. M. Adam:

> Contemporary biblical interpreters reflect a . . . specifically modern outlook when they work vigorously to distinguish themselves from the interpreters who have gone before them; only the most recent scholarship carries compelling rhetorical weight in biblical studies, and the more recent, the better. Articles in the *Journal of Biblical Literature* or *Interpretation* are likely to cite sources only from the last twenty years or so. Like the first moderns, modern biblical scholars set themselves over against their past, and defend the newness of their own conclusions. (1995, 3)

The way the assumptions of modernity relate to the interpretation of the Gospel of Mark should be clear. The consensus has shifted. According to modernity's axiom of intellectual progress, the new consensus must be better. "In all areas of life—and study of the New Testament is no exception—there is a psychological pressure to accept *current* orthodoxy" (Hall 1990, 2). It would be counterintuitive to suggest that scholars of a previous generation got something right, whereas the present generation has gone astray. But it is sometimes necessary, especially in the humanities, for the questions asked (and ostensibly answered) by one generation to be posed anew by the next generation.

4. SOCIOLOGY OF KNOWLEDGE

Closely related to the assumptions of modernity is the sociology of knowledge, or more colloquially (and pejoratively), "group think."[14] More formally: "The sociology of knowledge is the study of the way in which the production of knowledge is shaped by the social context of thinkers."[15] People have a tendency to learn in groups and, thus, to think in groups. There are mavericks, of course, but when mavericks break away and find like-minded friends, they tend to form new groups in which to think. Although scholars of early Christianity are a diverse lot, there is still a tendency toward "group think" on certain issues. An individual scholar may think, for example, that Paul wrote the Epistle to the Ephesians, but such a person probably would not deliver a paper that makes that assumption at a professional meeting, given the majority opinion that regards Ephesians as pseudonymous.

A generation of New Testament scholars has now been taught and, in turn, has helped perpetuate the majority view on Mark 16:8. As this happens it becomes increasingly difficult to espouse the contrary view and maintain credibility in the guild. The point is not that lost ending theorists are a persecuted minority, but simply that they are swimming upstream, and the current in this case may be driven more by fashion than by evidence. Ideally, hard data and critical analysis provide the foundation of scholarship. But most scholars would acknowledge that theories sometimes gain a mass and momentum disproportionate to the evidence. One generation's heuristic assumption thus becomes the next generation's axiom. When scholarship functions freely and self-critically, there will be a feedback loop such that opinions will be subject to reevaluation on the basis of both the original data and newer, more thorough spadework and analysis. Such a reexamination of the conclusion of Mark's Gospel is now due.

5. THE ZEITGEIST OF THE TWENTIETH CENTURY

I conclude with a fifth development whose influence is admittedly more subtle, but which, I believe, is still a contributing factor. The ending of Mark at 16:8 was apparently dissatisfactory to other first-century evangelists (note the modifications made by Matthew and Luke), to second-century scribes (note the addenda of the long and short endings), and to most modern scholars of the critical era up to about 1970. Readers both ancient and modern expected a happier ending, a resolution that Mark 16:8 did not provide.

But in the twentieth century, particularly following two world wars, the zeitgeist, or mood of the era, of the Western world changed in ways that may have made acceptance of this ending easier. The defeat, silence, and lack of closure at Mark 16:8 may have been more acceptable to the jaded and gloomy mood of the post-depression and post–World War II era. Such political and socioeconomic realities unquestionably influenced art and literature during this time.

> This pessimistic Modernist conception of the world and human nature was reflected in their *art*. If the cosmos is fractured and fragmented, if life is chaotic and meaningless, if the self is a congeries of irrational and uncontrollable impulses, art must reflect this broken and disharmonious reality. . . . The Modernists sought to create an art that would embody and communicate their disturbing perception of reality as fractured and chaotic, or at best paradoxical.[16]

The pessimism and alienation of modern life were reflected in such genres as film noir and theater of the absurd. Film noir, characterized by a fatalistic and cynical mood, was popular in the 1940s and 1950s. It gave expression to the widespread sense of the meaninglessness of human existence. Theater of the absurd, perhaps most famously exemplified by Samuel Beckett's *Waiting for Godot* (1952), portrayed human beings as the victims of inscrutable forces. A similar zeitgeist can be found in the existentialist dramas and novels of such writers as Jean-Paul Sartre and Albert Camus. The characters in these stories must have courage to confront a life that is full of anguish and loss, but void of meaning.

The ways that novelists composed the *endings* of their stories, in particular, underwent change in the twentieth century. Marianna Torgovnick has discussed the twentieth century's tendency toward an open-ended narrative technique, sometimes called "anti-closure." As one might expect, a bias in favor of such endings accompanied their development. Torgovnick cites Alan Friedman's study of the way novels end.

> For Friedman, the "truer ending" is one that endorses "either an ever-widening disorder or a finally open 'order' which embraces all the opposed directions on whatever ethical compass it has brought along for the trip." Thus, endings in which characters and readers

finish with an "open stream of conscience"—with an expanding, unresolved moral consciousness—are, for Friedman, "good" endings. Since such endings are more characteristic of Modernist than of nineteenth-century novels, we must devalue a significant number of nineteenth-century texts if we accept Friedman's vague, polemical criteria. Indeed, the Modernist bias of critics like Friedman has virtually destroyed the usefulness of the terms "open" and "closed" to describe endings, by making "open" a term of approbation, and "closed" a term linked with unadventurous and narrow didacticism. (1981, 9-10)

At the end of her book Torgovnick returns to this theme.

When Alan Friedman asserts in *The Turn of the Novel* that twentieth-century endings are "truer" and more interesting than those in nineteenth-century novels, he provides the best-known and most highly developed statement of the position in favor of recent fiction. But although he is the most vulnerable critic holding this view, Friedman is not alone. [Barbara Herrnstein] Smith and [Frank] Kermode occasionally seem to suggest that Modernist "open" endings deserve fuller discussion than older endings do, if only because they are both in the process of defining the "open" ending. Lightly made comments by otherwise perceptive critics reinforce the same misconception. . . . All these critics implicitly invoke a deceptive standard for discussing and evaluating endings—the criterion of newness.[17]

In these quotes we see the combination of two factors: the new cultural zeitgeist of disorder and irresolution and the assumption of modernity, that is, recent is better. Given these developments in literary criticism and the influx of literary critical thinking into the guild of biblical studies in the mid–twentieth century, it is not unreasonable to suggest that the changing academic environment could have affected the way Mark's ending was viewed.

Although we can rarely draw direct lines from the cultural zeitgeist to the interpretations of biblical scholars, there are some instances in which its effects seem likely. Donald Juel remarks that "A few bold interpreters have compared Mark to modern existentialist writers whose point is that life is endlessly disappointing" (1990, 233). Tom Wright observes that modern scholarship not only proposes that Mark intended to end with 16:8, but attempts "to wallow in the dark uncertainty that results. Mark, we are told, is a book of mysteries . . . a strange brooding puzzle" (2001, 223). A. E. Harvey waxes melodramatic on this point: "The mystery remains—a fitting reminder, perhaps, that though we may feel that we have begun to lay bare some of Mark's secrets, his little book contains far more mysteries than we shall ever be able to give an account of, and will continue to keep its readers fascinated and even a little mystified for as long as it continues to be read at all" (1977, 54). J. L. Houlden maintains that the conclusion of Mark "baffles exegesis at almost every level." Houlden offers a litany of nine bewildering and unanswered questions concerning Mark's conclusion and insists that none has a final answer. Indeed, writes Houlden, "there is something salutary in simply feeling *their cumulative enigmatic force.*"[18] Randolph Tate characterizes Mark as "the mysterious labyrinthine playground . . . , where the beginning never points to the end, but the end always points back to the beginning. Here is a world where forms fade almost imperceptibly into all other forms and every form is turned on its head; insiders are outsiders, purity is impurity, orthodoxy is heresy, death is life, and absence is presence" (1994, 74). For Harvey, Houlden, and Tate, Mark's Gospel has apparently come to represent the literary embodiment of Winston Churchill's famous description of the Soviet Union: "a riddle wrapped in a mystery inside an enigma."[19]

I must confess to being very skeptical about all of this. When literary critic Frank Kermode compares Mark's riddling narratives to those of Franz Kafka, I prefer to think that biblical scholarship should perhaps wake up and *smell* the Kafka. Mark is a Gospel, a proclamation of good news; not a brooding, inexplicable, existentialist riddle.[20]

The above factors, in my opinion, played a larger role in the sea change of scholarly views about the end of Mark's Gospel than did the introduction of new evidence. The task for chapter 4, then, will be to lay out the positive case for the mutilation of Mark's Gospel.

NOTES

1. LaVerdiere (1999, 2:329). In a similar vein, France (2002, 670 n. 1) muses, "It is tempting to wonder how far this 'modern' swing of opinion derives from a closer understanding of Mark's world and how far from a change in twentieth-century literary fashion."

2. While there might appear to be a conservative British cluster in Manson, Moule, France, and Wright, this is offset by the presence of liberal scholars (Bultmann, Vielhauer) and by the absence of several conservative scholars who incline toward 16:8 as Mark's intended ending (Achtemeier, Brown, Carson, Dunn, Garland, Lane).

3. The division according to gender is interesting. Women have opted almost without exception for Mark 16:8 as the intended ending of the gospel. The only published opinions that I have been able to find from women who think that Mark's Gospel lacks its original ending have been those of Eta Linnemann (1969) and Jane Shaberg (2002, 293). I suspect that the reasons for this have to do with the era in which women entered the field of New Testament studies and with the methodologies that they usually employed.

4. See Hall (1990, 4): "In study of the New Testament it is important to ask whether the views of modern scholars, where they differ from the views of earlier scholars, are based on superior technical know-how or simply on a change in attitudes and presuppositions."

5. Wimsatt (1954). On New Criticism, see Moore (1989, 9 and 181) and the discussions in Eagleton (1983, 47-53) and Poland (1985, 65-97).

6. Beal, Keefer, and Linafelt (1999, 2:80).

7. Note that "final form" (from the author's hand) and "extant form" (the canonical form found in a modern text) are usually regarded as approximately equal. In the case of a manuscript that has become truncated in the course of transmission, however, the difference between the two could be significant.

8. See Beal, Keefer, and Linafelt (1999, 2:83): "The leading figure of reader-response criticism in North America is S[tanley] Fish, who has most vigorously argued that the reader completely creates the meaning of a text. . . . the reader replaces the text as a primary locus of meaning." Similarly, Hooker (1999, 2:130) "Some literary critics have little need to ask questions about authorial intentions; they cut the Gospel loose from its original moorings and examine it in its own right, so that its meaning now depends on its impact on the reader. . . . It is easy to see how subjective such interpretations must be: The reader is acknowledged to be more important than the writer."

9. Morgan and Barton (1988, 7).

10. Beal, Keefer, and Linafelt (1999, 2:83).

11. Mark Allan Powell (1990, 92) notes that "Narrative unity is *not* something that must be proved from an analysis of the material. Rather, it is something that can be *assumed*. . . . From the perspective of the implied reader, it will make no difference whether the narrative form was created accidentally or intentionally. It is there, and the reader must deal with it." (My emphasis.) But as David Lee (1999, 136-37) observes, "At this point the supposedly empirical text-centred critical approach appears to be taken over by an *a priori* ideological concern. . . . [T]he first generation of New Testament narrative critics seem strangely un-disconcerted by the actual Gospel narrative text. Whatever the text includes, it always displays a self-consistent unity!"

12. Hall (1990, 3): "The 'upward still and onward' approach makes sense in those fields of study that depend on technical know-how."

13. Famously in the words of Wink (1973, 1): "Historical biblical criticism is bankrupt." In 1975 Edgar Krentz favorably cited R. P. C. Hanson's earlier statement: "the battle for the acceptance of historical criticism as applied to the Bible has been won" (Krentz, 1975, 3; citing Hanson 1970) and further stated: "The utility of historical criticism can no longer be questioned. It has arrived, so to speak (Krentz, 1975, 87). In 1993 he all but retracted those statements: "[Biblical criticism's] triumph on the American scene took place in the period between the two world wars, only to disintegrate in the biblical generation after the 60s" (Krentz, 1993, 345). See also Moore (1989, xiv and n. 2).

14. For bibliography on the sociology of knowledge, see Camery-Hoggatt (1992, 208).

15. Hess, Markson, and Stein (1991, 621).

16. Hobbs and Duncan (1992, 399).

17. Torgovnick (1981, 203). See also Wallace Martin (1986, 81-85).

18. Houlden (1987, 32-33); my emphasis.

19. Compare Martin Dibelius's often-quoted saying that Mark is a "book of secret epiphanies." See Dibelius (1934, 203) and Dahl (1976, 54). This alleged quality of Mark is effectively exploited in a pastoral reflection by Willson (1994, 277): "[Mark] refuses to tie the loose ends of the gospel into a tidy bow of fleeting consolations. The final verses are ambiguous: a promise greeted by fear; a pledge that . . . we will "see him" swamped by our own uncertainty and dread. What Mark's ending lacks in romance it makes up for in sheer realism. Isn't this the world we live in? No enchanted world of thinly fabricated happily-every-afters [sic], but a world in which we hold tightly to the promise and fearfully tread our way through a tangle of doubts and amazements."

20. For the comparison of Mark and Kafka, see Kermode (1979, 33, 45) and Juel (1994, 117-21). For a vigorous statement of the simplicity and transparency of Mark, see Gundry (1993, 1).

FOUR

THE GAPING WOUND

"The lion (the ancient symbol for Mark) . . . has turned around and bitten off its own tail."[1]

The fundamental reason that Mark 16:8 is not likely to be the author's intended ending is the jarring lack of closure that this verse presents. *Closure* has been defined as "a sense of completeness, integrity, and coherence, both formal and thematic, that the reader experiences at the end of the work."[2] This sense of completeness derives from "the satisfaction of textually generated expectations."[3] Mark 16:8 lacks both aspects of closure: formal and thematic.[4]

Formal closure refers to language that appropriately rounds off the narrative. Such language may itself be narrative, or dialogue, or authorial commentary. Excellent examples of formal closure can be seen in the other Gospels. Matthew ends with Jesus' commissioning words and promise (28:18-20). Luke contains similar words, followed by a terse narrative of the ascension and the disciples' return to Jerusalem (24:46-53). John famously has two

endings, both with suitable formal closures: a summary and purpose statement in John 20:30-31, and the attestation of the
beloved disciple followed by another summary in John 21:24-25. I
am *not* suggesting that Mark must have originally contained statements equivalent to these found in the other Gospels. Mark could
have closed his Gospel in a variety of ways. But the stark abruptness of his ending, not resembling any recognizable form of closure and seeming to many readers to be a partial sentence, begs
for an explanation.

Thematic closure pertains to content. When a work has thematic closure, it fulfills the expectations that the work has generated, sometimes recapitulating motifs from the narrative,
sometimes providing an inclusio with the beginning of the work.[5]
It might alternately be forward-looking, furthering a trajectory that
has been anticipated by the story up to that point. Matthew's conclusion highlights that Gospel's themes of authority, mission, the
nations, and Jesus as a teacher. In addition, "I am *with you* always"
(28:20) is often seen as an inclusio with "they shall name him
Emmanuel, which means, 'God is *with us*' " (1:23). Luke's ending
recalls the strategic prominence of Jerusalem in his Gospel as well
as the importance of the Spirit. Scenes of worship and prayer form
bookends for this Gospel (1:8-10; 24:52-53).[6] John's first ending
recalls the importance of signs, belief, life, and the titles Messiah
and Son of God. John's second ending provides the final mention
of the beloved disciple, as well as the themes of testimony and
truth.

With regard to *thematic* closure, Mark obviously had even
greater freedom vis-à-vis the other evangelists than with formal
closure. The Second Gospel does not by any means have to end
like Matthew, Luke, and John. It should, however, end in a way
that is appropriate on its own terms. In other words, if Mark's
Gospel "ought" to have one or more appearance stories, the
"oughtness" derives not from comparison with other Gospels, but
from the expectations that the Gospel of Mark itself has generated. It is entirely reasonable to expect Mark to have supplied a
suitable closure to his work, provided that "suitable" is defined in
Markan terms.

The absence of narrative closure, both formal and thematic, can
be elaborated in several ways. Most of the following arguments

have been previously suggested over the century-long investigation of the Markan ending. The aim of this chapter is to marshal those arguments as forcefully as possible and to corroborate them with new research. Chapter 5 will critique the various literary solutions that have been proposed to explain "the gaping wound" at Mark 16:8.[7]

1. THE WORLD ACCORDING TO GAR: THE ARGUMENT FROM STYLE

As I pointed out in chapter 2, much of the early debate about Mark 16:8 centered on the stylistic awkwardness of ending a gospel with the words "for they were afraid." The postpositive (never occurring first in its clause) Greek conjunction, *gar* ("for"), seems unlikely as the last word in a paragraph, let alone an entire work. The flavor of the Greek has been approximated in the translation, "They were afraid, you see. . . ."[8] It should not be thought that the word is necessarily dangling in midair, as if it were completely lacking its clause. It is not equivalent to the English: "They were afraid, for. . . ." *Gar* in Mark 16:8 logically introduces "they were afraid," not some other clause that is missing. But *part* of the "fearing" clause may be missing, and the abruptness of this ending understandably raised suspicion. Could this have been the way Mark intended to conclude?

As mentioned in chapter 2, a flurry of articles in the first few decades of the twentieth century addressed this question, many of them offering grammatical parallels for Mark 16:8. These articles established beyond any doubt that sentences and paragraphs could end in *gar*. A frequently cited article by P. W. van der Horst reprised the debate in 1972 with further parallels.[9] But the smattering of ancient texts that were adduced as parallels up through van der Horst's article are now dwarfed by the results of computer research. Steven Cox's 1993 dissertation utilized such technology and found that just over one thousand sentences in ancient Greek literature ended with *gar* followed by a period and roughly five hundred with *gar* followed by a question mark (1993, 152). Further advances in the encoding of Greek texts make possible even more expansive searches. The newest version of the *Thesaurus Linguae Graecae* (TLG CD ROM-E) now contains virtually all extant ancient Greek texts from Homer to C.E. 600, and several from C.E. 600 to the fall of Byzantium in 1453. A search of this data bank yields new statistics: 1,884 sentences ending in *gar*-period; 786 sentences ending in *gar*-question mark.[10]

The relevant question is no longer, can *gar* end a sentence? but rather what *kinds* of sentences end with *gar*? Obviously, such sentences must be short, usually two or three words long. Less obvious is the fact that such sentences occur most often in certain kinds of literature. Short sentences ending in *gar* reflect an informal oral or conversational style.[11] They often have the parenthetical quality of an aside. The text almost always continues. Sentences ending in *gar* are much less common in narrative. For example, the historians Herodotus, Thucydides, Appian, Procopius, Josephus, and Diodorus Siculus together use *gar* more than 12,000 times. Not once is the word followed by a period. Other major writers of narrative prose offer only sparse examples: Philo, 1; Polybius, 1; Dio Cassius, 2; Dionysius of Halicarnassus, 2; Plutarch, 2; Xenophon, 2. (These authors use *gar* more than 28,000 times.)

On the other hand, relatively larger numbers of sentences ending in *gar* are found in works having a more oral style. Perhaps most remarkable are the works of Plato, in which *gar* is followed by a period 158 times and by a question mark 182 times. Plato wrote philosophy, but in what form? Dialogues. Other literary genres with relatively high numbers of final *gar* sentences include comedy, oratory, and symposia. Perhaps less obviously, technical works, such as scholia (interpretative notes usually written in the margins of a manuscript), grammatical and lexicographical works, and commentaries have relatively high numbers of such clauses. Such technical works tend to have a choppy, disjointed quality. It is noteworthy that when *narrative* authors have sentences ending in *gar*, they are often found in speeches.[12] The *Life of Apollonius*, a quasi-biographical narrative often compared to the Gospels, has a total of eight sentences ending in *gar*-period. *All* eight are in dialogue.

The most significant parallels to Mark 16:8 are probably those found in Plotinus, a third-century C.E. Neoplatonist, and Musonius Rufus, a first-century C.E. Stoic philosopher. Van der Horst's article adduced the 32nd treatise of Plotinus (*Ennead* V.5) and claimed that "Here we really have a book ending with γάρ [gar]" (1972, 123). But Plotinus's works were not intended for publication and have a disjointed quality. Classicist E. R. Dodds notes, "Many of [Plotinus's] essays give the impression of a man thinking aloud or discussing difficulties with a pupil. Owing to bad eyesight, Plotinus never revised what he wrote . . . and his highly individual style often reflects *the irregular structure of oral statement.*"[13] Moreover, as van der Horst himself acknowledges, the writings of Plotinus have been cut up and rearranged by his pupil, Porphyry. This "final *gar*" example actually did have a continuation prior to being edited. The 32nd treatise of Plotinus, therefore, is a dubious example of *gar* ending a book. A more noteworthy example is essay 12 of Musonius Rufus. This essay concludes with *gnōrimon gar* ("For [it is] known.") I would note that this is a philosophical discourse, not unlike a dialogue in some respects, but it does constitute at least an essay (within a collection) that ends in *gar*.[14]

So, can a book end with *gar*? Van der Horst says that we cannot deny this possibility, and he is right. Despite the harshness of the style, no rule of grammar or logic prohibits it. We cannot gainsay the *possibility* of *gar* ending a book. But to point out the obvious, all things that are *possible* are not equally *probable*. The limited use of "final *gar*" sentences in narrative prose and their extreme scarcity at the end of narrative works (I am not aware of any such instance) argues *against* the likelihood that Mark concluded his entire Gospel with such a clause. It must readily be acknowledged that statistics have limited value and always require interpretation. The observations I have made about literary genres and final *gar* do not *prove* anything. But they do suggest certain probabilities. The *gar* argument is not as formidable as some have claimed, but the parallels that have been adduced by no means deprive the argument of its entire force. It is still quite awkward for *a narrative* to end as the Gospel of Mark does. To the extent that the stylistic argument weighs into the debate, it must be said to give its *modest* force to the thesis of a mutilated text.

Before concluding the discussion of the argument from style, we must consider the rejoinder that 16:8, though admittedly harsh, is in keeping with Mark's diction elsewhere in the gospel. Is not Mark's Greek in general the least polished of the four evangelists? Could not the discordance of 16:8 be within his range of normal expression? Such judgments about style are necessarily subjective, but this argument is worth considering.

It must be asserted that Mark's Greek is best described as inelegant, not ungrammatical. Vincent Taylor warns that "It is possible . . . to overstress the 'barbarous' character of Mark's Greek" (1966, 52). Mark does not commit many glaring solecisms, but neither does his diction soar. Hengel (2000, 79) strikes a good balance when he describes Mark's Greek as "linguistically unobjectionable, though rhetorically simple." I would say that Mark was at his stylistic worst, if he intentionally ended his narrative with 16:8.[15] Even Etienne Trocmé, who was inclined to accept 16:8 as the conclusion of the gospel, admits the stylistic problem.

> It has rightly been stressed that none of the other pericopes in Mark ends so abruptly on a γάρ and that the second-last word, ἐφοβοῦντο ["they were afraid"], is too obviously the justification of the silence preserved by the women in spite of the angel's commands for it to be passed off as a subtle conclusion designed to end the Gospel on a "numinous" note. The author of Mark is usually more skilful than that, even if his literary pretensions are modest.[16]

I would also think that abrupt and harsh expressions would *a priori* be more likely *within a work* than at its beginning or conclusion, where stylistic care and clarity are especially important. In any event, the argument from style is a lesser one in the case for the mutilation of Mark's Gospel. More significant observations lie elsewhere.

2. NOTHING TO FEAR BUT FEAR ITSELF: THE ARGUMENT FROM GRAMMAR

Another argument that has cautiously been proposed and whose weight, like the stylistic argument, is modest but not inconsequential, concerns the verb *ephobounto*, "they were fearing." Some commentators have felt that the verb would normally have some kind of grammatical continuation: an accusative direct object, a clause introduced with "lest" *(mē)*, a clause introduced by the preposition *apo*, or some other complement. It would be unusual, though not impossible, say such interpreters, for *ephobounto* to be used absolutely, that is, grammatically independent.[17] While this is not a clinching argument, it is an intuitive impression that finds some support in the way the word is used in the New Testament.

Writers of ancient Greek had two basic choices in expressing action in past time. The aorist tense denoted simple, undefined action: "They were afraid" *(ephobēthēsan)*. The imperfect tense denoted continuous, linear action, something like, "They were fearing" *(ephobounto)*. Mark 16:8 uses the latter. The usage of these two tenses in the Bible is instructive. The imperfect tense of the verb *phobeomai* (to fear) is used eleven times in the New Testament. Ten times it has some kind of object; only once (apart from Mark 16:8) is it used absolutely.[18] The imperfect of *phobeomai* is used nine times in the Septuagint. Eight times it has an object; only once it is used absolutely. The biblical totals for *phobeomai* in the imperfect tense, then, are eighteen times with some kind of sequel; two times with none.

The aorist tense of *phobeomai* is used somewhat differently. In the New Testament the aorist is used eight times with an object and eleven times absolutely. In the Septuagint the numbers are forty-seven and thirty-five respectively, for biblical totals of fifty-five times with an object and forty-six times absolutely. Similar ratios occur when one examines participles of *phobeomai* in the Greek Bible.[19] Again, one must acknowledge the limitations of grammatical statistics, but it seems that biblical Greek seldom used the imperfect tense to say that a person or group "was fearing" without designating an object or specifying the fear in some way. When an author did use *phobeomai* absolutely, it was, by far, more common to use the aorist tense. This is probably not due to chance but rather is related to the nature of the two tenses. The imperfect tense describes the action and thus is well suited to a specific fear. The aorist tense leaves the action undefined and so easily lends itself to more generalized expressions of fear. As with the stylistic argument based on *gar*, the weight of this grammatical argument is modest, but it lends its modest force to the thesis of a truncated text.[20]

3. GOSPEL OF GLOOM? THE ARGUMENT FROM THEOLOGY OR MOOD

Some interpreters have thought that 16:8 is an unlikely conclusion for Mark's Gospel due to the melancholy mood of this final verse. Bruce Metzger confessed, "[I] cannot believe that the note of fear would have been regarded as an appropriate conclusion to an account of the Evangel, or Good News." British scholar Donald Guthrie echoed this sentiment: "It must be admitted that it is strange to find a gospel, a book of good news, ending with a note of fear."[21] Even English literature scholar Frank Kermode, who himself was disposed to read Mark in terms of its ending at 16:8, said that "it's hard to see why the gospel, which is a proclamation of the good news, should stop before it had fairly reached the part that seemed most important to Paul; by Mark's time it had been preached for an entire generation" (1979, 67).

The tone of Mark, if the evangelist did conclude with 16:8, is indeed gloomy, and almost irredeemably so. The male disciples have variously betrayed, denied, and ultimately abandoned Jesus. Their last action (apart from Peter's brief surveillance in the courtyard) was when "All of them deserted him and fled" (14:50). The last words Simon Peter speaks in the Gospel of Mark are, "I do not know this man you are talking about" (14:71). The female disciples are present at the crucifixion, the burial, and the discovery of the empty tomb, but are silent, fearful, and disobedient when the climactic revelation is given and they are commissioned by the young man at the tomb to go tell the others (15:40-41, 47; 16:1, 7-8).

Even Jesus is not fully rehabilitated by this ending. True, the resurrection is announced and a reunion is foreshadowed, but the news is not believed, and the directive is not heeded. Jesus is not seen or heard from after the crucifixion. His last words in the Gospel of Mark are "My God, my God, why have you forsaken me?" (15:34). It can even be argued that God and the narrator stand in need of rehabilitation, for the narrator has announced that Jesus "has been raised" (with God's action implied in the passive voice), and yet the fulfillment of this promise is never realized in the story.[22]

The gloomy effect of 16:8 would be mitigated if *ephobounto* had the meaning of "felt reverential awe." This was suggested by Willoughby C. Allen, who paraphrases verse 8c, "They were hushed into silence because they were overwhelmed by a feeling of reverential awe."[23] Although this meaning is certainly within the semantic range of *phobeomai*, it is unlikely here for three reasons. First, there is a significant concentration of words denoting fearful or astonished reactions in this passage. In 16:5, 6 we find *ektham-beō*, "be amazed, alarmed." In verse 8 we find two nouns in addition to the verb *ephobounto*, namely *tromos*, "trembling," and *ekstasis*, "astonishment, terror."[24] Although Mark has a well-developed vocabulary of amazement and fear (see also *ekplēssomai* "astound," *ekphobos*, "terrified," *existēmi*, "astonish," *thambeomai*, "be amazed," and *tarassō*, "unsettle"), nowhere else in Mark are four such terms concentrated in so few verses.

Second, the motif here is not simply fear. There is a threefold motif: The women "fled from the tomb . . . and they said nothing to anyone, for they were afraid." We have "fright, flight, mouth shut tight." Elsewhere in Mark flight is found in situations of genuine fear, even dread. It is a response to cataclysmic loss (5:14), apocalyptic peril (13:14), and fear of bodily harm (14:50, 52). Although it would be fruitless to argue over quantitative distinctions such as "were afraid" versus "were terrified," a translation of "felt reverential awe" is too weak and leaves unexplained why the women *act* afraid. In light of their actions it is difficult to construe *ephobounto* in 16:8 as a positive emotion.[25]

Finally, the context of 16:1-8, provides adequate grounds for fear. The young man who appears, dressed in a white robe, is probably to be understood as an angelic figure, although he is not explicitly designated as such. The scene is a quasi-divine epiphany, an experience that often evokes fear (cf. 6:49-50; 9:2-6). More important, the stone has been rolled away and the body is said to be gone, facts that might evoke reverential awe *if* faith and understanding accompanied the perception, but in the context of 16:1-8 these facts are confronted with utter bewilderment, foreboding, and a sense of loss. To the women, the vacant sepulcher is not a numinous sign of divine presence and power, but a dreadful sign of deprivation. The women are deprived even of the corpse of their Lord. Thunderstruck, they flee hurriedly, feeling as empty as the tomb is.

If Mark 16:8 is the gospel's intended ending, then the second evangelist has introduced a literary genre unparalleled in antiquity: "Gospel Noir." A tiny glimmer of hope might be seen in the announcement of 16:7, but this announcement is unheeded, disbelieved, and abandoned. If the gospel ends with 16:8, it ends in disobedience, disbelief, fear, and silence. There is little hope and no ultimate reconciliation within the gospel as it stands. If an ending has been lost, and there was originally a continuation beyond *ephobounto gar*, the sequel would surely mitigate this mood.

There is, then, a problem of theology or mood when flight, silence, and disobedience are the gospel's final word. Donald Juel has posed the frank question, "What sort of good news concludes with 'and they said nothing to any one, for they were afraid'?"[26] Perhaps good news that is truncated in midsentence.

4. WHY DIDN'T HE TELL? THE ARGUMENT FROM TRADITION

Why did Mark not narrate a postresurrection appearance of the risen Jesus? If the ending at 16:8 is intentional, Mark's silence at this point is a radical deviation from existing Christian tradition. The resurrection of Jesus was a key aspect of early Christian preaching, and an apostle seems to be defined, in part, as someone who was a witness to the risen Jesus (see Acts 1:22, 2:32, 3:15, 4:33, 10:40-41, 13:30-31, 17:31; Rom 6:4, 10:9; 1 Cor 15:3-8; 1 Thess 1:10, 4:14). Given that fact, C. E. B. Cranfield has argued that "it is highly improbable that Mark intended to conclude his Gospel without at least one account of a Resurrection appearance" (1959, 471). The argument here is *not* that Mark must look like the other Gospels in every detail, that he must have a resurrection appearance simply because they do. *Quite apart from the other Gospels*, we know that the resurrection was of profound importance for the liturgical, confessional, and evangelistic life of the church. Mark's failure to tell of the appearance of the risen Christ, beyond a terse announcement (16:7) that is effectively withdrawn in the next verse, is an omission that requires a compelling explanation.

> [A]lthough . . . the empty tomb would be a most significant fact if conjoined with appearances, no one, surely, could ever have supposed that taken by itself alone it would be particularly convincing. The reply that an adversary or doubter could make would be obvious, that the body had been removed. Indeed passages in all the other Gospels shew how naturally this would occur to the mind. It is most unlikely then that any early Christian writer would have stopped short at the discovery that the tomb was empty, and not have gone on to relate appearances *which were already part of the Church's tradition*.[27]

Moreover, although the other Gospels are not *determinative* for what *must* be in Mark, their evidence is not entirely irrelevant. It must be acknowledged that resurrection appearances, based on the evidence of the other Gospels, seem to be a critical, constituent element in the story of Jesus.[28] It is one thing to say that a particular Gospel lacks *a certain detail* that the other Gospels include. Examples of this could be multiplied a thousandfold. It is another thing to say that a *major structural component* is lacking in one but present in the others.[29] This fact, by itself, is not a probative argument, but it points in the same direction as several other arguments.

5. How Did He Hear? The Argument from Logical Coherence

The ending of Mark also has a problem of logical coherence. If the women fled from the tomb and spoke to no one, how did Mark learn of this last incident (16:1-8) so as to report it in his Gospel? Robert Fowler reflects on this oddity of Mark's conclusion.

> Taken at face value, this says that the discovery of the empty tomb was never reported! Mark's story ends with the referential axis of the story having broken down completely. Amazingly, Mark's Gospel, unlike each of the other canonical Gospels, comes to a halt before it narrates circumstances in which one could imagine something like the gospel of Mark being narrated. The story *in* Mark's Gospel seems to preclude the telling *of* Mark's Gospel. This Gospel is therefore a narrative hanging in mid-air, so to speak.[30]

Stephen Moore also recognizes the difficulty of this ending and describes it with an imaginative variety of mixed metaphors.

> Mark 16:8 seems to be saying that the discovery of the empty tomb was never reported. But if it was never reported, how can *Mark* know that Jesus has risen?
> . . . Mark's ending undercuts its beginning; it saws through the branch on which the book is perched. Outside the tomb, as the women flee and say nothing, Mark rips up its own birth record. In contrast to Matthew and Luke, each of which *begins* with a virginal conception (Matt 1:18; Luke 1:34-35), Mark *ends* with a virginal conception—its own. Its tomb becomes a miraculous womb.[31]

Some modern interpreters approach Mark, however, as a fictional work, and thus they may be able to avoid the messy problems that historical reportage involves. Could not such interpreters simply evoke the "omniscient narrator" who stands above the story and needs no ordinary source of information to compose the narrative? I am not convinced that an appeal to an omniscient narrator is entirely satisfactory here, for readers have a right to expect even a purely fictional story world to cohere at some basic level of logic. A fascinating parallel exists in nineteenth-century literature. By some blunder in the process of printing, Herman Melville's novel, *Moby Dick*, was printed in London without its epilogue. "British reviewers pointed out in extravagant outrage or mock indignation that if all hands went down with the Pequod then no one was left to tell the first-person tale!"[32] The Gospel of Mark is not told in first person, but if his narrative went down in the abyss of the women's silence, it likewise begs for a source. Particularly in the context of ancient storytelling (whether historical, quasi-historical, or fictional), I suspect that readers normally expected a story line to have a surviving communicant. Even if Mark 16:1-8 were sheer fiction, it would be logically confounded fiction. Thus, the argument from logical coherence may come into play regardless of how one assesses Mark's historicity.

Many interpreters, including some who argue for the textual integrity of Mark, feel obliged to explain that, of course, the women eventually broke their silence![33] One of the more elaborate explanations is given by William Arndt.

> The statement from Mark refers to the attitude of the women *while they were returning home*. They were so overawed that they did not stop at the houses of friends and acquaintances to report what they had seen and heard, but hastened back to their abode as quickly as they could. Mark certainly does not wish to create the impression that they did not inform the disciples of the message of the angels.[34]

Merrill Tenney has a similar viewpoint but provides a more ominous scenario for the women.

> [T]he episode at the tomb would have remained unknown had not the women reported it to somebody. Mark means that they did not tell anyone apart from the disciples, for they had a commission to

discharge and would be reluctant to discuss their experience with unsympathetic listeners. They would not dare to publish what they had witnessed, either because they would be regarded as religious fanatics or because their presence at the tomb would be a cause for suspicion of a plot. (1963, 60)

What must be admitted about all such explanations is that they simultaneously have the air of common sense but defy the plain meaning of the text. Can Mark 16:8, if it was truly the evangelist's concluding verse, be made to say what Arndt and Tenney want it to say? Logic and the course of Christian history insist that the women's silence must have been temporary, but the text does not seem to allow it. But if Mark's narrative continued in a now lost ending, the continuation could easily have made plain that the silence was not permanent.[35] The options, then, seem to be either that Mark is doing something incredibly subtle and devious or that he did not, in fact, intend his Gospel to conclude with these words.

6. WE WOULD SEE JESUS: THE ARGUMENT FROM NARRATIVE EXPECTATIONS

Probably the strongest argument for the thesis that Mark did not intend to conclude his Gospel with 16:8 is the glaring lack of thematic closure that would result. Mark has elaborately prepared the reader for a very different kind of ending through his heavy reliance on the plot device of prediction and fulfillment. Robert Gundry points out that "Mark has *repeatedly and in detail* narrated the fulfillments of Jesus' other predictions so far as those fulfillments occurred during Jesus' time on earth."[36] In fact, as N. R. Petersen observes, Mark's empty tomb scene occurs "in the context, indeed at the climax, of the greatest density of closural satisfactions in the entire narrative."[37] Mark's narrative has been gathering momentum through chapters 14 and 15. It rushes on toward an apex, but then suddenly plunges off the precipice of 16:8.

What, then, are the fulfillments of Jesus' words which Mark has provided up to this point? Gundry enumerates the following: (1) seeing God's kingdom as having come with power in the Transfiguration (9:1-8); (2) the finding of a colt (11:2-6); (3) meeting the man carrying a jar of water and being shown the upper room (14:13-16); (4) the betrayal of Jesus by one of the twelve (14:18-20, 43-45); (5) the scattering of the disciples (14:27, 50); (6) Peter's denial of Jesus (14:30-31, 66-72); and, most important, (7) the passion and resurrection, which themselves involve several particulars. The so-called passion predictions in Mark speak of Jesus' betrayal, condemnation, suffering, death, and resurrection in increasing detail (8:31; 9:31; 10:32-34), down to the fact of Jesus' being mocked, spat on, and flogged, details that are all fulfilled in the ensuing narrative.

One might argue, however, that the passion predictions speak of the resurrection but not of the appearances. What specific preparation has Mark offered with regard to postresurrection appearances? Jesus utters a prediction of a resurrection appearance in 14:28: "But after I am raised up, I will go before you to Galilee." This prediction is reiterated by the young man at the tomb in 16:7, the penultimate verse of the gospel: "But go, tell his disciples and Peter that he is going ahead of you to Galilee; there you will see him, just as he told you." Note the important modifications to 14:28. The prediction is not just restated; it is enhanced by the words "there you will see him." It is also explicitly grounded in the reliable words of Jesus: "just as he told you" (Gundry 1993, 1010). Finally, the tense of the verb, which was future in 14:28, is present in 16:7: "he *is going* ahead." The narrative is clearly in motion toward a reunion in Galilee. The reader is given every reason to expect that the reunion will be narrated—and soon.

Some interpreters have suggested that Jesus' prediction, reinforced by the young man at the tomb, should be sufficient. Jesus is a reliable character; the reader can trust that his words will be fulfilled.[38] But Mark's consistent habit is *to demonstrate the reliability* of Jesus' words by narrating their fulfillment, even when that narration is incidental to the flow of the main story. In Mark 7:29, for example, Jesus tells the Syrophoenician woman who came seeking healing for her daughter, "You may go—the demon has left your daughter." The reader can trust Jesus' words; the pericope can conclude. But it doesn't. Mark 7:30 says, "So she went home, found the child lying on the bed, and the demon gone." Similarly, in Mark 10:46-52, Jesus heals blind Bartimaeus. In verse 52a Jesus says, "Go; your faith has made you well." Surely Jesus' words will come to pass. Yes, we *know* they come to pass because Mark *tells* us they do in 52*b*: "Immediately he regained his sight and followed him on the way."[39]

Although the lack of a resurrection appearance is the most glaring loss from Mark's truncated text, there are other related promises that fall short of fulfillment if the end has been reached at 16:8. Three in particular deserve mention.

(1) The first of these is the intimation that the disciples will not only see Jesus but will be reconciled with him. Susan Garrett mentions four passages in Mark that "hint that the disciples, who fled from Jesus at his arrest, would return to see Jesus and follow him in the period after the resurrection" (1998, 143). The first of these is Jesus' promise to Simon and Andrew that he would make them "fish for people" (1:17). This promise is "not adequately fulfilled within the framework of the narrative" (Garrett 1998, 143). The full realization of this metaphor would occur in the postresurrection era.[40] The second passage in Garrett's list is Jesus' prediction that James and John will share a fate like his own (10:39). This prediction of witness and martyrdom clearly awaits fulfillment after the disciples' failure narrated in the coming chapters. The third and fourth texts are the references already mentioned to "going ahead to Galilee" (14:28; 16:7). These texts imply more than a resurrection appearance. Garrett calls 14:28 "nothing less than a prophecy of reconciliation between Jesus and his disciples: he will 'go before them,' which implies that they will 'follow' him in the way" (1998, 144-45). Finally, 16:7 reiterates the prophecy that the disciples, highlighting Peter's inclusion, will return to follow Jesus.

(2) A second related prophecy that lacks fulfillment within Mark's narrative is Spirit baptism. This is promised explicitly by John the Baptist (1:8) and implicitly by Jesus (13:11). The Holy Spirit is not even mentioned in Mark's Gospel after 13:11. In contrast one can see how Matthew's Gospel promises the Spirit (Matt 3:11) and implicitly fulfills the promise (28:19). In Luke, the promise (Luke 3:16) is fulfilled at Pentecost and repeatedly thereafter (Acts 2:3-4). In John, the promise (John 1:33) is fulfilled in the so-called Johannine Pentecost (20:22). The point here is *not* that Mark must have some element because the other Gospels do, but rather that it is remarkable how well the other evangelists keep

their promises (and how well *Mark himself* does elsewhere), whereas certain climactic promises in Mark are not fulfilled.[41]

(3) A third promise in Mark that lacks fulfillment is the disciples' proclamation of the gospel after the resurrection. Especially noteworthy here are Jesus' words immediately following the Transfiguration (9:9): "As they were coming down the mountain, he ordered them to tell no one about what they had seen, *until after the Son of Man had risen from the dead.*" This highly suggestive verse receives further support from 13:10 and 14:9, which speak, respectively, of the gospel being proclaimed "to all nations" and "in the whole world." C. H. Dodd hazards the guess that in view of Mark 13:10 and 14:9, the lost ending of Mark probably contained something like the great commission of Matthew 28:19*a*.[42] Note that precisely such a fulfillment is supplied for Mark by the "Shorter Ending" and by 16:15.

Thus Mark fails to satisfy the expectations that he himself generated concerning a resurrection appearance and certain related themes. Russian dramatist Anton Chekhov said, "If you hang a gun on the wall in the first act, you must fire it by the third."[43] Mark repeatedly displays a gun, but never discharges it. This remarkable *non*-fulfillment of explicit and implicit promises, supported by textual, stylistic, grammatical, theological, and other literary arguments, strongly suggests that the Gospel of Mark has suffered damage.

7. MARK AS NONCONFORMIST STORYTELLER? THE ARGUMENT FROM LITERARY CONVENTION

If Mark ends his Gospel at 16:8, he defies the general expectations of ancient storytelling. This applies to both ancient fiction and ancient biography. Hellenistic fiction in particular shows a strong tendency toward resolution of the basic, underlying tension of the plot. There are five fully extant Hellenistic novels. Their plots have a basic, shared pattern. "Boy and girl fall in love. . . . Either before marriage . . . or soon after . . . they are separated and survive storms, shipwreck, imprisonment, attempted seduction or rape, torture, and even what readers and characters believe to be death [the apparent death motif], before reunion at the book's end."[44] Although the five extant novels vary this pattern in certain ways, the reunion is an essential component in all five. The protagonists in Hellenistic fiction "invariably overcome all their tribulations, to live happily ever after (the happy-ending feature being very much after the taste of the general public)."[45]

In this respect, ancient fiction does not always correspond to modern fiction. The latter does not always provide resolution; it may tease, goad, and ultimately undercut the reader's expectations. Hellenistic fiction shows less diversity. "With its low birth and unofficial status, the ancient novel does not know the many-faceted resolutions of the modern novel."[46] In Hellenistic fiction, a suspended ending in which lovers are separated and never reunited is unknown. Similarly, an ending in which the protagonist (apparently) dies and never again appears is not to be found. Separation of the central characters is the basic tension of the plot, and it is never left unresolved. Mark's Gospel fails at this point, suggesting either that he was indifferent to this conventional principle of storytelling or that 16:8 is not his intended ending. The Gospel of Mark does not necessarily belong to the literary genre of the novel; in all likelihood biography is a better generic classification for Mark's Gospel.[47] But if the second evangelist was acquainted at all with traditional narrative motifs and with the general expectations of readers, it would have been quite unusual for him to conclude his entire work with a pericope like 16:1-8.

Although the Gospel of Mark more likely fits the genre of biography, it is not at all clear that biography provides a parallel for the kind of provocative, suspended ending sometimes attributed to Mark. Several decades ago a study comparing Mark's ending with those of ancient biographical works was done by Wilfred Lawrence Knox (1942, 13-23). He examined dozens of Jewish and Greco-Roman biographical writings, identified a variety of techniques for concluding such writings, and provided examples of each. A partial list includes the following: (1) a description of the person's burial (Joshua, 1 Samuel, the Testament of Abraham, and several of Plutarch's *Lives*); (2) a summary description of a person's final prosperity, when the plot of the story did not extend to the person's death (Tobit, Judith, 3 Maccabees); (3) a summarizing panegyric or laudatory statement (Plato's *Phaedo*, Deuteronomy, Lucian's *Life of Demonax*, and several of Plutarch's *Lives*); and (4) a formal concluding statement such as "And here ends the story of King So-and-so" (Numbers, Philo's *Life of Moses*, 2 Baruch, Jubilees, 2 Maccabees, and several of Plutarch's *Lives*). The upshot of Knox's study was that some sort of rounded off ending, namely "closure," appeared to be the consistent practice of writers of biographies and similar narratives (1942, 17). Mark's conclusion at 16:8, therefore, "appears to be unparalleled in ancient literature of the narrative type, even when it is of the most sophisticated character. To suppose that Mark originally intended to end his Gospel in this way implies both that he was totally indifferent to the canons of popular story-telling, and that by a pure accident he happened to hit on a conclusion which suits the technique of a highly sophisticated type of modern literature."[48]

More recently Ben Witherington has stressed the connection between biographical works and literary closure.[49] As an ancient biography, Mark's Gospel presents "a vivid portrait through the chronicling of words and deeds of some great ancient person—in this case Jesus" (Witherington 2001, 42). But if 16:8 is the close of Mark's Gospel, then the readers are deprived of "the final key christological moment where the central character one final time appears on the stage confirming the main theme of the work" (2001, 43). Readers justifiably expect "one final revelatory moment at the end of the Gospel where Jesus' true identity would be made known to the disciples" (2001, 47). As it is, the last words spoken by Jesus in the Second Gospel are the anguished cry of dereliction, "My God, my God, why have you forsaken me?" Witherington goes on to show how biographical works of Plutarch (e.g., *Caesar*) and Tacitus (e.g., *Agricola*) had well-rounded, often laudatory, endings that provided proper closure. "Judged by ancient biographical standards," Witherington concludes, "[Mark] 16:8 does not provide a suitable ending, and likely would not have been seen as such by Mark's audience" (2001, 44).

The complex issue of closure and the Gospel of Mark has also involved comparisons to epic, tragedy, and other ancient genres, not to mention analogies to modern literature. The subject will come up again in chapter 5, especially in the context of examining J. Lee Magness's important study. For the present, it will suffice to say that Hellenistic fiction and biography do not provide an analogy of a radically suspended ending such as we have at Mark 16:8 in which climactic and constituent narrative traditions that are well known, preexisting, and that have been hinted at throughout the story, are not recounted.

8. DISSATISFACTION WITH MARK 16:8: THE ARGUMENT FROM TEXTUAL ADDITIONS

Many readers of Mark, beginning in the first century, have found the ending at 16:8 dissatisfying. As John Dominic Crossan observes, "redoing the ending of Mark became a small industry in the early church" (1991, 416). As we saw in chapter 2, significant discontent with the ending continued well into the twentieth century and persists today, although with less intensity. Does this dissatisfaction across the centuries constitute evidence for the thesis of Mark's mutilation? On the one hand, *modern* scholarly opinion is not evidence per se. In other words, the fact that many scholars hold a particular view is not necessarily evidence for that view. One must look behind scholarly opinion to the *grounds* thereof to find evidence. On the other hand, *ancient* dissatisfaction may constitute evidence and be especially revealing since it suggests that early readers did not recognize the ingenious literary strategy that some modern interpreters allege that Mark used. "[I]t is far more likely that the earliest readers would understand the literary conventions of documents such as Mark's Gospel than we do at almost two thousand years' remove, and that they would know when a narrative did not have an appropriate closure" (Witherington 2001, 46). So as a final argument, I include this point: the discontent with Mark's conclusion in the early period.[50]

The early readers whom I have in mind are particularly the other synoptic evangelists, namely, Matthew and Luke, who augmented Mark in their own versions of the gospel, and the second-century scribes who augmented Mark's Gospel even more intrusively by appending the various endings to 16:8. These reactions to Mark complicate the theory that the second evangelist composed a provocative, suspended ending of a sort that was common in antiquity. If this had been the case, why would Matthew, Luke, and the second-century scribes not have recognized it? It is perhaps conceivable that Matthew and Luke recognized Mark's literary strategy and simply chose for their own theological reasons to add further material, but why would scribes, whose task is to preserve texts (relatively) unaltered, have so flagrantly added to a document that was allegedly complete? Was it not precisely because Mark did *not* appear complete to them?[51]

Scholars sometimes speak of a "non-recognition" motif in the resurrection stories, the fact that Jesus was not always immediately recognized by his followers (e.g., Luke 24:15-16). There seems to be a much more serious "non-recognition" problem when it comes to Mark's ingenious, suspended ending. Larry Hurtado wryly observes, "If Mark did end his Gospel here, it would be an unusually clever and subtle device, so clever and subtle that perhaps no one detected his intent until modern scholarly research succeeded!" (1983, 272). Perhaps modern scholars are such good detectives because they employ the tinted magnifying glass of twentieth-century literary criticism.

In this chapter I have tried to set forth the positive case for the mutilation of the ending of Mark's Gospel. I have not attempted to address every potential objection to the thesis, and there have been many such objections and alternative explanations, especially over the last thirty years. In chapter 5 I will discuss in roughly chronological order the various alternative ways that have been proposed to bandage "the gaping wound." But first, I conclude the present chapter with a brief excursus on an intriguing, ancient reference to Mark.

EXCURSUS: *KOLOBODAKTYLOS* AND THE MUTILATION OF MARK'S GOSPEL

Hippolytus, an early third-century theologian of the Roman church, refers to Mark as the *kolobodaktylos* (*Refutation of All Heresies* VII.30.1).[52] The word is a compound of *koloboō* (dock, mutilate, shorten) and *daktylos* (finger), so etymology would seem to suggest a meaning like "stump-fingered." The difficulty lies in determining the nature and cause of the imperfection, whether the word was intended literally, and, indeed, whether it applied to the evangelist or to his Gospel!

Ancient opinion favored a literal meaning. Latin prologues to the Gospel of Mark variously explained the unusual epithet as referring to a congenital peculiarity or a self-mutilation so as to avoid the priesthood.[53] Swete thinks there is no reason for doubting that it describes a physical peculiarity about Mark, but he is agnostic about its cause (1927, xxvii). A metaphorical, but still personal, interpretation is found in the suggestion that the term may have meant "shirker," supposedly originating in the practice of self-mutilation to avoid military service.[54] Thus, whether Mark literally so inflicted himself or not, he might be called this on the basis of his defection from the Pauline mission (Acts 13:13; 15:36-38).[55]

Other scholars, including some recent ones, prefer to construe *kolobodaktylos* in terms of the body of the gospel rather than the body of the evangelist. Vernon Bartlet proposed this view about a century ago:

> [S]urely . . . Hippolytus cannot have meant in such a solemn, argumentative context to introduce suddenly and without explanation a reference to "a personal peculiarity which had impressed itself on the memory of the Roman Church". . . . Surely the term is meant in a self-explanatory sense, obvious to all who knew Mark's Gospel, transferring to the Evangelist himself an epithet proper to his work, which seemed but a "curtailed" account of Christ's ministry, when compared with the fuller Matthew and Luke—curtailed especially at the extremities, the beginning and the end. . . . Thus I think we may bid good-bye to these stories as to Mark's physical peculiarity.[56]

Inevitably, it has been suggested that *kolobodaktylos* is a *double entendre*, referring to both the evangelist as a "shirker" and the gospel as a "torso" (Streeter 1925, 336-37).

The interpretation of the word in reference to Mark's Gospel, whether in lieu of the personal meaning or in addition to it, is weakened by the fact that Hippolytus clearly understood it to refer to the evangelist. The context of the reference is a polemic against the heretic Marcion. Hippolytus observes that "neither Paul the apostle nor Mark the *kolobodaktylos*" corroborates the unorthodox ideas of Marcion. On the one hand, it is odd that an ostensibly pejorative epithet stands in parallel with "apostle." On the other hand, the same parallel excludes an association of the term with the Gospel, unless Hippolytus picked up the expression from a source and used it mistakenly.

What then does Hippolytus's peculiar nickname for Mark contribute to this study? Despite a number of ingenious explanations, there is no consensus as to precisely what the word means and whether it attaches to the writer or the writing. Even if a connection with the writing were certain, we would still be unsure whether it simply reflected an observation of the patent brevity of Mark's Gospel vis-à-vis the other Gospels or preserved some ancient awareness that the Second Gospel had been physically truncated. Ultimately, the epithet is intriguing, but neither probative nor corroborative of the thesis of this book.

NOTES

1. Tate (1994, 141).

2. Fusillo (1997, 210).

3. Petersen (1980, 152). B. H. Smith (1968, 2) describes closure as "a confirmation of expectations that have been established by the structure of the sequence . . . the sense of stable conclusiveness, finality, or 'clinch' which we experience."

4. B. H. Smith devotes entire chapters to "Formal Structure and Closure" and "Thematic Structure and Closure." See Smith (1968, 38-95 and 96-150, respectively).

5. *Inclusio* is a rhetorical term referring to the use of the same or similar words at both the beginning and ending of a unit so as to enclose or bracket the material and provide thematic unity. The unit may be anything from a paragraph to an entire writing.

6. See M. A. Powell (1998, 92).

7. Thus B. H. Streeter (1925, 336) referred to the truncation of Mark at 16:8.

8. Juel (1994, 115) quoting Kermode.

9. See van der Horst (1972). See also Danker (1963–1964), which adduces a parallel from Menander's *Dyscolos*.

10. Information about the *Thesaurus Linguae Graecae* can be found at www.tlg.uci.edu.

11. The very fact that nearly 30 percent of sentences ending with *gar* are interrogative sentences suggests the oral/dialogical quality of this style.

12. The only other New Testament example of a sentence ending in *gar* occurs in dialogue (John 13:13).

13. Dodds (1970, 847); my emphasis.

14. Two other "final *gar*" sentences could be mentioned: Pseudo-Demetrius, *Formae Epistolicae* § 21, line 8; and the Life of Aesop § 67. The work by Pseudo-Demetrius does, in fact, end with *gar*, but this is deceptive. *Formae Epistolicae* is a guide to letter-writing that lists 21 types of letters and gives examples of each. The alleged final *gar* actually concludes a four-sentence sample letter which comes at the end of the work. The letter amounts to a memo in the first and second person, more dialogical in nature than narrative. The Life of Aesop (see Perry 1952, 56 and 93), on the other hand, is a narrative. However, its final *gar* occurs

in a very short, paragraph-length fable *contained within* the larger narrative, and the writing continues after it. Moreover, the final clause of the fable is dialogue, and the direct object (which the penultimate verb lacks) can be supplied from the clause immediately preceding it; indeed, one manuscript eliminates the final *gar* by adding a direct object.

15. See Blunt (1929, 268): "Mark is no stylist; but could even he end his work with v. 8?"

16. Trocmé (1975, 67). Trocmé's solution is to attribute 16:8 to a slavish editor, a solution that strikes me as much less likely, all things considered, than the thesis of mutilation. On the stylistic question, see also P. Parker (1953, 120): "For all the compiler's rough Greek, moreover, it still is hardly credible that he closed his book with *gar*"; and Edwards (2002, 2-3): "The spate of recent scholarship devoted to Mark has succeeded in laying to rest, I believe, the pejorative judgments of earlier scholars that Mark was a clumsy and artless writer."

17. According to this view, not just the narrative of Mark is incomplete, but the final sentence as well. So Burkitt (1911, 172): "the clause is unfinished, γαρ should have no stop after it at all and it should have a grave accent." Vincent Taylor (1966, 609) calls a "lest" clause "the natural sequel." See also Metzger (1992, 228).

18. It must be admitted that the only other absolute use is Mark 10:32. This verse does, however, have a textual variant that omits *phobeomai*, and its exact meaning is baffling. See the appendix in Wrede (1971, 276-78).

19. The participle does not, of course, occur in the imperfect tense, but a comparison of the present tense participle of *phobeomai* with the aorist passive participle (the aorist middle does not occur in the Bible) is a comparison of verbal aspects identical to comparing the imperfect indicative with the aorist passive indicative. In the Bible the present participle of *phobeomai* occurs 105 times with an object (LXX, 91; NT, 14) and only 5 times absolutely (LXX, 4; NT, 1 [1 John 4:18]). The aorist passive participle occurs seven times with an object (LXX, 5; NT, 2) and 8 times absolutely (LXX, 5; NT, 3). A reasonable inference is that while the aorist is serviceable for both specific and general expressions of fear, the present participle is generally preferred for expressions that specify the object or content of the fear.

20. A second argument from grammar has been put forward by Gundry (1993, 1010). He argues that the women's silence was not understood by the evangelist as so permanent as to constitute disobedience to the young man's command. Gundry notes that verse 8 is introduced with the paratactic (linking) conjunction *kai* (and) rather than the adversative (indicating contrast or opposition) *de* (but). The latter is what Mark consistently uses to introduce disobedience to a command (1:45; 7:36; 10:14, 22, 48; 15:23, 37).

21. Metzger (1992, 228); Guthrie (1990, 91). See also Balz and Wanke (1974, 211): "On theological grounds, too, fear and silence can hardly be the last word of the εὐαγγέλιον Ἰησοῦ Χριστοῦ." Similarly, McDonald and Porter (2000, 290-91): ". . . it seems strange to end a Gospel about the triumph of Jesus on a note of fear and fleeing. . . . It would be difficult to construct the logic of the good news from this kind of conclusion," and Godwin (1979, 130): "*Afraid* (v. 8) does not appear to be a good word to end an account of good news."

22. Petersen (1980, 161) rightly says that "we expect the disciples to come to their senses—because the reliable narrator led us to believe that the reliable Jesus assumed, intended, and expected that they would. But when they do not the characterization of Jesus is transformed and the purpose of the narrator becomes suspect." See also Hester (1995, 61-62). In contrast, Tannehill (1979, 83-84) implies that Mark actually ends on a note of potential restoration and faithfulness since the evangelist has portrayed Jesus' words as trustworthy. We are to expect that what Jesus promised in 14:28, reiterated and clarified by 16:7, will prove true. But while the perception of Jesus' reliability as a character is surely sound, the failed promise of 16:7 is a glaring exception to this characterization. If the reader is supposed to understand that the promise of reunion in Galilee was fulfilled, why did the evangelist not narrate its fulfillment as he has done repeatedly for other predicted events?

23. Allen (1946, 48; 1947, 201-3). For other interpreters who construe this fear positively, see Lightfoot (1950, 88), M. J. Harris (1983, 16), O'Collins (1988, 499-500), and those listed in Lincoln (1989, 286 n. 8). For the standard translation, "they were afraid," see BDAG (2000, 1061).

24. Although Mark uses *tromos* only in 16:8, the related verb, *tremō*, is used in 5:33 to describe the reaction of the woman with a flow of blood. Even Allen (1947, 202) admits that this is possibly a reaction of fear.

25. Lincoln (1989, 285-87) observes that fear in Mark usually has negative connotations. See also Danove (1993, 176-78). Note also how the first evangelist has strenuously redacted this verse. In Matthew 28:8, the women "left the tomb quickly" (vs. "fled"), "with fear and great joy" (vs. "fear" only), and "ran to tell his disciples" (vs. "said nothing to anyone"). Matthew clearly understood Mark's tone as austere and felt obliged to remedy it. See also Williams (1994, 197-99).

26. Juel with Ackerman and Warshaw (1978, 170). Juel, however, accepts 16:8 as the gospel's intended ending.

27. Stanton (1909, 2:201); my emphasis.

28. Hedrick (1983, 262): "The unified witness of the canonical tradition after Mark is that 'Gospels' conclude with postresurrection appearances. Even in the textual tradition of Mark's Gospel one does have such endings to Mark." James R. Edwards notes that post-resurrection appearances are also prominent in gospel-like narratives found in the NT Apocrypha and Nag Hammadi documents. He cites fifteen such works (2002, 502 and n. 21).

29. In other words, what a Gospel could be expected to contain can be gleaned both from early traditions that preceded the written Gospels and from the broad outline of the Gospels themselves. While every gospel has many unique details and omissions, there is a kind of macrostructure common to the four. Mark's lack of resurrection appearances at the very least raises suspicion, and *when combined* with textual, stylistic, grammatical, logical, and literary arguments, it suggests something is awry with this Gospel. Although Lührmann (1987, 268-69) argues that we should free ourselves from the impression that a Gospel must in every case end with reports of resurrection appearances, I would assert that this "impression" is pressed upon us by the Gospels themselves.

30. Fowler (1986, 14). In the next sentence, Fowler goes on to call Mark "a crafty piece of narrative discourse." But given this extremely peculiar ending and the general simplicity of Mark's narrative otherwise, I would prefer to speak of a *truncated* piece of narrative discourse.

31. Moore, in Anderson and Moore (1992, 86); original emphasis.

32. Parker and Binder (1978, 131).

33. See Morison (1873, 466), Nicklin (1926–1927, 429), Creed (1929–1930, 177-78), Arndt (1955, 86), Moule (1955–1956, 58-59), Cranfield (1959, 469), Tenney (1963, 60), Campenhausen (1968, 61), Catchpole (1977, 6), Schüssler Fiorenza (1983, 322), and Brooks (1991, 275 n. 6).

34. Arndt (1955, 86); my emphasis. By referring to the messenger (singular) as "angels" (plural), Arndt is guilty of a little gospel conflation. See Matthew 28:2 and Luke 24:4.

35. One may compare here Mark 16:8 to 1:44. In the latter passage, Jesus tells the newly cleansed leper, "See that you say nothing to anyone; but go, show yourself to the priest." The first clause is quite similar to the penultimate clause of 16:8. Jesus' words to the leper clearly mean, "Don't advertise this along the way." Jesus does not exclude speaking to the priest, who is an obvious exception to the prohibition. It has been argued by Catchpole (1977, 6), Schüssler Fiorenza (1983, 322), and Magness (1986, 100) that the disciples are the implied exception in 16:8. Lincoln (1989, 290 n. 17) disagrees: "It is precisely the specific qualification of the general statement that allows 1:44 to be understood in this way, and such a qualification is absent from the description of the women's response in 16:8." I'm confident that Mark's lost ending contained some such qualification.

36. Gundry (1993, 1009); my emphasis. See also Williams (1994, 199-200 and n. 4).

37. Petersen (1980, 155). Petersen does *not* concur with my thesis, but part of his research, I believe, offers support for a lost conclusion.

38. G. Stanton (1989, 56). See also Kingsbury (1989, 113): "Predictions and promises made by Jesus are reliable and certain. . . . Since in the world of Mark's story Jesus' word is firm and sure, the reader is invited to postulate that also Jesus' promise about seeing the disciples in Galilee comes to fulfillment. To be sure, Mark does not narrate a scene describing this fulfillment. Nevertheless, he obligates the reader to project it." Kingsbury goes on to discuss three things that Mark would have the reader project: (1) an appearance to the disciples that involves reconciliation; (2) the disciples' coming to understand about Jesus; and (3) the disciples' coming to understand about the servant nature of discipleship. One can only say that, if Mark expects the reader to do all this, not only without any assistance but also over the obstacle of 16:8, then he has radically departed from his own custom of narrating fulfillments, and this at what would seem to be the most critical part of his story.

39. See also the cursing of the fig tree; Mark 11:12-14, 20-22.

40. One might consider the disciples' Galilean mission (6:7-13, 30) a fulfillment of the saying in 1:17; so Gundry (1993, 67). This is possible, but the connection is less explicit than with other Markan fulfillments of Jesus' words.

41. Gundry (1993, 38-39) suggests that Jesus' public ministry, particularly his

exorcisms, fulfilled 1:8. Again, this is possible, but Mark's pattern of prediction/fulfillment is usually more overt.

42. Dodd (1953, 440 n. 1). Raymond Brown (1994, 132) notes that "[t]he absence of a reference to *seeing* in 14:28 has led some interpreters to stress another aspect of the disciples' predicted encounter with the risen Jesus, namely, hearing and receiving his commission to teach the Gentile world." Brown, however, finds this interpretation "too subtle."

43. Quoted in Reedy (1972, 197).

44. Bowie (1996, 1050); see also Reardon (1989, 7).

45. Giangrande (1970, 739). See also Reardon (1989, 2): "[F]idelity to one's partner, together often with trust in the gods, will ultimately guarantee a happy ending," and Hansen (1998, xiv-xv): "A central trait [of popular literature], I suggest, is straightforwardness, the contrary of subtlety and indirection. . . . [A popular audience] likes plots that make their way logically and chronologically toward a happy ending."

46. Fusillo (1997, 226). Fusillo is quick to point out that closure in ancient novels is not always consolatory, nor does it exclude tension and contradiction. Yet it remains the case that no extant Greek novel concludes without narrating the reunion of the protagonists.

47. On the subject of the generic classification of the Gospels, see Talbert (1985), Aune (1987, 17-76), Burridge (1992).

48. Knox (1942, 22-23). Knox's method and conclusion are, I believe, quite sound, although he does occasionally overstate the closure-quality of Mark's pericopes: "[Mark's] endings follow the usual 'form' of popular stories which demands that you must round off your incident properly, *leaving nothing to the imagination*" (14-15; my emphasis).

49. Witherington (2001, 40-49; see also 416-18).

50. Gundry (1993, 1012) speaks of "massive dissatisfaction with an ending at v 8, a dissatisfaction best explained by knowledge that Mark did not originally end there." The dissatisfaction is evident. I suspect that the knowledge that Mark was incomplete was of an intuitive sort.

51. I am tempted to add the scribe of Codex Vaticanus to the list of those discontent with 16:8. At Mark 16:8 in that manuscript, the scribe concludes the gospel and leaves the remainder of that column *and the next column* blank, a phenomenon not found anywhere else in the manuscript. Could the scribe have suspected an ending was lost and left space for its possible restoration? See Westcott and Hort (1882, 2. Appendix, 29).

52. For a critical text, see Marcovich (1986, 311). For an English translation, see Black (2001, 116). Detailed discussions can be found in Bartlet (1904–1905), North (1977), and especially Black (2001, 116-24).

53. See Swete (1927, xxvi-xxvii), Hennecke and Schneemelcher (1963–1965, 2:68), North (1977, 499-500), and the explanatory note in Marcovich (1986, 311).

54. For a discussion of the ancient sources, see North (1977, 503-5 and notes). North makes the ingenious suggestion that *kolobodaktylos* was a Greek translation of an original Latin pun on Mark's name. The Latin word *murcus*,

meaning a coward who cuts off his thumb to avoid military service, is only one letter different from Mark in Latin (Marcus). This explanation is possible, but the sole reference to *murcus* is from Ammianus Marcellinus, a fourth-century C.E. Latin historian. The practice of self-mutilation to avoid military service existed at an earlier date, but the key word in North's explanation is late.

55. Streeter (1925, 336), citing Wordsworth and White's edition of the Vulgate. See also North (1977, 502 n. 6).

56. Bartlet (1904–1905, 123-24). See also Hanson (1962, 202), who thinks the word "very likely" referred to the state of Mark's Gospel. Jefford (1992, 4:558) observes that modern scholars often prefer the meaning "shortened" as a reference to "the abbreviated nature of the gospel text itself (when compared to the other NT gospels) or in support of the manuscript tradition that concludes the gospel at Mark 16:8."

FIVE

AN ASSORTMENT OF LITERARY BANDAGES

"Nowadays . . . you can always find somebody willing to argue that an ending, however irresponsible it seems, is right. There are so many professional interpreters around, and most of them continue to assume that if a text appears to lack coherence it is their business to demonstrate that the reality is otherwise."[1]

A few years ago I was reading scholarship essays for my institution's admissions department. Eager students, hoping to win significant financial awards, had submitted essays on an assigned topic to be judged by several members of a committee. Most of the essays were about two pages long. I began to evaluate one essay and noticed curiously that it was a single page in length. This struck me as odd. Then I noticed that the last line on the page ended in the middle of a sentence. Clearly a page was missing. I called this to the attention of the Financial Aid Director, who quickly found the missing page, but also noted that the incomplete version had gone out to the entire committee, and at least one reviewer had already graded and returned the essay without noticing that it lacked the second page. It is apparent that readers can sometimes make "sense" out of incomplete writings.

In this chapter I will examine the interpretations of several persons who, like my colleague on the scholarship committee, have succeeded in making sense out of a document that is, in my opinion, defective. In some academic quarters, this admission might seem to end the discussion and obviate this entire study. If Mark's Gospel can be adequately interpreted in its extant form, why would we entertain the possibility of its mutilation? First, let me explain why I concede that Mark's Gospel *can* be interpreted in its extant form. For starters, the resourcefulness of interpreters makes it possible. As Frank Kermode said in the above quote, there are so many interpreters at work nowadays that "you can always find somebody willing to argue that an ending, however irresponsible it seems, is right." The glut of professional biblical interpreters has increased in the years since Kermode wrote those words. Moreover, as suggested in chapter 3, the specializations of many of these interpreters tend to lie in the areas best suited to overcoming just such interpretive problems. A good reader-response critic can make sense out of a moth-eaten scrap of poetry from E. E. Cummings. Second, the preservation of the majority of the Gospel of Mark makes it possible. Even by my theory, perhaps 95 percent of Mark's Gospel is extant. One can construe even the authorial meaning of such a text with at least some degree of accuracy. Finally, even if we assumed that *full* textual integrity was prerequisite to discerning the intention of an author, that intention, as shown in chapter 3, is by many persons no longer considered the necessary yardstick of interpretation. So, of course, we *can* make sense of Mark's Gospel as it stands. The question is, at least for historical-critical interpreters, are we getting *Mark's* sense when we do so?[2]

We must acknowledge that there is a psychological tendency to impose closure. The human mind seeks order, and when that desire for order is reinforced by the visual stimulus of a writing's end, there is an even stronger impulse to find closure. Barbara Herrnstein Smith observes that "we tend to impose closure on what is known, independently, to be the terminal point of a sequence. If we hear a bell tolling the hours and know from a watch that it is ten o'clock, the tenth tone will be heard as slightly louder or longer." Since a writing is usually experienced, at least in modern times, from the printed page, "no matter how weak the forces of closure are, the simple fact that [the writing's] last line is followed by an expanse of blank paper will inform the reader that it is concluded" (Smith 1968, 41 and 211). Given the disruptions that often occurred in the transmission of ancient texts, however, we should remain open to the possibility that such a visual stimulus may be a sheer accident, masked by a neatly printed and punctuated modern text.

Advocacy for the integrity of Mark's Gospel, namely that the evangelist wrote 1:1 to 16:8 and no more, stretches over more than a century and can be roughly divided into three phases. In the nineteenth century and through the first quarter of the twentieth century, promoters of this view were few in number, negligible in influence, and often ignored. But in the second quarter of the twentieth century, their number and influence began to grow. There was a particular focus on the Greek conjunction *gar*, with which the gospel ends. This was the heyday of *gar* parallels. Adducing such parallels weakened the stylistic argument for mutilation. Finally, by midcentury, scholars favoring Markan integrity had become a formidable force, and sometime, probably during the 1970s, the consensus shifted in their favor. I have already broadly surveyed this shift in scholarly opinion in chapter 2. In this chapter I examine in more detail the third phase of this shift, the last few decades of the twentieth century. During this time, scholars proposed various literary solutions (narrative, rhetorical, reader-response) for the problem of Mark's ending and gradually won over the majority of New Testament scholars. I will here highlight the proposals of several major interpreters in approximate chronological order.

1. LITERARY CRITICISM AT THE BIBLICAL GATE: FRANK KERMODE

The history of biblical scholarship in the last third of the twentieth century is largely one of cross-disciplinary enrichment (or chaos, depending on one's point of view). Methodologies that were developed in large part for the analysis of secular literature (epic, novels, tragedy, etc.) came to be applied to biblical texts. Two broad streams flowed together here: scholars of religion who imported these methods into their own discipline, and secular critics who ventured outside the literature department of the university into the domain of biblical writings.[3] During the decade of the 1970s the Gospel of Mark was a particularly intense focus of literary analysis, and the ending of Mark naturally drew much attention.[4] Frank Kermode was a pioneer during this era.

Kermode was a professor of English at Cambridge University with particular expertise in the novel. Several of his publications touch on biblical texts; a few specifically treat the ending of Mark's Gospel. In *The Genesis of Secrecy* Kermode writes that "Mark is never more enigmatic, or never more clumsy, than at the end of his gospel" (1979, 65). Note the alternatives that Kermode has given us. Mark was *either* enigmatic, that is, subtly crafting a sort of nonending that is only appreciated by equally subtle readers, *or* Mark was clumsy, that is, ineptly concluding his Gospel in a way that many readers found dissatisfying. Kermode ultimately opts for "enigmatic," but it should be observed that these alternatives preclude the possibility of 16:8 *not* being intentional. Indeed, Kermode briefly mentions but never reckons seriously with the possibility of textual damage to the gospel. He writes, *"Let us pass by* the theories which say the book was never finished, that Mark died suddenly after writing 16:8, or that the last page of his manuscript fell off, or that there is only one missing verse which ties everything up, . . . or that Mark had intended to write a sequel."[5] Some of these possibilities are less likely than others, but it is noteworthy that four alternative hypotheses are swept aside in a single sentence. Elsewhere Kermode implies that such hypotheses do not come into consideration because they "will never be validated" (1978, 148). If by "validated" Kermode means "proved true beyond a reasonable doubt," then one can only agree but also assert the same about Kermode's solution and conclude that all interpreters should follow the example of the women at the tomb and "say nothing to anyone." But if "validated" means "shown to be likely or plausible," then Kermode may have erred and too quickly dismissed solutions that contravene a twentieth-century literary predisposition.

A preliminary question for historical-critical interpretation is whether the Markan text that we have is the one the evangelist intended. Just as we identify secondary additions with the aid of textual criticism, so we must be alert to the possibility of textual losses through the analysis of style and literary coherence. While some interpreters may, for methodological reasons, choose to bracket the question of textual integrity,[6] those who seek meanings informed by the author's intentions will want at least to entertain the question of integrity. Remarkably Kermode affirms this principle but does not apply it to Mark. He cites examples of how misprinted texts have given rise to ingenious interpretations. One critic interpreted William Butler Yeats's poem, "Among School Children," assuming that a misprinted phrase, "*Soldier* Aristotle," was correct. (The text should have read "*Solider* Aristotle.") Kermode says that we may applaud such ingenuity, but ultimately "the text to interpret is the one the author would have recognized as his own." Moreover, Kermode asserts that "we ought not to ignore available evidence to the effect that there has been at some stage corruption in the transmission of a text" (1978, 147). I would agree heartily, but it is precisely such "available evidence" regarding the corruption of Mark's ending that Kermode has ignored. The gospel that Mark "would have recognized as his own" probably was *not* one ending at 16:8.

2. MARKAN POLITICS AND THE ABSENT JESUS: JOHN DOMINIC CROSSAN

In a collection of essays on Mark's passion narrative, John Dominic Crossan contributed a study of the empty tomb story (16:1-8).[7] The study sought to show that this tradition is entirely Mark's creation. Crossan's thesis has three interdependent arguments, which effectively outline the essay: (1) there are no versions of the empty tomb tradition prior to Mark; (2) all post-Markan versions derive from him; and (3) the empty tomb pericope in Mark is completely consistent with and required by Markan theology (1976, 135).

In his first argument, Crossan discusses various New Testament passages that have been alleged as preserving pre-Markan traditions. If Crossan meant here that no *narrative* accounts of the empty tomb predated Mark, he would find considerable agreement. By the general scholarly consensus of gospel relationships, Mark's is the earliest story. But Crossan's thesis goes beyond that. He denies that Jesus' body was buried in a manner anything like what Mark has narrated. Neither are there any traces (let alone narrative accounts) in the New Testament that suggest any pre-Markan awareness of the discovery of the empty tomb "on the third day" (1976, 136-38). This first argument involves discounting the straightforward sense of several New Testament texts, even texts that describe wholly natural and plausible actions. His understanding of Jesus' burial ultimately relies on reading alleged subtexts and finds no explicit support in any New Testament passage.

Crossan's second argument asserts that all other empty tomb stories in the New Testament are adaptations of Mark. Mark is thus the "Big Bang" of the empty tomb tradition. Nothing preceded Mark, and everything after Mark owes its existence to him. While this is certainly possible for portions of Matthew's and Luke's Gospels, given their likely use of Mark, it is far from certain that John's empty tomb story derives from Mark. Indeed, Crossan's reasoning depends on a purely hypothetical intermediate step between Mark and John, the so-called Gospel of Signs, a theoretical source for John's Gospel that is itself much disputed. Source criticism of the Fourth Gospel is notoriously difficult, highly subjective, and seldom capable of supporting the weight of a separate interpretive scheme.[8] Crossan is trying to traverse a lake on lily pads.

Where this second argument especially strains credibility is Crossan's attempt to construe such features as the presence of the apostles, the guards, and Jesus at the tomb as redactional creations of the respective evangelists *in reaction to Mark*. Matthew's guards (Matt 28:4, 11-15) may certainly be his own redactional creation, but Crossan argues that they were created in order to address a Jewish polemic *that arose specifically in reaction to the Markan story*. Why this is more likely than a Jewish polemic against a pre-Markan tradition is not clear. Similarly, according to Crossan, the apostles appear at the tomb (Luke 24:12 and John 20:2-10), as does Jesus (Matt 28:9-10 and John 20:14-18), as redactional creations of their respective evangelists, reacting again to Mark's narrative, even though Mark has no trace of the apostles or Jesus at the tomb. In two different cases, then, different evangelists operating independently of one another remarkably create similar traditions *ex nihilo*, that is, without any oral or literary precedent. The usual scholarly explanation for similar but independent traditions is that they share a common source. But Mark cannot function as a source here, for he lacks these traditions entirely. For Crossan, Mark's narrative somehow prompts the creation of these traditions in two independent authors. The more usual solution strikes me as more likely: Matthew, Luke, and John got their shared (non-Markan) traditions from a common (written or oral) source that by necessity was independent of Mark.

The third argument alleges that Mark had to create his empty tomb story *just as he did* in order to conclude his Gospel. Crossan presupposes here "that [Mark] created the genre Gospel, and thereby created Gospel as we know it" (1976, 146). Although the latter half of this statement underestimates the contributions of the other evangelists, the first half would find broad agreement. But in the ensuing words, Crossan defines "Gospel as we know it" in a manner so freighted with further assumptions that it must be seen in full to be appreciated. "Gospel as we know it" is

> an intra-Christian polemic against theological opponents character-ized by (1) interest in miracles and apparitions rather than in suf-fering and service; (2) very little sympathy with the Gentile mission especially insofar as this questioned the validity of the Law; (3) an appeal to the authority of the Jerusalem mother Church, based both on the family of Jesus and on the original disciples of Jesus: the twelve, the inner three, and Peter in particular. (1976, 146)

Gone are the days when *gospel* simply meant "good news." Now it is a polemic that reveals the factious character of early Christianity at every turn. Given that Mark's opponents were apparition-loving, Gentile-snubbing, Jerusalem-hugging, Petrine sectarians, Crossan argues that Mark could not have concluded his Gospel with a miraculous apparition of Jesus to Peter (following the minimal outline Paul provides in 1 Cor 15:3-5*a*). This would have thwarted the polemic to which his entire gospel was allegedly devoted, a polemic that downplayed the miraculous and de-emphasized Peter and the apostles. What he created instead was an antitradition that countered the opponents' tendencies point for point. Thus Mark's Gospel virtually has to end at 16:8 with an absent Jesus, the Lord who "is not here."

There are several problems with this third argument. To begin with, how averse to the miraculous could a Gospel be that includes the baptism scene, the transfiguration, a leper cleansing, healings of the disabled, the deaf, and the blind, exorcisms, at least four nature miracles, and the resuscitation of a dead child? Second, Crossan does not seem to consider the import of Mark 14:28 and 16:7, which clearly refer to a postresurrection appearance. (Perhaps Crossan understands these verses as referring to the Parousia [Second Coming]. This unlikely thesis will be discussed later in this chapter.) Moreover, this appearance will be to the disciples, presumably including the eleven apostles, and to Peter, who is singled out as in some way an exceptional recipient of the appearance. How does this square with an anti-apostle, anti-Peter polemic? Third, although Mark has no equivalent to Matthew's, "Lo, I am with you alway" (Matt 28:20 KJV; cf. 18:20), it may not capture the full Markan truth to say that the Lord is absent until the Parousia. The Markan Jesus promises that the Holy Spirit will speak through the disciples after he is gone (13:11). Finally, Crossan argues that Mark's lack of a resurrection appearance is wholly in keeping with his theology. I find this dubious for reasons given in chapter 4, but even if we granted this, it would not follow that Mark created *ex nihilo* the empty tomb tradition. This is simply a non sequitur: "It was useful to him, therefore, he must have made it up."

Crossan acknowledges that his thesis is tripodal, that is, that all three of the above arguments must hold for the thesis to be sustained. In fact, all three are vulnerable. The first rests on idiosyncratic interpretations of several texts; the second on a hypothetical reconstruction and an elaborate schema of tradition-history; the third on a jaundiced view of early Christianity and gospel composition. The whole interpretation privileges allegorical and political meanings over historical and pastoral ones. At several points Crossan's essay anticipates what N. T. Wright would later call the "hermeneutics of paranoia." The simple meaning of the text is set aside; political maneuvering and theological polemics are smoked out behind every verse. In particular, "if an event or saying fits a writer's theological scheme, that writer invented it."[9] It hardly needs to be said that many scholars have found a much more straightforward reading of Mark 16:1-8 to be quite plausible. Some modest historical core of the women's visit on Sunday morning and their discovery of the empty tomb is the best explanation of both Mark's narrative and the other New Testament traces of this tradition.[10] Most important, the momentum in Mark has been building toward a reunion with Jesus in Galilee, granted, a reunion that is preceded and presumably followed by Jesus' physical absence. The final words of the young man at the tomb are not, "He is not here," but "there you will see him, just as he told you."

3. IRONIC CLOSURE: N. R. PETERSEN

Petersen begins his essay on the ending of Mark with a quote from Frank Kermode, who remarks, "we are left with a choice between saying that Mark was simply incompetent, or that the ending, though strange, is right if rightly (finely) interpreted. We have to explain why a book that begins so triumphantly and makes promises of a certain kind ends in silence and dismay, without fulfilling the promises" (Kermode 1978, 148). Petersen argues that the ending of Mark must be considered in terms of literary closure. Closure here refers to "a sense of literary ending derived from the satisfaction of textually generated expectations." The aim of Petersen's essay is to consider the closural qualities of Mark's ending and thereby "to determine whether it is an incompetent ending or a competent one when 'rightly interpreted'" (Petersen 1980, 152).

Dissatisfaction with Mark 16:8, says Petersen, stems from its juxtaposition with 16:6-7. The latter verses contain the directions of the young man to the women at the tomb. Jesus is going before them to Galilee where they will see him. The women are instructed to go and tell Peter and the disciples of this. But suddenly the text stops. The narrator's "unexpected *withdrawal from communication* with the reader is such that the reader is compelled *by the narrator* to respond."[11]

Petersen rightly observes that Mark 16:8 not only fails to drop the second shoe but also tells us to forget it. "The narrator creates an expectation and then cancels it, leading the reader to wonder why he raised the expectation in the first place." For early Christian readers, Mark 16:8 created "an intolerable discontinuity in the narrative and in the readerly expectations generated by it." This is particularly odd in the Gospel of Mark because, as Petersen notes, Mark's "principal plot device is one of prediction and fulfillment." Moreover, 16:8 "occurs in the context, indeed at the climax, of the greatest density of closural satisfactions in the entire narrative (Mark 14–16)."[12]

How then should the reader understand 16:8? Petersen suggests that there are two alternatives. If 16:8 is interpreted literally, then the women did not tell Peter and the disciples anything, and they (the disciples) are left ignorant, unrehabilitated, and ultimately repudiated by the author.[13] The problem with a literal reading, says Petersen, is that it reflects ill on the previous story in its entirety. It leads to a complete inversion of all that has gone before. The disciples never come to their senses; the explanation of the young man at the tomb is undermined; the reliability of Jesus as a character is in jeopardy; even the motives of the narrator become suspect. Mark 16:8, read literally, has a toxic effect on the whole gospel!

Petersen rejects this. The alternative, he says, is an ironic reading of Mark 16:8 (1980, 162-63). The narrator does not mean what he says in the closing verse. The readers must recognize the irony of 16:8, look back to the promise of 16:6-7, and themselves provide the proper closure to the story. The narrator thus provides only "an artfully penultimate closure," one which must be followed by the ultimate closure in the reader's imagination.

The weaknesses of this interpretation are its extreme subtlety and modernity. Because a straightforward reading is too devastating, we must assume a continuation that Mark has given us little reason to assume. Petersen's article, to my mind, actually makes a better case for denied closure than for this subtle, reader-supplied closure. In what he writes about author-generated expectations and the lack of satisfaction in 16:8, Petersen sounds as though he is arguing the mutilation case! He makes all the right observations, but reaches an unlikely conclusion because he has ruled out the most plausible solution. When Petersen speaks of the narrator's "withdrawal from communication" and the way that the reader is "compelled by the narrator" to respond, he begs the question. The expressions, "withdrawal from communication" and "by the narrator" obviously assume authorial intent. But if the gospel is mutilated, the reader's response may be "compelled" by no more than the accidental state of the text.

Petersen's essay is engaging and provocative as a "new critical" interpretation of the ending of Mark, and as an interpretation of *the effect of the extant text,* it is plausible. As an interpretation of the intent of Mark, *the author,* it fails. It fails because Petersen (along with Kermode) has assumed a false dichotomy of interpretive options from the very beginning. The alternatives are not just twofold (i.e., Mark's incompetence or a mysterious but appropriate ending). A third option is that Mark was a victim of misfortune, that the gospel bearing his name suffered accidental damage. When Petersen writes that "the text-critical evidence indicates . . . that Mark's narrative text *originally ended* at 16:8," he has assumed a literary starting point on the basis of textual criticism.[14] But textual criticism cannot deliver this; it can only indicate the *earliest recoverable* text of Mark. Whether or not 16:8 is the author's intended ending is a *literary* question. Textual criticism is incapable of answering this question, and most of the literary arguments that Petersen adduces suggest that the answer to that question is negative. It is precisely Mark's *lack* of closure (based on expectations generated *by Mark himself*) that explains the dissatisfaction so often experienced by both ancient scribes and modern readers.

4. MARKAN NARRATIVE TECHNIQUE: BOOMERSHINE AND BARTHOLOMEW

Thomas E. Boomershine and G. L. Bartholomew wrote an influential article on Mark's ending in which they analyzed the narrative technique of Mark's final verse. They identified three specific techniques used in Mark 16:8: extensive narrative commentary, intensive inside views, and short sentences (1981, 214).

By "narrative commentary," the authors mean explanatory comments by which the narrator interrupts the reporting of events in order to clarify something. One of the specific grammatical forms of narrative commentary used by Mark is the *gar* clause, almost always used to explain confusing or surprising events which have just been reported. In Mark 16:8 *gar* clauses explain first the women's flight ("for terror and amazement had seized them") and then their silence ("for they were afraid"). Boomershine and Bartholomew compare 16:8 to two earlier passages in Mark in which explanatory narrative comments come at the end of a unit: 6:45-52 and 14:1-2. Like 16:8, say the authors, these *gar* comments explain the previous clause but leave open many questions. Mark 6:45-52 is the story of Jesus' walking on the water. It ends with the description of the disciples: "And they were utterly astounded, for *(gar)* they did not understand about the loaves, but their hearts were hardened." The questions remain: What is the meaning of the loaves? Why were their hearts hardened? Are the disciples like Pharaoh whose heart was hardened? Mark 14:1-2 concerns the plot to kill Jesus. It reads, "The chief priests and the scribes were looking for a way to arrest Jesus by stealth and kill him; for *(gar)* they said, 'Not during the festival, or there may be a riot among the people.' " Questions immediately arise, say Boomershine and Bartholomew. Will the authorities be unable to proceed with their plan? Will Jesus escape death? The authors assert that the narrative function of the *gar* clauses here is identical to the function of the *gar* clause in 16:8. They do not wrap up the story tidily, but rather they leave loose ends "which invite the audience to do some work."[15]

I do not find the parallels here persuasive, however, because these two examples (6:45-52 and 14:1-2) are not stylistically abrupt at all. Entire clauses follow *gar* in both cases, in contrast to 16:8 where the *gar* clause is dead last. But more important, the questions that are raised are in most cases answered precisely because the narrative continues. Boomershine and Bartholomew admit this in reference to the first story: "The questions raised at the end of this story [6:45-52] are then illuminated in the rest of the narrative" (1981, 216). Apparently, the "work" that the audience is poised to do, Mark plans to do for them. The same is all the more true regarding 14:1-2: the ensuing narrative answers the questions. Mark 16:8 undoubtedly raises questions: Do the women never tell their story? Do the disciples ever go to Galilee? Will they see Jesus again? But if anything, Mark's earlier narrative technique leads us to believe that critical questions like these *will be answered!* There is a difference then, between the end of a *medial* unit and the end of an entire narrative. The former can have greater openness precisely because the story is not finished.[16]

The second narrative technique, intensive inside views, refers to the narrator's description of the inner perceptions or emotions of a character. Mark 16:8 contains two examples of inside views of the characters' emotions: "for terror and amazement had seized them" and "for they were afraid." Boomershine and Bartholomew then examine three other passages in Mark to show that it is characteristic of Mark's narrative style "to end a story with a climax of insight into the feelings of the characters" (1981, 218). After finding this technique at the end of the story about paying taxes to Caesar, the second passion prophecy, and the story of Jesus walking on the water, the authors conclude: "Thus Mark is *consistent* in the way he uses inside views to end stories. *In all four cases* they describe emotional reactions to Jesus' surprising words or actions."[17] Strictly speaking, this is not true about 16:8, for in that verse the women are reacting to the words of the young man, not the words of Jesus. But more important is the question of Mark's consistency in the use of this technique. Boomershine and Bartholomew compare four passages, but in a previous footnote they cited fifty-eight "representative instances" of Mark's use of inside views (1981, 218 n. 12). An examination of all fifty-eight passages shows that Mark uses inside views, both for emotions and for perceptions, at the beginning of passages, in the middle of passages, and at the end of passages. Indeed, the most common location for this narrative technique is in the middle. Looking specifically at thirty-six passages that Boomershine and Bartholomew have identified as revealing "thoughts/feelings," I find that the inside view occurs at the beginning of the passage in four cases, in the middle in twenty-two cases, and at the end in ten cases.[18] It is simply not true that Mark is "consistent in the way he uses inside views to end stories." Boomershine and Bartholomew have used a selective sample and reached a skewed result.

The third narrative technique examined by the authors is "short sentences." Boomershine and Bartholomew assert that gospel stories end on several occasions with a simple and relatively brief sentence and that Mark does this three times as often as the other evangelists. But the authors have a sense that they are sledding uphill here, for they acknowledge that neither the standard Greek texts nor a wide variety of English translations treat *ephobounto gar* ("for they were afraid") as an independent sentence in Mark 16:8.[19] A comma or semicolon regularly precedes these words. It is by no means impossible for a *gar* clause to introduce an independent sentence, but by the nature of the case (*gar* usually being a subordinating conjunction), it more often introduces dependent clauses.[20] The latter seems to be the case in Mark 16:8. Both *gar* clauses provide the reasons for the immediately preceding actions of the women at the tomb. Part of the authors' argument for construing the words, "for they were afraid," as an independent sentence depends on highly subjective reflection on how the verse might have been read aloud in the early church. They reason that since the words, "they said nothing to anyone," prompt the readers to ask, Why were the women silent? the narrator must have paused to allow the listeners "enough time to ask the question themselves. In order to allow that time, [the narrator] needed to come to a full stop" (1981, 222). Orality and aurality come to the rescue of grammar and supply the punctuation that was in doubt. More precisely, orality and aurality trump grammar in a dubious argument that appeals to the inner thought processes of ancient readers and listeners.

In summary, although Boomershine and Bartholomew present an interesting study of Mark's narrative techniques, the data do not support their conclusion. There is no question that Mark uses narrative commentary, inside views, and short sentences, but these phenomena are by no means limited to or even concentrated in closing verses of pericopes.[21] Narrative analysis of Mark provides just as much evidence for the thesis of a lost ending.

5. Mark's Apostolic Commission: Thomas Boomershine

In a second article contained in the same issue of the same journal, Boomershine extended his thesis by arguing that Mark 16:8 is "the climactic reversal in the motif of the messianic secret and that it emphasizes, in Mark's characteristic style, the same theme as the endings of the other gospels, namely, the apostolic commission to proclaim the gospel" (Boomershine 1981, 225). The "messianic secret" has been a concept in Markan studies for over a century.[22] It refers to the repeated injunctions in the Gospel of Mark to silence and secrecy regarding Jesus' identity, especially Mark 8:29b-30: "Peter answered him, 'You are the Messiah.' And he sternly ordered them not to tell anyone about him." (See also 1:34, 44; 3:11-12; 5:43, etc.) The methodology of this article, like the previous one, is narrative analysis. The bulk of the article consists of Boomershine's examination of three different interpretations of Mark 16:8.

The first is the positive interpretation of 16:8 as "Holy Awe." The outstanding proponent of this view was R. H. Lightfoot (1958, 80-97, 106-16). Boomershine argues that fear is not always negative for Mark. Earlier in the narrative there are a few instances in which fear is an appropriate response (2:12; 4:41; 5:42; 9:6).[23] On the other hand, Boomershine notes that the connotations of *flight* are shown by the previous narrative to be strongly negative (14:50-52). Finally, the women's *silence* in 16:8 compounds the negative evaluation of their action, for it is "the most blatant form of disobedience to a divine commission."[24] Boomershine thus (rightly) interprets the tone of the ending as chiefly negative.[25]

The second interpretation of Mark's ending is as theological polemic. John Dominic Crossan is the representative of this view. As discussed above in the treatment of Crossan's article, he sees Mark as engaged in a polemic against the Jerusalem church and its fondness for the miraculous, a divine, triumphant Jesus, and a mission focusing on Jews rather than Gentiles. The women, a group which includes the mother of Jesus (see 15:40, 47; 16:1 and cf. 6:3), represent the Jerusalem church, and their silence represents the failure of the Jerusalem church to accept the call of the exalted Lord communicated through Mark. Thus, in Crossan's words, "The Gospel ends in juxtaposition of Markan faith in 16:6-7 and of Jerusalem failure in 16:7-8."[26] According to this view, then, the readers are distanced from the Jerusalem disciples, both men and women, who are presented as negative role models. But Boomershine rightly insists that the portrayal of the women is "extremely sympathetic." After all, they are "the only followers of Jesus who risked being witnesses and mourners at his death and burial" (1981, 232). Throughout the passion narrative, the characterization of the women constitutes an appeal for identification with them. The "norms of judgment," says Boomershine, are conflicting (1981, 232). As readers we criticize the women's flight and silence, but we praise their devotion and faithfulness and are sympathetic to their plight. Since Crossan's polemical interpretation requires a highly negative characterization, Boomershine rightly rejects it: "The characterization of the women is in no sense a polemical characterization. . . . Mark's negative norms are directed against the women's *response* of flight and silence rather than against the women themselves. A valid interpretation of the ending, therefore, must account for the predominantly sympathetic characterization of the women."[27]

The third interpretation of Mark's ending, advocated by W. Marxsen and Reginald H. Fuller, finds in it a reversal of the Messianic secret motif. Throughout the gospel Jesus has silenced testimony about his identity and ministry. Now suddenly the women are told to "go, tell his disciples and Peter that he is going ahead of you to Galilee." This reversal was foreshadowed earlier in Mark 9:9: "As they were coming down the mountain, he ordered them to tell no one about what they had seen, *until after the Son of Man had risen from the dead*." The problem with this analysis of Mark's conclusion, however, is the final verse, 16:8. Mark 9:9 does, indeed, promise an end to the secrecy motif, to the containment of the news, and 16:7 seems to herald that end. But 16:8 retracts it. If this is the last verse of Mark, there is no reversal of the silence, only an unfulfilled promise of one.

In addition to the reversal motif, Boomershine sees the meaning of 16:8 as an apostolic commission to proclaim the gospel, an ending similar to the close of the other Gospels but in Markan terms. The women experience "the powerful conflict between responsibility and fear which is implicit in the commission to announce the resurrection" (1981, 237). The ending is a call to repent of fear and accept the responsibility of proclamation. Boomershine emphasizes that Mark is here developing the same theme as the later evangelists. This deserves closer scrutiny.

It is doubtful that the command to the women in Mark 16:7 is truly parallel to the apostolic commission found in various forms in the other Gospels. By way of review, Matthew has the classic call to "Go therefore and make disciples" (Matt 28:19); Luke's commission urges "that repentance and forgiveness of sins is to be proclaimed in his name to all nations" (Luke 24:47); and John has two commissioning scenes: one to the disciples, "As the Father has sent me, so I send you" (John 20:21) and a threefold commission to Peter alone, "Feed my lambs" (John 21:15-17). Mark 16:7 is not truly parallel to these commissioning scenes for at least three reasons. First, consider the scope of the command to the women. They are instructed to tell the disciples and Peter. This does not have the universal scope of the other Gospels' commissions; it appears to be an "in-house" message. Second and more important, it is not clear that the resurrection is the primary thrust of the message that the women are to bear. Of course, they will share that news, but the command of the young man is for the women to announce "that he is going ahead of you to Galilee." The content is not chiefly the evangel, the good news. The content is rather specific. The women are to remind the disciples of Jesus' earlier words ("just as he told you," cf. 14:28) promising a reunion in Galilee.[28] Finally, there is still the problem of the last verse. If 16:7 is an apostolic commissioning, then it is aborted by 16:8. The reversal of the Messianic secret promised in Mark 9:9 does imply that the news will be released, that the ban will be lifted, but we have not seen it happen by 16:8. Both the promise of 9:9 and the command of 16:7 suggest that Mark had more to tell. I believe he told it, and sheer accident has deprived us of it.

6. AN UNCERTAIN FUTURE: RHOADS AND MICHIE

David Rhoads, a New Testament scholar, and Donald Michie, a professor of English, collaborated in a monograph-length study of Mark as narrative. A major feature of their study is the analysis of Mark's plot and the conflict that drives it. Conflict in Mark occurs in various relations: between Jesus and the demonic, between Jesus and the authorities, and between Jesus and the disciples. The latter is especially important as the story draws to a close. Although the disciples make some progress in understanding Jesus' identity and fate, ultimately "[t]hey fail at renouncing self and taking up a cross" (Rhoads and Michie 1982, 96). The penultimate verse of the gospel holds out hope, however, in that the women are commanded to tell the disciples and Peter to go and see Jesus in Galilee. "Everything about this statement suggests the possibility of restoration." But then the ultimate verse of the gospel calls this into doubt. Although the earlier promise of Jesus (14:28) would seem trustworthy, "[t]he end of the story leads the reader to conclude that the disciples will not go to Galilee, will not therefore see Jesus or be restored. So the reader remains uncertain." By reviewing the narrative, however, the reader finds a variety of "clues about the fate of the disciples in the future of the story world."[29] Jesus has made prophecies concerning the future ministry of the disciples (10:39; 13:9-13), and he has issued "conditional warnings" that suggest the disciples may jeopardize their fate (8:35, 38; 9:42; 13:13). If the narrator had ended the story with the promised reunion, then the reader would be assured of the disciples' fate. Since the narrator did not do this, Rhoads and Michie argue, "the reader can *only* conclude that the narrator has *deliberately* left the future of the disciples uncertain."[30] The final resolution of conflict only comes when the rule of God is established in power.

There is much about the narrative analysis of Rhoads and Michie and other similar analyses that I find insightful and complementary with my own approach. Narrative critics have shown us not just *what* stories mean but *how* they mean. My only contention with their analysis, as I've summarized it above, is the statement that "the reader can *only* conclude that the narrator has *deliberately* left the future of the disciples uncertain." Even here my main concern is only to draw attention to the presupposition lying behind such a statement. The reader must conclude this *only if the reader assumes the vantage point of a narrative critic*. Axiomatic to this vantage point is the presupposition of the integrity of the text.[31] If readers are open to the possibility of textual damage, then they may reach the end of Mark and conclude that, in fact, it is *not* the end!

7. SUSPENDED ENDINGS IN ANTIQUITY: J. LEE MAGNESS

The monograph of J. Lee Magness is one of the most significant works in the shifting opinion about the interpretation of Mark's ending. His special contribution to the debate is the attempt to substantiate "suspended endings" as an ancient literary device. He acknowledges that Mark's Gospel stops short of describing the resurrection and offers no postresurrection appearances. Even Mark 16:7 "must be identified as an announcement in discourse form and distinguished from an account in narrative form." Thus, a seemingly essential component is omitted, which many have thought deprives the gospel of wholeness (Magness 1986, 2). "[T]he definitive place of the resurrection and appearance accounts in the kerygma [the core of early Christian preaching] and the paradosis [the body of Christian tradition handed down from one generation to the next] . . . makes Mark's omission striking" (1986, 4). Magness thus admits the oddity of this ending, but he challenges the assumption that full narrative closure is characteristic of all ancient writing.

Magness's second chapter examines modern literary theory on the phenomenon of "suspended endings." It is a complex and technical chapter, replete with references to Frank Kermode, Wolfgang Iser, Paul Ricoeur, and others. The gist is that communication involves both revelation and concealment, both statement and allusion. The act of reading informs and modifies the reader's perceptions, but it also leaves gaps. It "forces readers into a future of which the text is the foundation but they themselves are the builders" (1986, 17). The conclusion of a story is a critical part of communication, but not everything communicated by a conclusion has to be explicit.

The potential peril of such theory in a book on ancient literature is obvious: anachronism. The way modern authors, particularly novelists, communicate may not be comparable, certainly not in every respect, to the way ancient authors, particularly evangelists, communicated. The modernity of such literary theories, and specifically on the point at issue (endings), is unmistakable in Magness's discussion. Note the following four excerpts:

> Novelists and critics alike have stressed effective conclusions. *Well into this century* full closure was taught, practiced, and evaluated as the ideal.

> But it is *the modern novel* which has not only recognized the inevitability of the ending which does not end but has also exploited the power of the absent ending.

> The *modern novelist* E. M. Forster . . . bears witness to this tendency [for unchecked, expanding endings]. 'Expansion. That is the idea the novelist must cling to. Not completion. Not rounding off but opening out.' . . . [Literary critic Alan] Friedman . . . sees this yearning as *a particularly modern one.*

> It is not unusual for *the modern novel* to end with hero and reader

lost, the quest unfulfilled, and more questions raised than answered.[32]

But Magness is well aware of the danger. He acknowledges that "the leap from twentieth century literary theory to first century gospel is an abrupt one. Only if these principles are clearly present in the ancient literary context of which Mark was a part can we confidently claim that our assessment of Mark's suspended ending is anything other than a modern imposition on an ancient text" (1986, 24). The burden of proof lies on Magness, therefore, to demonstrate that *ancient* authors also used the device of suspended endings. His next few chapters examine literary endings in classical literature, the Old Testament, and the New Testament.

Epic literature, namely Homer's *Iliad* and *Odyssey* and Virgil's *Aeneid*, is the first testing ground of the hypothesis. Magness observes that the plot of the *Iliad* is set in the context of the much larger story of the Trojan War.[33] The plot of the *Iliad* begins in the ninth year of the Trojan War and ends with the death of Hector. Magness points out that events that are crucial to the war's beginning and ending are omitted. The abduction of Helen, the near sacrifice of Iphigenia, the Achaean victory, and the fall of Troy are all events insinuated by the author and known to the reader, but never narrated. The famous Trojan horse episode is not even mentioned. Magness concludes that "real beginnings and the real ends are not narrated; the cause of the war, the course of the war, and the outcome of the war are barely mentioned" (1986, 31). Surely, in the *Iliad* we have a classic example of a suspended ending.

Not necessarily. The critical question here is, What *is* the story of the *Iliad*? This must be answered before we can say whether the ending is open or not. If the *Iliad* is the story of the Trojan War, then without question, the ending is open. The final book of the *Iliad* does not provide closure on the war. But judging from the clues the author has given us, the *Iliad* is *not* the story of the Trojan War! As the opening invocation in Book One makes clear, it is the story of the "wrath of Achilles," and that story is quite fully concluded when the greatest hero of the Greeks (Achilles) slays the greatest hero of the Trojans (Hector). The *Iliad* employs typical closural strategies in the burial of Hector, the lamentation over him, and the Trojan funeral rites. "This is the end *of the limited subject* chosen by the poet [namely, the wrath of Achilles]."[34] Only if we understand the "story" to be the whole mythic tale of Troy, can we speak of the *Iliad* as having an open ending. If the ending of the *Iliad* were a true parallel to the Gospel of Mark, Achilles would have been commanded to go and meet Hector on the battlefield, but he would have changed his mind at he last minute and fled.

A modern analogy might be helpful here. One might say that Steven Spielberg's movie, *Saving Private Ryan*, had a suspended ending because it did not relate the conclusion of World War II. It began with D day, a point quite well into the war, and concluded with the saving of Private Ryan. But, of course, this would be to misunderstand the movie completely, which by both its title and the trajectory of its plot is clearly the story of one soldier's rescue. No informed viewer of *Saving Private Ryan* would think it had a suspended ending because the story did not extend to VE Day.

The other great Homeric epic, *Odyssey*, has an even stronger closural strategy. The far-reaching adventures of Odysseus come to an end. He is reunited with his wife and father. He exacts revenge on the suitors who have overtaken his home. This is a "closed and harmonious ending."[35] Of course, one can always point to forward-looking elements. There is, for example, a prophecy about Odysseus's new journey, and there are allusions to the later life, old age, and death of Odysseus. But the test of a suspended ending cannot be the reader's ability to ask what happened next, for this is always possible. Even the formulaic fairy-tale ending "they lived happily ever after" can be followed by questions: Where did they live? How happily? How long was "ever after"?[36] If an open ending is one that does not fully narrate the whole conceivable story, then *all* endings are open, and the category becomes meaningless. Magness begs the question when he says, "Even the ending that appears to include full closure can only close but not end" (1986, 34). The *Odyssey* has closure in that it narrates the fulfillment of the basic plot, the subject matter chosen by the author.

It is not possible to discuss every individual example adduced by Magness, but the critique given above would apply in some degree to the other genres of classical literature. The ancient tragedians, Sophocles, Aeschylus, and Euripides, used a variety of techniques to conclude plays without the usual enactment. Murders often occurred offstage, a scream and a messenger's report taking the place of the action. There were also prophecies and predictions of events that are not enacted. The effect of such nonenactment, however, was to provide the same certainty of outcome that enactment would. In Euripides' *Medea*, which Magness calls "perhaps the most dramatic example of . . . suspension" (1986, 38), the climactic action of the story is the death of Jason's and Medea's children at the hands of their mother. Although the heinous deed is not enacted on stage, there is no doubt that it occurs. We hear the boys' offstage screams; we hear the report of the chorus; we see Medea carry away the bodies in the chariot of Helios. Magness concludes, "The narrative has satisfied the expectations it created. Medea is avenged and Jason is broken. But the satisfaction is accomplished by a suspension—by a refusal to let us see the deed we have expected from the beginning" (1986, 39). The first two sentences are true; the third is questionable. The audience has surely been led to expect the deed *to occur*. But given tragedy's use of indirect revelation, the audience has *not* necessarily expected *to see* the deed. *Medea* has closure; it does not provide a parallel to the Gospel of Mark, whose culminating action is not only not seen but also never referred to as accomplished. Indeed, its accomplishment is called into question by the final words of the gospel.

Magness next considers suspended endings in the biblical canon. Again, the examples are too numerous to discuss in detail, but representative texts may be examined to assess their value in interpreting Mark's ending. A shorter narrative adduced by Magness is the miracle story of the widow's oil in 2 Kings 4:1-7. A widow's children are about to be sold into slavery because of the debts of the woman's deceased husband. The prophet Elisha instructs her to take a jar of oil, the woman's sole possession, borrow vessels from all her neighbors, and then, inside her house, begin to fill the vessels from the jar. The woman fills all the vessels available to her, and then the jar runs empty. Finally, Elisha instructs her to sell the oil and pay her debts. Magness observes that "the story closes with no word of the actual performance of the action or of the results of the action. Did she go? Did she sell? Did they live on in peace?" (1986, 55). Magness rightly intuits that the prophet's command suggests the outcome and substitutes for its narration. So should we speak of this as a suspended ending? Was not the obstacle to the woman's well-being overcome in the miracle such that the performance of the prophet's final directions can obviously be assumed? Magness would appear to join me in making this assumption, but if so, the story does not provide a true parallel to the ending of Mark. The problem of Mark's ending is precisely the fact that the narrative does *not* allow us to assume the actualization of the young man's promise (16:7). The outcome is left very much in doubt.

The example of the good Samaritan (Luke 10:30-35) suffers from similar weaknesses. Magness argues that questions remain at the end of this story: "[D]id the [wounded] man recover, did he complete his journey, did the Samaritan complete his journey? In short, we are left, at least on one level, still asking the question, 'What happened?' " (1986, 78). One can ask such questions, but they are not the questions that the story invites. Sometimes the perception of "openness" may, in fact, be a misperception of the story's purpose. Like the person who hears the punch line of a joke and asks, "And then what happened?" readers sometimes ask inappropriate questions.

Again, a modern analogy may be useful. Innumerable crime dramas in both movies and television have used a kind of ending that might be called suspended, but in fact provides closure. An odious villain eludes capture by the police again and again while committing a series of crimes. The story ends with the apprehension of the villain at the scene of a crime. The police handcuff him and lead him away. If the story has been well crafted, viewers will not need to ask, Will he stand trial? Will he be found guilty? Will he be sentenced? The apprehension of the criminal allows viewers to assume this (provided that the story has not shown the criminal repeatedly capable of evading conviction or escaping from custody). A truly suspended ending, one that would constitute a meaningful parallel to Mark, would be an ending that leaves the reader in doubt about the outcome of the basic plot, not about peripheral details concerning which the reader might be curious or about logical consequences that the reader can obviously assume.

Finally, two canonical examples of longer narratives deserve discussion. Jonah in the Old Testament and Acts in the New Testament are cited by Magness as instances of whole writings with suspended endings. I will treat them here in reverse order. The book of Acts ends with Paul in Rome under house arrest. The closing words of the book are: "He lived there two whole years at his own expense and welcomed all who came to him, proclaiming the kingdom of God and teaching about the Lord Jesus Christ with all boldness and without hindrance" (Acts 28:30-31). Magness no doubt echoes other readers of Acts in observing, "The tantalizing mention of the 'two whole years' impels us to ask, 'What happened then?' " (1986, 84).

The ending of Acts has occasioned a huge amount of speculation and interpretation which I cannot begin to summarize here.[37] Explanations have ranged from the death of the author to a planned third volume to the extension of the narrative to the author's day. It will have to suffice to make a few observations. I would grant that a reader could very plausibly have unanswered questions upon reaching the end of this writing. In that sense it might be perceived as having an open ending. But a good argument can be made that Luke has reached his goal at this point and that nothing is lacking. Acts is not a biography of Paul; it is a theological depiction of the spread of the gospel through key figures, according to a geographical plan that is as much a literary scheme as an actual chronicle of events. Acts 1:8 famously describes the goal of the apostles' witness (and simultaneously the plan of the book) as extending "to the ends of the earth." The arrival of the foremost Christian missionary in Rome is surely Luke's understanding of the achievement of that goal. Acts may not have the well-rounded ending that some readers would like, but its ending provides thematic closure on Lukan terms and, unlike Mark 16:8, is unmistakably triumphant in tone.[38]

The book of Jonah admittedly has an abrupt ending.[39] God addresses the prophet, condemning his misplaced anger and affirming divine providence and care over all creation, including Nineveh's residents and livestock. The most essential components of the plot have been fulfilled: Jonah eventually went to Nineveh and preached his message. We learn of Nineveh's repentance and of Jonah's response to Nineveh's repentance. The concluding exchange between God and Jonah allows the author to make a final point about God's mercy. The only omission is the prophet's response. Did Jonah learn from God, or was he hardened in his bitterness? Did he remain stranded outside Nineveh or did he return to Israel? We must, however, ask questions about these questions! Are they evoked by the work itself (in which case the omission of their answers is significant), or do they stem from modern curiosity (in which case the author has no obligation to answer them)? In other words, has the narrator generated the expectation of Jonah's response? The book of Jonah is indeed puzzling, including the question of just how much of a puzzle it is. The writer has presumably told us all that he or she thinks we need to know about Jonah. God's question that remains at the end is, therefore, probably addressed to the reader as much as to the prophet. For this reason, some readers might view Jonah as a biblical example of open-endedness. The book breaks with conventions in a number of ways; its ending may be one of them. Nevertheless, while the ending of Jonah may not have the nicely rounded closure that some readers would like, neither does it subvert the book's trajectory and constitute an anticlimax as Mark 16:8 does.

This discussion of Magness and suspended endings must itself come to an end. His study is learned and far-reaching, but I dispute his conclusion that suspended endings were a common phenomenon in antiquity. Endings of whole and independent narratives that leave the fulfillment of an essential narrative component in serious doubt are definitely *not* common. The closest possible parallel would be the book of Jonah, and even it has been called into question. Knox's influential article concluded that the book of Jonah could not be considered a precedent for such an ending as Mark 16:8 since Jonah's author had completed his story. The Gospel of Mark, on the other hand, stops just before the story's climax. It fails to reach its resolution (1942, 22). In conclusion, I would recall Magness's acknowledgment that the ancient use of suspended endings must be demonstrated. Otherwise, the construal of Mark's ending in this way would only be "a modern imposition on an ancient text" (Magness 1986, 24). I fear that the perception of Mark 16:8 as a provocative, open ending is just that, an anachronistic reading.[40]

8. PROMISE MINGLED WITH FAILURE: ANDREW T. LINCOLN

Andrew T. Lincoln's important essay attempts to correct certain imbalances in previous interpretations of Mark's ending by giving equal stress to 16:7 and 16:8. Previous interpreters have often allowed one of these verses to override the other (1989, 283-84 n. 2). In addition, Lincoln insists that the pattern that emerges from these two verses must be linked to similar patterns earlier in Mark. Finally, the content of 16:7-8 must be connected with major Markan themes, including the theme of the messianic secret.

The effect of verse 8, Lincoln rightly observes, is to undermine earlier expectations. Lincoln points to Mark 9:9 as an indication that the messianic secret has a temporal limit: the resurrection. So in 16:7, when the resurrection is announced, and the women are commanded to go and tell, the reader expects to see the fulfillment of 9:9. But the cunning narrator "has carefully created such an expectation only to shatter it immediately."[41] Lincoln sees Mark's ending as the supreme example of irony. Earlier injunctions to silence were disobeyed by persons who disclosed the news; now an order to disclose the news is disobeyed by persons who keep silent.[42] But the crushing failure of verse 8 is rescued, Lincoln says, by verse 7, which points to a time beyond the women's disobedient response to a time of restoration. "[T]he silence of the women was overcome by Jesus' word of promise. The word was fulfilled. Jesus did meet with his disciples and Peter, and they did regroup for mission to Gentiles" (1989, 292).

As attractive as this is, I do not think it works. The failure of verse 8 comes *after* the promise of verse 7, and the order is critical. It is true, as Lincoln says, that the promise of verse 7 is a promise of restoration after failure, but this refers to *earlier* failures: the disciples' abandonment of Jesus, Peter's denials, and so forth. The promise of restoration can undo all that, but it is contingent upon the proclamation of the news and the journey to Galilee to see Jesus. Lincoln appeals to "the Gospel's narrative world," which extends beyond 16:8 and has been foreshadowed in such passages as 13:9-13 (1989, 283). The implied reader trusts that Jesus' words will be fulfilled, and the actual reader knows that Christian history did not grind to a halt on Easter Sunday.[43] But 16:8, if it is Mark's intended ending, throws a monkey wrench into the machinery. It makes the implied reader wonder, Was Jesus wrong in his long-range predictions? It makes the actual reader wonder, How then did I hear the message? The gospel, therefore, would end with uncertainty for the implied reader and incoherence for the actual reader. A story is linear, and the final note of a story is critical to its interpretation; the alternative on which the series ends is all important.[44]

Perhaps, though, the negative ending forces the reader back into the narrative, searching for hope. Lincoln suggests this: "a recalling of the earlier threefold cycle [of passion prophecies] and knowledge of the fulfillment of its predictions will reinforce for the reader that the end of the narrative need not be the end of discipleship and that on the basis of the earlier story there will always be the possibility of discipleship's renewal" (1989, 294). Perhaps, but the earlier narrative might also lead a reader to believe that the promise is nearing exhaustion, particularly since the resurrection was supposed to signal a new era (9:9; 16:7), yet failure continues (16:8).

For Lincoln, the final word of Mark is not the word of failure, but the juxtaposition of promise and failure, a juxtaposition that he finds elsewhere in the gospel, especially in 8:27–10:52. For Lincoln, this pattern is descriptive of Christian discipleship, and Mark's use of it shows both his realism and pastoral concern. I will not argue that the gospel *can* be read this way; I have no quarrel with the basic theological outlook of this interpretation, but I do not think this represents the trajectory *of the evangelist*. Lincoln concludes his article by referring to the gospel and his own analysis of it in these words: "There is at least some plausibility about a story without a straightforwardly happy ending leading to a reading without a straightforwardly positive conclusion" (1989, 300). It seems that the good news has become ambiguous news. Was this Mark's intent?

9. READER TO THE RESCUE: DANOVE AND HESTER

Paul L. Danove's published dissertation combines linguistic, structuralistic, rhetorical, and reader-response methods in its interpretation of Mark's ending. It is an exceedingly technical work, in effect, generating its own "narrative grammar" by which to analyze and present the structure of Mark's plot. Although several portions of the monograph are jargonistic and tedious, Danove has, nevertheless, made a vigorous case for 16:8 as Mark's intended ending.[45]

Danove believes that Mark's ending should be interpreted liter- ally. When the women fled, they maintained their silence. The message they received from the young man at the tomb was *not* delivered. Their reaction was one of fear, not reverential awe. By the end of the gospel both the male disciples and the women have failed. Mark 16:8 thus frustrates the reader's expectations and engenders "a crisis of interpretation." The coherence of the story world is deconstructed, "leading to the entrapment of the implied reader" (Danove 1993, 208, 220).

But according to Danove, the gospel as a whole gives the reader hope that the failure of the disciples, both men and women, is not final. The narrative has shown repeatedly in earlier episodes that failure does not nullify the disciples' relationship with God. In Mark's large, central section (8:27–10:52) the disciples exhibit obtuseness in three consecutive scenes: Peter's rebuke of Jesus, the debate about who is the greatest, and the audacious request of James and John. Each of these scenes is followed by Jesus' further instruction, designed to bring the disciples to a fuller understand- ing. Jesus' unflagging commitment to them is thereby confirmed. The reader who has attended faithfully to these earlier episodes recognizes that the failure of the story is not equivalent to the fail- ure of the plot. The women's failure to report the message can be remedied if an alternate disciple steps in to fulfill the task (1993, 220). Enter . . . the reader!

Danove's solution then has similarities to other reader-oriented interpretations in which the readers, implied or real, must con- clude the story. There are at least two thorny problems with solu- tions of this kind: anachronism and inconsistency. But before elaborating these criticisms, I should examine one more study that inclines in a similar direction.

J. David Hester's study of Mark's ending is appropriately enti- tled "Dramatic Inconclusion." It is a narrative-critical study which, despite a heavy dose of the jargon typical to that methodology, offers many insights into how Mark's conclusion works in narrative and rhetorical terms. He analyzes the characters of the women in the crucifixion, burial, and tomb scenes (15:40-41, 47; 16:1-8) and the young man at the tomb (16:5-7). The special focus of Hester's study is the use of irony, not the traditional irony that pits the knowledgeable *implied* reader over against ignorant characters in the story, but a "higher order of irony" in which the *actual* reader knows more than both the characters and the implied reader.[46] Actual readers, who would include all modern interpreters, are in a position to "intervene and rescue the story" (Hester 1995, 86).

Rescue is needed because of the dire and contradictory circumstances of the ending. Mark 16:7 introduces the young man's commission to go and tell. The expectation of narrative closure is strong at this point "due to the trustworthiness of the implied author, and to the important and repetitive theme of prediction/fulfillment by which the reader has come to expect that Jesus will meet with the disciples in Galilee. . . . [T]here is nothing in the narrative dynamics of the story to suggest that the commission will go unfulfilled" (Hester 1995, 80-81). The failure of the narrative in 16:8, then, comes as a complete surprise, and the reader feels deceived for trusting that narrative completion was at hand. The sense of betrayal then escalates, for "if the implied author is unreliable, not only the disciples, but also Jesus must be unreliable. Actual readers are led to believe that they have been duped, and the whole story is a mockery and a swindle." Hester says that at this point the actual readers must

> enter into the story, search out clues to help them on the track towards fulfillment, and "go to Galilee" to see the risen Jesus. The story remains unfulfilled; it does not end this way because Mark has no need to go any further. I suggest that to such actual readers Mark fully intended to end the story this way. The author *did* mean what is not said, because it brings about closure *only* by forcing actual readers to finish it in their own interpretive way.[47]

In other words, Hester's view is that, in one respect, the evangelist intended 16:8 as the ending (in the sense that the evangelist neither wrote more, nor intended to write more); but in another respect, Mark did *not* intend 16:8 to be the ending, for he intended to prompt actual readers to complete the narrative beyond that point and thus to rescue the story from failure.[48]

Explanations like those of Hester and Danove are liable to the weaknesses that adhere to all reader-response interpretations. They are ingenious, methodologically rigorous, and utterly modern. If they purport, as it seems, to explain the deliberate plan of the first-century evangelist, then they are anachronistic in the extreme. It is beyond belief that Mark, a writer with modest literary pretensions even for the first century, could have had such a plan in mind. The highly nuanced distinctions of implied versus actual readers and story versus plot are thoroughly modern. As the ending of Mark stands, it certainly *is* ironic, but sheer accident is a far more likely explanation for it. This criticism need not diminish the ingenuity and rigor of such interpretations. They are valid, modern-day ways of making sense of the extant form of this ancient text. But this "sense" can hardly be ascribed to the evangelist. The locus of textual meaning has shifted over the last several decades from author to text to reader. While modern interpreters can certainly bracket the historical author when engaging in interpretation, they should do so with self-consciousness of their own historical perspective.[49]

The second problem with solutions like Hester's and Danove's is the resulting inconsistency in Mark's narrative technique. Danove rightly observes that Jesus is persistent earlier in the gospel, and this persistence could be construed as offering hope that the disciples' failure is not irreversible. But 16:8, interpreted literally, dashes that hope. At a point in the narrative that would seem to be most critical, Mark has not even allowed the promise of reunion and restoration to be heard by the full group of disciples. The hope that previously has followed failure is here not just unfulfilled, it is denied, and this at a time when readers have been led to expect its fulfillment (9:9). It is also unclear how the readers could serve as surrogates for the women. If the women had been told to proclaim the news of the resurrection *to the world* and had failed, one could perhaps find an implied call for the readers as alternate disciples to take upon themselves the evangelistic mantle and complete the plot. (One would still face the problem of anachronistic interpretation.) But the women are told to report *to the disciples and to Peter* (16:7). How could Mark's original readers, let alone anyone thereafter, have fulfilled this precise mandate?

10. APOSIOPESIS AND MARK 16:8

It has occasionally been suggested that what we have in Mark 16:8 is something akin to the rhetorical device of aposiopesis.[50] Aposiopesis is a technique of oratory in which some brief background matter is alluded to or assumed but not fully related, usually for reasons of modesty or passion.[51] The speaker in these situations edges toward but ultimately avoids saying something that might be offensive to the gods or to the audience. Sometimes the omission of details creates the impression that the truth is even greater or more egregious than an explicit statement would have suggested. Compare the modern politician who says, "I won't even go into the *personal* life of my opponent." At first blush it might sound as if Mark 16:8 could be categorized as aposiopesis, but a closer examination calls this into question.

First of all, this rhetorical device is not characteristic of the New Testament writings. One standard Greek grammar insists that "[a]posiopesis in the strict sense, i.e. a breaking-off of speech due to strong emotion or to modesty, is unknown in the NT."[52] In addition, aposiopesis reflects a degree of rhetorical sophistication that would particularly be out of place in Mark.[53] But beyond these general considerations, there are several intrinsic reasons why it would be a mistake to classify Mark 16:8 as aposiopesis. (1) Wrong genre: Mark is narrative, not oratory. While some rhetorical techniques, first developed for oratory, may be used in narrative works, aposiopesis seems distinctively to be a strategy of speech. It is not the same as the modern *narrative* technique of a suspended ending. (2) Wrong scope: Aposiopesis involves the omission of incidental information, invariably a single thought or sentence. The alleged aposiopesis in Mark 16:8 involves a major narrative component of critical importance: the conclusion to the entire story. (3) Lack of explicitness: Aposiopesis as an ancient rhetorical technique is unambiguous. The speaker explicitly says that he or she is passing over a certain unpleasant fact or unnecessary remark. In effect, orators tell us when they are using aposiopesis. (4) Lack of continuation: Aposiopesis is an omission in the course of speaking; the orator continues on after the exclusion of some detail. It would be virtually unprecedented for an entire work to conclude in this way. Whatever the evangelist is doing in Mark 16:8 (if indeed it is intentional), it is not aposiopesis.

11. THE PAROUSIA SOLUTION: ERNST LOHMEYER

Ernst Lohmeyer's novel interpretation of Mark's ending effectively solves the problem of a lack of resurrection appearances.[54]

He construed the language of Mark 16:7, "he is going ahead of you to Galilee; there *you will see him*," as a reference not to the resurrection, but to the Parousia. The primary basis of Lohmeyer's thesis is the similarity of language between Mark 16:7 and passages that refer unmistakably to the second coming (especially Mark 13:26 and 14:62). In particular, the middle (deponent) voice and the future tense, "you *will* see" (Gr. *opsesthe*), is the appropriate form for referring to the Parousia, a technical expression according to Lohmeyer. Resurrection appearances, says Lohmeyer, generally use the passive voice, "he was seen" or "he appeared" (Gr. *ōphthē*). This interpretation, while by no means sweeping the field, has had some followers.[55]

This view disintegrates, however, on closer inspection. Robert Stein and others have argued the case against Lohmeyer.[56] First, it is by no means clear that "you will see" is a technical expression for the Parousia. Matthew used the same future tense Greek word in referring to resurrection appearances (Matt 28:7, 10) and clearly understood Mark 16:7 in this way. The reason why references to the Parousia employ the future tense is obviously because it was understood as a future event, whereas the resurrection was understood as having occurred already. Moreover, the active voice of "to see" is also used for resurrection appearances (John 20:18, 25; 1 Cor 9:1). The Greek word used here for "see," like its English counterpart, is an exceedingly common word. The object of the seeing and thus any possible technical meaning would derive entirely from context.

Second, the language that truly characterizes the unmistakable references to the Parousia (Mark 8:38; 13:24-27; 14:62) would be such terms as "Son of Man," "clouds," "coming," "heaven," "power," "angels," and other celestial phenomena. This entire cluster of terms is *completely lacking* in 14:28 and 16:7.

Third, we must pose the question, Why Galilee? The mention of Galilee in both 14:28 and 16:7 undermines the Parousia interpretation, for the coming of the Son of Man is not associated with Galilee. Although the Parousia seems to be understood as a cosmic event to be experienced by all humanity (see especially Mark 14:26-27), if specific geography plays a part at all, the event is associated with Judea (see Mark 13:14).

Fourth, the corollary question arises, Why are the disciples and

THE MUTILATION OF MARK'S GOSPEL

Peter singled out? The Parousia "surely involves a manifestation to the world, and strange indeed would be a parousia selectively directed to the disciples and Peter."[57] The mention of Peter (contextual in 14:28 but explicit in 16:7), or even the disciples, is never a characteristic of the Parousia passages, whereas it is definitely characteristic of the resurrection appearances (1 Cor 15:3-5; Luke 24:34). Robert H. Stein points out that when the Gospel of Mark was written, Peter was almost certainly dead and the Parousia was still yet to be fulfilled. What would be the meaning of Mark writing in the late 60s about a meeting in Galilee of the recently deceased Peter with the returning Son of Man?[58]

Finally, the change in verb tense between 14:28, "I *will* go before you," and 16:7, "he *is going* before you," "indicates that what was in the future before the resurrection . . . is now a present reality for the disciples immediately after the resurrection" (Stein 1974, 449). This change favors the interpretation of 16:7 as a reference to a postresurrection appearance.

In sum then, the construal of Mark 16:7 as a reference to the Parousia is a very weak thesis. Mark's interest in Galilee is largely motivated by much more mundane reasoning. Seán Freyne's authoritative study of Galilee reaches the following conclusion.

> A consideration of the geographical data of Mark's gospel does not suggest that Galilee was important to him because it was the place of the expected Parousia or because it was an influential Christian centre in his day. Rather it was significant as the place of the first ministry of Jesus, which was an integral part of the gospel story, and had to be included in any authentic proclamation by the later church. (1980, 359)

12. CONCLUSIONS

There are many other scholars whose interpretations I have not surveyed. Most of their arguments are similar to one or more discussed above.[59] Perhaps the most common characteristic among them is a new emphasis on the reader's contribution to meaning. The abrupt ending of Mark is seen as a means to bring about a certain effect in the reader. The austere note of fear and silence with which the gospel concludes forces the reader to take a more active role, pondering such questions as, Who will report the good news?

Will I succeed where the disciples have failed? This reader-oriented emphasis is seen again and again, especially among interpreters of the last ten to fifteen years. Note this motif in the following excerpts.

> [Mark] wanted his readers/hearers to continue the story in their own lives. By stating that the women told no one, he challenged his readers/hearers to assume the responsibility of telling the good news to everyone.
>
> Mark's abrupt ending leaves it up to his readers to "complete" his Gospel in their lives.
>
> The women's flight challenges the reader of Mark to complete the story . . .
>
> The ending would call the audience to *continue* the story, expecting both successes and failures. The lack of closure helps to involve the hearer in the continuation of the story.
>
> The reader must decide how the story will continue, and whether it will continue in his or her own life.[60]

There is no question that Mark wanted his Gospel to have an *effect* on readers, not just a latent and abstract meaning for curiosity seekers. The question is, How did Mark hope to achieve this effect? Did he intend to use a harsh and disconcerting ending that left the outcome of the plot uncertain at its climax and, in effect, required the reader to do Mark's work for him? Or did Mark intend a more hopeful, complete ending that would fulfill the expectations generated by the narrative and offer restoration to the wayward and despondent disciples? Reader-response critics, such as Wolfgang Iser, speak of "gaps" in texts, lacunae that must be filled in by readers for meaning to be actualized. One scholar opined that "Mark's open ending is the quintessential Iserian gap, one to be filled by each reader" (Tate 1994, 141). This may very well describe the text in its extant form, but I doubt that it was Mark's intention. The "gap" at Mark 16:8 is much more than a simple assumption required of the reader, a filling in of information passed over by the author. Mark 16:8 is not a gap, but a dismemberment; the gospel does not need stitches, but a prosthesis.

The jarring force of Mark's ending must not be glossed over. One recent interpreter speaks of Mark's preparation in the passion predictions, in 14:28, and finally in 16:7. The final verse is construed (implausibly) as a note of "awe and astonishment." Then comes the surprising comment, "The promise given by Jesus . . . is about to be fulfilled. There is nothing more to be said" (Stanton 1989, 55). But Mark, by this writer's own accounting, has given us numerous indications that there *is* more to be said, that he is *not* finished telling the story. The difficulty with this explanation is that it requires us to trust or distrust the evangelist in a rather selective and capricious way. We are to *believe* Mark fully up to 16:7, so fully that we are propelled ahead in the direction of the narrative, like lemmings off a cliff, even when that narrative stops. But then we are required to *disbelieve* Mark in 16:8 when he tells us the fulfillment did *not* happen. Remember, 16:8 does not just fail to give us the expected fulfillment, but positively retracts it. The story is not told. The ending is fear, not joy. The revelation is stifled, not proclaimed. Whether that is Mark's intended ending or not, readers are left scrambling to make sense of it, to remedy by some means the deficit in the storyline. But can we attribute such a strategy to Mark?

I return to Kermode's alternative explanations of Mark's ending, "clumsy" or "enigmatic," and add the one that he omitted. The possibilities, then, are threefold: (1) Mark is an incompetent storyteller. He elaborately generates expectations throughout the gospel, especially in the passion narrative, and then clumsily fails to carry out his own plan. (2) Mark is a protomodernist. Two thousand years ahead of his time, Mark has hit upon the style of a twentieth-century novelist: a mysterious, suspended ending that teases the reader, first promising a denouement, then deviously retracting it. Or (3) Mark is the victim of accidental damage.[61]

So what is this Gospel? Maladroit, modernistic, or mutilated? The well-crafted quality of the gospel up to 16:8 argues against "maladroit." Logic and ancient literary conventions argue against "modernistic." As I demonstrated in chapter 4, several strands of evidence suggest that the peculiarities of 16:8 are most easily explained neither by authorial incompetence nor anachronistic genius, but by an accident befalling the manuscript.

If the ending is lacking, there are three possible explanations:

(1) Suppression of the ending due to something about its content; (2) Mark's failure to complete the manuscript due to his death or other misfortune; or (3) Physical damage to the manuscript, either a torn scroll or the loss of a codex leaf. Solutions 1 and 2 unnecessarily complicate the thesis. The suppression hypothesis requires not only a truncated gospel, but early Christian factionalism over resurrection appearance stories, allegedly due to their location (Galilee) or the manner of their portrayal (alternately too "spiritual" or too "material").[62] That such a controversy existed at such an early stage and reached such a pitch that bowdlerizing scribes would have intentionally suppressed a story are all unsupported hypotheses. Indeed, the preservation of Galilean appearance stories (Matthew 28, John 21) and of varied portrayals of the Jesus' resurrection body in other Gospels and Acts (Luke 24, John 20 and 21, Acts 9) argues against these hypotheses. Moreover, scribes who would have been so bold as to excise an offensive passage would probably have done so at a different point in the text, perhaps even supplying an ersatz ending of their liking. Solution 2 also complicates the thesis by requiring the evangelist's ill-timed death, or perhaps I should say, *perfectly* timed death, for the theory to work. While it is entirely plausible that the author of the Second Gospel died sometime in the 70s or 80s of the first century, solution 2 requires that Mark experienced a fatal stroke or was arrested by Roman soldiers just as he penned the words *ephobounto gar*. As John P. Meier reminds us, "A basic rule of method is that, all things being equal, the simplest explanation that also covers the largest amount of data is to be preferred" (1991, 67). By this rule, known as Occam's Razor, solution 3, accidental loss, is the most likely of the three explanations. In addition to this intrinsic probability, there are other corroborating data that make the third option most likely. These will be taken up in chapter 6.

NOTES

1. Frank Kermode (1978, 144). Kermode is here paraphrasing Parker and Binder (1978, 133), who wrote that, "However uncomfortable a bolus it proves, almost any ending can be swallowed by a modern critic determined to prove the unity of a novel, even when . . . events in the writer's life or sheer passage of time made the book conclude in a different vein than it had begun." The ingenuity of interpreters is also reflected in the statement of Paul Valéry (quoted in Wallace

Martin, 1986, 85-86): "There is no discourse so obscure, no tale so odd or remark so incoherent that it cannot be given a meaning."

2. Wedderburn (1999, 144) rightly cautions, "Mark's ending may undoubtedly be enigmatic, but that does not entitle me to claim his authority for my own existential interpretation of the enigma."

3. In the former category, prominent figures would include William A. Beardslee, John Dominic Crossan, Alan Culpepper, Jack Dean Kingsbury, Edgar V. McKnight, James Muilenberg, Norman Perrin, Charles H. Talbert, Dan O. Via, and Amos N. Wilder. In the latter group, Robert Alter, Roland Barthes, Harold Bloom, Jacques Derrida, Northrop Frye, and Frank Kermode especially come to mind. For a survey of this period, see Moore (1989, xiii-xxii and 3-13).

4. Moore (1989, 7).

5. Kermode (1979, 67); my emphasis.

6. This is typically done by narrative critics. See chapter 3, p. 43 n. 11.

7. Crossan's 1976 essay was followed by a similar article in 1978 that appeared in the journal, *Semeia*. Although I focus on Crossan here, his thesis was anticipated by Neill Q. Hamilton (1965) and echoed by Badham (1982, 23-24).

8. The same hindrances to source and redaction criticism of John arise in the case of Mark's Gospel. Even so, O'Collins (1988, 492-93) asserts, "I do not know any scholar who has examined Mark 16:1-8 to distinguish the source(s) from the Markan redaction, and who then argues that for these eight verses Mark had *no source* but freely composed the narrative on his own. . . . Redaction criticism supports the existence of a pre-Markan source and not the . . . thesis that Mark composed *ex nihilo* the entire empty tomb story."

9. See Borg and Wright (1999, 18).

10. See the references in Gundry (1993, 995). For other criticisms of Crossan's interpretation, see Alsup (1976), Longstaff (1976), and Craig Evans (1978).

11. Petersen (1980, 153); my emphasis.

12. All the quotes in this paragraph are from Petersen (1980, 154-55).

13. This literal reading is derived from Weeden (1971). Petersen presses it further to show that it necessarily leads to a hermeneutical inversion.

14. Petersen (1980, 152); my emphasis.

15. Boomershine and Bartholomew (1981, 217). Gundry (1993, 1018) disagrees, however, and argues that 6:52 and 14:2 do *not* leave questions unanswered, and neither passage presents the reader with the jarring contradiction of command versus silence that 16:8 does.

16. Indeed, Hedrick (1983, 267) asserts that none of Mark's major units ends inappropriately or with an explanatory comment. He concludes that Mark "tends to follow the conventions of ancient popular narrative elsewhere in the gospel."

17. Boomershine and Bartholomew (1981, 219); my emphasis.

18. I use the same unit divisions that Boomershine and Bartholomew (1981, 215 n. 7) used, namely, the paragraphs in the United Bible Societies Greek NT. The inside views coming at or near the beginning of a paragraph are 6:2; 8:11; 10:32; and 11:21. Those falling within the paragraph are 2:6; 3:5; 5:29, 30, 33, 42; 6:19-20, 26, 34; 9:6, 10; 10:14, 24, 26, 41; 12:15; 14:4, 19, 33; 15:43, 44; and 16:5.

Those occurring at or near the end of a passage are 4:41; 6:6, 50-52; 7:37; 9:32; 10:22; 11:18; 12:17; 15:5; and 16:8. In a few cases there might be disagreement about what constitutes the end of a unit (the last verse?), but my point would not be affected by the shifting of a few verses from one category to another. For those instances of inside views revealing "perceptions," the numbers I find are: beginning of a unit: 3; middle of a unit: 17; and end of a unit: 2. These observations are consistent with Gundry's remark (1993, 1011) that Mark sometimes closes a pericope on a note of fear, but more often he strikes this note earlier.

19. To the Revised Standard Version, New English Bible, and the Jerusalem Bible, cited by Boomershine and Bartholomew, one can add the King James Version, New International Version, Today's English Version, New Revised Standard Version, and Today's New International Version.

20. Boomershine and Bartholomew (1981, 221 n. 23) list several passages in Mark where *gar* introduces independent sentences. My own survey using the UBS Greek NT, 2d ed., found Mark's *gar* clauses following a comma 25 times, a dot above the line (semicolon/colon) 21 times, a period 12 times, a question mark 7 times, and a dash 1 time. Thus, according to these modern editorial decisions, *gar* clauses introduce *dependent* clauses more than twice as often as independent sentences (46 to 20). I also note that those *gar* clauses most similar in content to 16:8 are punctuated as dependent clauses (6:20, 50, 52; 9:6; 11:18).

21. Gundry (1993, 1020) points out that the brevity of some of Mark's *gar* clauses that do *not* end pericopes "demolishes the argument" that 16:8 exemplifies a prominent Markan technique. As in the case of "inside views," Mark uses short sentences in several different positions within pericopes. Moreover, I would point out that the allegedly complete two-word sentence ending 16:8 is shorter by half than all the "short sentences" that Boomershine and Bartholomew (1981, 219 n. 15) cite in Mark. The latter average over five words in length.

22. W. Wrede wrote the classical study of this topic in 1901. For an English translation, see Wrede (1971). C. M. Tuckett (1992, 4:797-800) provides an excellent, brief introduction to the issue. Wrede's thesis has rightly been criticized. See, for example, Moule (1978).

23. A more negative and, I think, more accurate interpretation of "fear" in Mark's Gospel can be found in Lincoln (1989, 285-87).

24. Boomershine (1981, 229). Boomershine construes (correctly, no doubt) the young man at the tomb as a divine messenger.

25. See above, chapter 4, part 3: "Gospel of Gloom? The Argument from Theology or Mood." Williams is even less sanguine (1994, 197): "Every aspect of the women's response in Mk 16.8 is negative."

26. Boomershine (1981, 230). Boomershine (1981, 231 n. 20) points out, however, that only Mary is a relative of Jesus, and she is the only woman who has been characterized prior to 15:40. Moreover, "a Marcan polemic against the mother of Jesus seems somewhat improbable."

27. Boomershine (1981, 233); original emphasis.

28. See Lincoln (1989, 297 n. 36) and Williams (1994, 202 n. 1).

29. Last three quotes, Rhoads and Michie (1982, 97).

30. Rhoads and Michie (1982, 99); my emphasis.

31. See chapter 3, page 43, note 11. See also David Lee's criticism of Rhoads in Lee (1999, 137 n. 55).

32. Magness (1986, 20-21); my emphasis in each case.

33. The distinction between plot and story is important to Magness, who emphasizes that the two are not coterminous. I do not find this language particularly helpful. I would prefer to speak of story versus mythic or historical context.

34. Fusillo (1997, 213); my emphasis.

35. Fusillo (1997, 214).

36. See Richter's comments on this fairy-tale ending and the question of openness in general (1974, 1-21).

37. See any recent critical commentary on Acts, such as Witherington (1998, 807-16) or Johnson (1992, 473-76). Fitzmyer (1998, 791-92) has an especially helpful discussion of the ending.

38. Acts 28:30-31 can certainly be seen as providing formal closure since it amounts to a summary statement of the type used frequently in Acts. Metzger (1994, 444) speaks of the "artistic literary cadence of the concluding phrase" and of the "powerful note of triumph expressed" by the final word. This is scarcely analogous to Mark 16:8.

39. On Jonah and closure, in addition to critical commentaries, see Crouch (1994) and (2000, 177-92).

40. I thus agree with R. T. France (2002, 671 n. 6), who concludes, "It must be for the reader to judge whether any of Magness's examples are really parallel in terms of literary effect to the supposed impact of Mark's 'absent ending', but my own impression is that (quite apart from the question of how far it is literarily appropriate to compare Mark with, say, a Greek tragedy, epic, or romance) few if any of them give quite the same jolt and sense of having been cheated which I feel when I reach Mark 16:8 and find nothing to follow."

41. Lincoln (1989, 290-91). Reader-response critics would argue that the forming of expectations followed by their undermining is a common way in which an author "educates" a reader. See Lincoln (1989, 295 n. 31). The critical question is whether this was a practice among *ancient* authors.

42. On irony in Mark, see the authors listed in Lincoln (1989, 291 n. 20), as well as Via (1988), Camery-Hoggatt (1992), and Hester (1995).

43. The "implied reader" is a technical term of narrative criticism. It is a theoretical construct referring to a reader who is informed and shaped purely by the text. The implied reader accepts the assumptions of the text (e.g., Jesus can perform miracles) and knows only what the text communicates (e.g., the implied reader of Mark does not know that Jesus is born of a virgin). In contrast, an actual reader may share or resist the assumptions of the text and will have knowledge from other sources. For example, an actual reader of Mark in the twenty-first century knows that the news of the resurrection was reported, whether by the women or by someone else.

44. It is, therefore, hard for me to accept Juel's conclusion (1994, 116) that "Mark's Gospel ends with both hope and disappointment." If we understand 16:8 as the intended ending, it would seem to crush, or at the very least, cast great doubt over the hopefulness of the message.

45. See the critique of Danove in France (2002, 673 n. 12). My summary draws chiefly from Danove's eighth chapter (1993, 203-30).

46. See note 43 above for the distinction between implied readers and actual readers.

47. This and the previous quote, Hester (1995, 83); original emphasis.

48. This interpretation has some similarity to that of Camery-Hoggatt (1992, 11): "the ironies of the final verse leave the reader with an enormous residue of unfinished readerly work."

49. Danove asserts that there are scriptural precedents for Mark's entrapment of the reader, and thus "the proposed interpretation, despite its dependence on modern theories of narrative analysis, is fully consonant with the conventions available to the real author" (1993, 225). In particular, Danove appeals to Nathan's parable of the rich man (2 Sam 12:1-12) and the book of Jonah. I am not at all convinced that these examples substantiate the claim. Nathan's story is transparently designed to entrap King David. It has nothing of the alleged openness and subtlety of Mark's ending. Even Jonah, although admittedly abrupt in its ending, has made its point quite completely. Neither of these stories has the glaring irresolution of Mark's Gospel, and neither requires readerly work to complete the essential narrative.

50. Magness (1986, 26-28), for example, sees aposiopesis and other rhetoric devices as part of the background for Mark's ending.

51. See Smyth (1956, 674 § 3015), Blass and Debrunner (1961, 255 § 482), and Lausberg (1998, 394 § 887-89). References to the ancient rhetoricians are given in Lausberg.

52. Blass and Debrunner (1961, 255 § 482).

53. Balz and Wanke (1974, 9:211) say that "aposiopesis . . . can hardly be presupposed in M[ar]k."

54. See Lohmeyer (1936, 10-14) and (1951, 356).

55. See Marxsen (1969, 83-95), Weeden (1971,111-17), Perrin (1977, 26-27), and, tentatively, Fenton (1990, 590). See also the list in Stein (1974, 445 n. 2).

56. Stein (1974, 445-52); reprinted in Stein (1991,135-45). See also Burkill (1963, 255-57), Taylor (1966, 608), Strecker (1968, 421-42), Stemberger (1974, 427-29), Pesch (1976, 2:540), O'Collins (1988, 495-96), Lincoln (1989, 285), and Brown (1994, 132-33).

57. Brown (1994, 132). On this point, see also Burkill (1963, 256).

58. Stein (1974, 450). As Stein rightly argues, the possible symbolic significance of "Peter" does not remove this difficulty. Whatever else Peter might have been to Mark, he was a historical person.

59. For instance, Collins's interpretation (1992, 119-48) is similar in several respects to Crossan's. Juel's (1994, 107-21) is indebted to Kermode and Lincoln.

60. Respectively, Brooks (1991, 275), van Linden (1983, 85), Perkins (1992, 36), Dewey (1994, 156, original emphasis), and Boring (1990, 69). See also Reddish (1997, 106): "The ending of the Gospel is continually being written"; W. Reiser (2000, 215): "each of us supplies an ending and brings the Gospel to completion as we seek to live Mark's text day by day"; and Hays (1996, 93): "Mark's Gospel ends without closure, requiring readers to supply the imaginative completion of the message in their own lives."

61. Like Kermode, Magness (1986, 12-13) envisions the first two alternatives when he asks, "Is [Mark] an unpolished writer who does not know how to end a narrative or a skillful impressionistic writer adept at suggestion and surprise?"

62. See the discussion of all three possibilities in Branscomb (1937, 310-11) and Creed (1929–1930, 175-76). Deliberate suppression of the ending is favored by Rohrbach (1894), Goguel (1909, 301), Lowrie (1929, 554), Williams (1951, 44-45), and Vielhauer (1975, 348). Burkitt (1903–1904, 342) argues for accidental mutilation over deliberate suppression on the basis of the odd location of the break.

Six

FRONTAL DAMAGE

A whole is that which has a beginning, middle, and end. A beginning is that which does not itself follow necessarily from something else, but after which a further event or process naturally occurs.[1]

Dionysius of Halicarnassus, a rhetorician in Rome during the waning years of the first century B.C.E., wrote an essay on Thucydides in which he noted that some critics faulted the great historian for the arrangement of his work. They complained that Thucydides "neither chose the beginning of the history that was needed, nor did he fit it with a suitable ending." These critics insisted that "by no means the least important part of good arrangement was to choose a beginning, prior to which there would be nothing, and to conclude the matter with an ending in which nothing seemed to be lacking."[2]

If we overlook for the moment the significant differences in literary terms between Thucydides' history and the Gospel of Mark, we might find it remarkable how the same criticism has been leveled against the author of the Second Gospel. The oddity of Mark's ending at 16:8 has often been observed, as the previous chapters have shown, but the Gospel's beginning is also inauspicious. Does Mark, like Thucydides, suffer from faulty arrangement? This chapter will examine the beginning of Mark's Gospel and propose, or in truth, recall and corroborate, a rather pedestrian explanation of its many peculiarities.

1. AN INAUSPICIOUS START FOR A GOSPEL

We may begin by considering two independent descriptions of Mark's beginning given by eminent scholars writing fifty years apart. First, T. W. Manson, writing shortly before the midpoint of the twentieth century, observed: "The opening of Mark has long been as difficult a problem to commentators as its close, in some ways even more difficult. Verse 1 offers a subject with no predicate; verses 2 and 3 a subordinate clause with no main clause; and verse 4 gives a statement of fact about John the Baptist, which seems to have some links in thought with what has gone before, but no obvious grammatical connexion."[3] Manson thus highlights grammatical, logical, and stylistic difficulties.

Much more recently John P. Meier described the problems of Mark's opening with these words: "From the initial words of v 1 onward, the entire pericope is plagued with minor problems of grammar and syntax, medium problems of text criticism, and major problems of overall meaning."[4] The syntactical problem that Meier has in mind is similar to those pointed out by Manson. How does Mark 1:1 connect with what follows? The textual problem he mentions concerns the precise wording of verse 1, primarily how many and which modifiers attach to the word "gospel." The larger interpretive problem is the determination of precisely what the evangelist means by "the beginning of the gospel." These remarks by Manson and Meier call attention to three types of problems in Mark's beginning. I will begin with the textual problem.

2. THE TEXTUAL PROBLEM

The textual problem in Mark 1:1, although overshadowed by the more famous problem related to the gospel's ending, has nevertheless received a significant amount of attention.[5] It is unfortunate, however, that the textual issue of Mark 1:1 has frequently been oversimplified as a choice between the presence or absence of the words "Son of God." While it is true that most of the textual witnesses support one of these two possibilities, there are several other variant readings, and the "Son of God" reading is divided against itself since there are two variations of it. In fact, there are not two, but at least nine textual variants for Mark 1:1. The standard edition of the Greek New Testament presents the following six options with their supporting evidence from Greek manuscripts, early versions, and quotations in early church writers.[6]

1. *archē tou euangeliou*, "The beginning of the Gospel," Irenaeus, Epiphanius

2. *archē tou euangeliou Iēsou*, "The beginning of the Gospel of Jesus," codex 28

3. *archē tou euangeliou Iēsou Christou*, "The beginning of the Gospel of Jesus Christ," codices ℵ and Θ, some Coptic, Armenian, and Georgian manuscripts, Origen, Jerome, and others

4. *archē tou euangeliou Iēsou Christou huiou theou*, "The beginning of the Gospel of Jesus Christ, Son of God," a corrector of codex ℵ, codices B, D, L, W, and 2427

5. *archē tou euangeliou Iēsou Christou huiou tou theou*, "The beginning of the Gospel of Jesus Christ, Son of [the] God," codex A and a very large number of other Greek manuscripts, some Ethiopic, Georgian, and Slavic manuscripts

6. *archē tou euangeliou Iēsou Christou huiou tou kuriou* "The beginning of the Gospel of Jesus Christ, Son of the Lord," manuscript 1241

A seventh variant is found in three Vulgate (Latin) manuscripts which read: *Initium evangelii domini nostri Iesu Christi filii dei*, "[The] beginning of the gospel of our Lord Jesus Christ, Son of God."[7]

115

These Latin manuscripts presuppose the following Greek original:

7. *archē tou euangeliou kuriou hēmōn Iēsou Christou huiou theou*,
   "The Beginning of the Gospel of our Lord Jesus Christ,
   the Son of God"

An eighth variant has been either overlooked or incorrectly cited in many editions of the Greek New Testament. In the Palestinian Syriac version Mark 1:1 lacks the word *beginning* and adds "Lord" to Jesus' name. Thus the Syriac version would suggest the following Greek variant:[8]

8. *Euangelion tou kuriou Iēsou Christou*, "The Gospel of the Lord
   Jesus Christ"

Finally, Peter Head notes that an Arabic manuscript preserves an unusual form of Mark 1:1 which has previously been overlooked.[9] This variant, which brings the total to nine, would be the following in Greek:

9. *archē tou euangeliou Iēsou tou huiou tou theou tou zōntos*, "The
   beginning of the Gospel of Jesus, the Son of the living God."

When the textual problem is falsely reduced to the presence or absence of the words "Son of God," the readings are usually explained in one of two ways. Either the words were original and were omitted due to an error of the eye, or they were absent from the original and were added due to the tendency of scribes to expand titles or quasi titles. The likelihood of such words being omitted, it is argued, would have been increased by the scribal practice of *nomina sacra*. *Nomina sacra*, or "sacred names," were special abbreviations of divine names and related terms: God, Son, Lord, Jesus, Christ, and so forth. They were contracted by writing only the first and last letters of the word and placing a superscript line above them. While this practice *might* have led to the omission of the words "Son of God" from some manuscripts of Mark 1:1, Peter Head reminds us that *nomina sacra* were not simply time-saving devices. Indeed, since they were written with a special superscript line, the practice was "apparently designed to draw attention to and protect the highlighted terms."[10]

Another consideration is even more important. Peter Head and Bart Ehrman, in independent studies, have argued that an accidental error would be particularly unlikely *in the very first line of a text*. Ehrman's comments are worth quoting at length:[11]

> It should strike us as somewhat odd that the kind of careless mistake alleged to have occurred here, the omission of two rather important words, should have happened precisely where it does—within the first six words of the beginning of a book. . . . [I]t seems at least antecedently probable that a scribe would begin his work on Mark's Gospel only after having made a clean break, say, with Matthew, and that he would plunge into his work with renewed strength and vigor. So that this does not appear simply to be the romantic notion of a twentieth-century critic, I should note that recent manuscript analyses have indeed demonstrated that scribes were more conscientious transcribers at the beginning of a document.

This observation and others, Head and Ehrman contend, make the shorter text, that is, the one lacking the words "Son of God," more likely original, and if we were faced with a simple choice of the presence or absence of these words, the arguments of Head and Ehrman would compel this decision. But I would apply their observation to the entire textual problem of Mark 1:1 in all its complexity. Given the tendency for scribes to be particularly conscientious when beginning a work, how do we explain not just the omission or insertion of two words in some manuscripts, but the diverse array of nine different readings for the opening verse of this Gospel? If the original reading was "The beginning of the Gospel of Jesus Christ," how do we account for the abbreviation of the text in variants 1 and 2? How do we explain the alterations (not simply expansions) of variants 8 and 9? The most basic canon of textual criticism dictates that the reading which provides the most plausible explanation of the origin of all the other readings is most likely original. This canon seems to be thwarted when applied to the beginning of Mark's Gospel. The textual evidence could be construed as suggesting that Mark 1:1 lacked a stable form when it first began to circulate.[12]

3. THE GRAMMATICAL AND STYLISTIC PROBLEMS

One of the difficulties facing modern editors and translators of Mark's opening is the matter of punctuation. Should Mark 1:1 be followed by a period and thus set off as a title, leaving verses 2-4 as the first full sentence in the gospel? Or should 1:1 and 1:3 be followed by commas, treating verses 2-3 as a parenthesis and verse 4 as the continuation? Or should there be no punctuation at all after verse 1 such that it is regarded as the subject of a verbless clause whose predicate is verses 2-3? These are just a few of the ways that have been proposed for construing verse 1 and its relationship with what follows. Allen Wikgren surveyed the problem and identified six categories of interpretation (1942, 11-12). C. E. B. Cranfield somewhat more expansively lists ten different explanations (1959, 34-35). How can there be such diversity of opinion over so short and seemingly straightforward a verse? When one additionally recalls the significant textual problem in the same verse, one can see the merit in James Moffatt's suggestion of a "primitive disturbance or corruption" (1914, 230).

Since a detailed consideration of ten interpretive options would be wearisome, let us consider two simple alternatives: Does Mark 1:1 stand alone syntactically or connect in some way with what follows? Several specific interpretive possibilities fall into each of these categories, but these two will suffice to show the serious difficulty entailed in this verse. Let us consider each in turn.

Construing the opening words as syntactically independent, that is, as a title, is the choice of "the overwhelming majority of translations and commentators."[13] This is also the choice of the standard editions of the Greek New Testament. This alternative has merit. As was pointed out earlier, verse 1 is a verbless phrase, and it is by no means clear how it would connect with verse 2 as a smooth and natural continuation of the thought. Moreover, the Greek word *archē*, "beginning," lacks the definite article, an omission that is more intelligible in a title than an opening sentence. On the other hand, it is odd for a title to speak of a beginning. Does *archē* refer only to the opening section of Mark, or does it refer to the entirety of Mark's work, such that one must understand "gospel" as denoting the ongoing Christian mission of which the earthly career of Jesus serves as the "beginning"?

The awkwardness of verse 1 increases when we consider a second fact: Verse 2 is a subordinate clause that lacks a main clause. Construing verse 1 as a title makes verse 2 the beginning of a sentence, indeed, the beginning of the entire gospel. But this is unlikely. *Kathōs gegraptai*, "as it is written," is a fixed formula that requires a certain kind of construction. This was first noticed by Friedrich Spitta a century ago. Spitta observed that, "According to the unvarying practice in the New Testament, the citation formula καθὼς γέγραπται ["as it is written"], as well as all similar formulas, is never the introductory clause, but rather always follows a report of something seen as the fulfillment of a prophetic word."[14] This means that the report of a "prophecy-fulfillment" sequence actually follows the order of "fulfillment," then the citation of the "prophecy."

T. W. Manson picks up on Spitta's observation, as does G. D. Kilpatrick in a different context. Kilpatrick insists that "the position of καθὼς [*kathōs*, "as"] clauses in the New Testament is much more subject to rule than scholars allow."[15] He goes on to demonstrate that *kathōs* clauses nearly always follow their main clauses in the Synoptic Gospels. But then he observes, "There is, however, a further consideration. Where καθὼς introduces a following quotation in the New Testament it *invariably* follows its main clause."[16] This fact constitutes a serious obstacle for those who would interpret Mark 1:1 as a title and Mark 1:2 as the beginning of the text proper.[17]

Synoptic comparisons strengthen this observation. Both Matthew and Luke seem to have felt the abruptness of Mark's use of *kathōs gegraptai*, "as it is written," without any preparatory main clause. Both of these evangelists, working independently, inserted brief narrative material about John the Baptist before the quotation. Matthew 3:1-2 prefaces the Isaiah quotation with a temporal indicator ("in those days"), a reference to John's activity and location (preaching "in the wilderness of Judea"), and a brief quote summarizing John's preaching. Luke 3:1-3 introduces the quote with an elaborate temporal indicator containing the names of five political rulers and two high priests. A statement of John's reception of the word follows, again locating the event in the wilderness. Finally, the location is more precisely identified as the area surrounding the Jordan River, and the content of John's preaching is characterized. All of these details Matthew and Luke place *before* their parallels for Mark 1:2. This is a strong indication that Mark, as it stands, violated the expected literary order of "fulfillment," *then* citation of the "prophecy."

The alternative, then, is to take verse 1 as continuing in verse 2,

or somewhat less probably, in verse 4 with verses 2-3 as a parenthesis. But neither is this solution without its problems. It recognizes that verse 2 is extremely awkward as the beginning of a
sentence and surely requires a preceding main clause. It construes
verse 1 in this role, but this short phrase, being verbless, does not
even constitute a clause! Those who would connect verse 1 with
what follows must presuppose the omission of a verb, presumably,
"was." Thus one would read, "The beginning of the Gospel of Jesus
Christ [was] just as it has been written." The omission of the verb
"to be" is common enough, but it occurs largely in predictable situations.[18] These include proverbial statements, expressions of duty
and obligation, and predications with certain adjectives. Mark 1:1-
2 does not fit any of these categories. Analysis of Mark's Greek
shows verbless sentences to be rare. Indeed, his style tends in the
opposite direction, as Nigel Turner (1965, 28) asserts:

> [T]here is a real stylistic difficulty about supplying "is" or "was" in
> any sentence written by St. Mark. In many writers of Greek, even
> biblical Greek, it would be easy enough. They regarded the copula
> verb as at best an encumbrance in a simple subject-predicate sen-
> tence, and in fact they went even further than this and sometimes
> omitted "is" or "was" when its meaning was stronger than a mere
> copula. St Mark is a notable exception. He was inclined to insert
> these words where more literary authors ignored them as weak cop-
> ulas. . . . This is a feature of his style and for that reason the gram-
> marian must feel considerable doubt about the interpretation, "The
> beginning of the gospel *is* or *was* as it is written in Isaiah."

It is unlikely, therefore, that we are dealing with an ellipsis of the
verb "to be" in the first two verses of the gospel.[19]

Hubert Grimme identifies a further difficulty in construing
verses 1-2 as a verbless sentence: their location at the beginning of
the writing. Greek hardly ever uses verbless sentences at the beginning of a section. It is much more common for such a sentence to
follow some statement whose temporal setting passes over to the
verbless sentence (Grimme 1946, 280). In other words, context
normally provides clues as to what verb and tense are to be supplied, but such a context is lacking in the case of Mark 1:1. If the
evangelist intended "was" to be supplied after verse 1, then he has
used an unusual and unparalleled verbless construction *in the very*

first sentence of his gospel.[20] Even if this were granted, one would still be hard pressed to see verse 1 as the fulfillment of the prophecy quoted in verses 2-3. By itself, Mark 1:1 does not predicate, let alone narrate, anything! Finally, if verse 1 is the start of a sentence that continues in verse 2, it is odd that *archē*, "beginning," lacks the definite article.

To sum up, then, Mark 1:1 is unlikely to be a title, grammatically independent of what follows, but it is equally unlikely to be a main clause, having its continuation in 1:2-3 (or 4). This dilemma might be solved, however, if verse 1 is a latter addition to the gospel. Before I proceed to consider briefly the third kind of problem with Mark's beginning, it would be appropriate to point out two stylistic peculiarities about Mark 1:1.

First, *euangelion*, "gospel," in Mark 1:1 is almost always interpreted as "oral proclamation of good news" rather than "gospel" in the sense of "a written record of Jesus' life." The former meaning is in keeping with Mark's usage elsewhere (1:14, 15; 13:10; 14:9), where *euangelion* is often the object of the verb *preach*. Moreover, this meaning fits a first-century context. *Euangelion* as "a written record of Jesus' life" has been shown to be a second-century usage.[21] Despite this, one finds occasional scholarly ambivalence about the meaning of *euangelion* in Mark 1:1. The standard lexicons cite this passage under the basic meaning of "God's good news to humans," but suggest other possible meanings: "details relating to the life and ministry of Jesus," or "a book dealing with the life and teaching of Jesus."[22] In his commentary on Mark, Robert A. Guelich is nearly self-contradictory when he writes that *euangelion* here "can hardly be taken as intended merely to name a literary genre" but rather "refers to the good news as proclaimed," and then three pages later declares that "Mark by designating his *written* account as the 'gospel' (1:1) broke with the traditional use of 'gospel' to refer to the *proclaimed* message of the Church's preaching."[23] Such ambivalence is excusable, however, given the fact that *euangelion* in Mark 1:1 seems to mean something it cannot mean. But what if Mark 1:1 stems from the second century when the literary meaning of *euangelion* came into vogue? If one considers the possibility that verse 1 is a second-century gloss, this meaning is immediately seen as contextually appropriate. Surely an important consideration for interpreting the words, "The beginning of the Gospel," ought to be the fact that these words *occur at the physical beginning of the Gospel!*

Second, the dual name "Jesus Christ" is peculiar in Mark. It is altogether likely that *"Christos"* here is not the title "Christ" ("Messiah") but simply part of a compound proper name. This is the judgment of many modern translations, lexical works, and theological studies.[24] But this meaning would be unusual to Mark, for whom the term is always a title. Of the other six instances of *Christos* in the Gospel of Mark, five have the definite article and are unambiguously titular, and the sixth is arguably so.[25] A further difficulty with "Jesus Christ" in Mark 1:1 is the fact that the dual name appears *only here* in Mark. Even though elsewhere in his Gospel Mark uses the name "Jesus" 78 times and the title "Christ" 6 times, only in 1:1 is the combined form found. These two stylistic observations by no means *compel* the judgment that Mark 1:1 is a later addition, but one has to admit that even this short phrase contains features that are not characteristically Markan.[26]

4. THE INTERPRETIVE PROBLEM

Finally, there is the interpretive problem with Mark's opening passage. What does the evangelist mean by "beginning"? What does he mean by "gospel"? Is "of Jesus Christ" an objective genitive ("the good news *about* Jesus") or a subjective genitive ("the good news *preached by* Jesus")? The interpretive problem is closely related to the problems of syntax and punctuation discussed above. Decisions made about one will necessarily influence choices about the other. The literature on the passage, if expanded to include the entire prologue, is considerable.[27] To give some order to the array of possibilities, I will examine the interpretive options related to the three main grammatical alternatives.[28]

First, those who place a period after verse 1 and construe it as a title usually understand "the beginning of the gospel" as referring to the entire book, or possibly, to the opening section. By either alternative, if the evangelist wrote verse 1, "gospel" would have to mean "the oral proclamation of Good News." Thus, the sense would be either "(the following narrative in its entirety represents) the beginning of the oral proclamation of the Good News about/by Jesus Christ (which continued on in the life of the Church)" or "(the following paragraph or two represent) the beginning of the oral proclamation of the Good News about/by Jesus Christ (which continued on in Jesus' public ministry)." The precise limit of the "beginning," according to the second alternative, is much debated. All of the following have been proposed: verses 1-8, verses 1-11, verses 1-13, and verses 1-15.[29] The first of these options would perceive John the Baptist (or his preaching) as the "beginning of the Gospel."[30] John could be "the beginning" in the sense of "precursor" but not in the sense of "first proclaimer," since Mark never explicitly associates John with the preaching of the Gospel. The other options would variously include Jesus' baptism, temptation, and the beginning of his Galilean ministry as part of the "beginning of the Gospel."

By any of these alternatives, questions arise: If Mark has given a title to the opening of his work, why are there no titles for other divisions? If, for Mark, the gospel has a beginning, why is there no mention of a continuation? As for the issue of objective versus subjective genitive, Mark 1:7-8 would fit the description "good news proclaimed *about* Jesus" (although this news is not explicitly identified as *euangelion*), but in 1:14-15 good news is clearly proclaimed *by* Jesus. Other uses of *euangelion* in Mark are somewhat ambiguous as to whether they imply good news "about" or "by" Jesus (8:35; 10:29; 13:10; 14:9). Was Mark being unusually subtle and exploiting both meanings of the genitive in 1:1? And whether verse 1 is Mark's original title for the opening section or for the entire work, how does one explain the melee in the textual tradition and the extreme grammatical awkwardness of verse 2 as the beginning of the text proper?

Second, those who would put a period after verse 3 and construe verses 2-3 as the predicate of verse 1 obviously forge a stronger link between "the beginning of the gospel" and the quotation. By this interpretation, "the beginning of the gospel (came about in a way that was) just as it has been written in Isaiah the prophet" (AT). This would implicitly limit the "beginning" to John the Baptist since the citation refers to him. Any such interpretation faces the grammatical improbability of a work beginning with a complex but verbless sentence, as well as the difficulty of explaining how verse 1 can function as a main clause to what follows, that is, how it is in any sense an event or fact that fulfills the prophecy of verses 2-3.[31]

Finally, those who would place a period only after verse 4 and construe verses 2-3 as a parenthesis offer the least attractive option.[32] This interpretation links "the beginning of the gospel" with John, not by means of a verb to be supplied, but by *egeneto* ("was" or "became") in verse 4. Thus, the meaning would be: "The beginning of the gospel of Jesus Christ . . . was John, the one baptizing . . . and preaching." But this interpretation leaves the *kathōs* ("as") clause of verses 2-3 without a supporting main clause either before or after. It also would be odd for verses 2-3 to be parenthetical given the fact that they are necessary in the logic of the passage and constitute the only instance in the gospel where Mark formally cites scripture. Finally, Mark's style is scarcely so baroque as to have subject and verb separated by thirty-four words.[33]

In addition to these basic interpretations, there have been other novel suggestions. These include *archē* as the "lemma" or "scriptural basis" of Mark's Gospel, *archē* as the "rudiments" or "essentials" of the gospel, a kind of catechism, *archē* as "norm" or "canon," and *archē* as a "summary."[34] Although these interpretations cannot be dismissed as wholly impossible, their sheer multiplicity and variety inspire suspicion rather than confidence. In sum, the beginning of Mark's Gospel is a seriously confused text that invites a new proposal that will explain its many textual, syntactical, and interpretive problems.

5. THE PROPOSAL

The proposal is simple: The beginning of Mark's Gospel, like its ending, is defective. Something originally preceded Mark 1:2 but has been lost. A superscription was added in various forms by redactors probably in the second century, not as a title but as a marker with the meaning, "the text of the Gospel begins here." Some such marker was necessary since a manuscript beginning with Mark 1:2 would have been intolerable on the grounds of grammar, style, and coherence. The addition of this marker had the unintended effect of a cosmetic repair. An otherwise abrupt and incoherent beginning was partially masked. At first glance Mark 1:1 could be mistaken, however improbably, for the evange-

ARK

list's opening words. But the considerable difficulties described above point to the likelihood of a textual defect. Consider the question, If an ancient text *were* mutilated at its beginning, what signs thereof would we expect? Would they not be precisely the indications we have at Mark 1:1: grammatical incompleteness, interpretive difficulties, stylistic abruptness, and a textual tradition marked by scribal repairs and clarifications? (These are precisely the indications we have that the ending of Mark is defective.)

The alert reader may remember that I said at the beginning of this chapter that I would "recall and corroborate" a solution to the many difficulties of Mark's beginning. As in the case of Mark's troublesome conclusion, I am not proposing something entirely new. Several scholars have previously suggested that the beginning of Mark's Gospel is defective. Besides Spitta and Manson, among the better-known scholars are C. F. D. Moule, Stephen Neill, and N. T. Wright.[35] Other scholars, such as Paul Feine, Gerhard Friedrich, Helmut Koester, Walter Schmithals, Henry Barclay Swete, and Nikolaus Walter, have suggested that verse 1 is a later addition without explicitly saying that the text beginning with verse 2 is defective.[36] But the hypothesis of *both* a redactional first verse *and* textual damage would account for all the difficulties of Mark's beginning.

But one might reasonably ask, What positive evidence is there that *archē* was used as a manuscript marker, a scribe's way of indicating the beginning of a manuscript? There is significant evidence of three different types: (1) simple references in one work of literature to the beginning of another work; (2) markers designating the beginning and end of lectionary readings (usually *archē* and *telos* abbreviated *arch* and *tel*);[37] and (3) superscriptions or manuscript markers appearing at the head of a writing or a division of a writing. Let us consider each of these.

(1) It is natural and rather unremarkable that *archē* would be used to refer to the beginning of a book. Dozens of such instances could be cited. A small sampling:

1. *en archē tēs Politeias*, "in the beginning of The Republic," Diogenes Laertius 7.32.

2. *en archē tēs Iliados*, "in the beginning of the Iliad," Dionysius of Halicarnassus, *Rhet.* 9.7.

125

3. *en archē tēs Geneseōs*, "in the beginning of Genesis," Justin, *Dial.* 79:4.

This usage of *archē* in a prepositional phrase is quite common. One naturally refers to the beginning of a work of literature by using the word "beginning." A related construction is equally common: using *archē* to refer to the first line of a literary work in lieu of using a title. In antiquity, especially early antiquity, Greek writings were often *not* furnished with titles. The common way of referring to a poem, essay, or play was to cite its opening words.[38] Examples:

1. *en tō iambō hou hē archē ou moi ta Gugeō*, "in the iambic poem whose beginning [is], 'The possessions of Gyges are nothing to me,' " Aristotle, *Rhet.* 3.17.16.

2. *kai toutou dithyrambos tis hou estin archē; Deut' en choron Olympioi*, "And [there is] a certain dithyramb of this fellow whose beginning is, 'Come to the chorus, Olympians,' " Dionysius of Halicarnassus, *Comp.* 22.

3. *ho hekatostos ogdoos psalmos . . . hou hē archē; Ho theos, tēn ainesin mou mē parasiōpēsēs*, "The 108th Psalm . . . whose beginning [is], 'O God, do not pass over my praise in silence,' " Origen, *Cels.* 2.11.

This usage was so common that it would not be exaggerating to consider *hou* (or *hēs*) *hē archē*, "whose beginning," a technical introductory formula.[39] This means that, whatever its other many uses, *archē* frequently was used to denote the opening words of a text.

(2) The second type of evidence is the well-known scribal practice of using *archē* and *telos* as lectionary markers. Such notations are found in many manuscripts, either in the margins or between the lines of the text itself.[40] They are found even in the early and important Codex Vaticanus, although by a later hand than that of the manuscript. The practice of inserting such markings probably began in about the sixth or seventh centuries.[41]

(3) The third type of evidence has the most significance for the present study: the use of *archē* and similar language for super-

scriptions or headings for entire books. These occur quite frequently in the manuscripts of the New Testament. The most common forms are *archetai* ("it begins") in Greek texts and *incipit* in Latin texts. Latin superscriptions are more common than the Greek and can be found in some manuscripts of almost every New Testament book. The Greek word *archetai* occurs in a combined closing note and superscription in codex D: *euangelion kata iōanēn etelesthē, archetai euangelion kata loukan*, "The Gospel according to John has ended; the Gospel according to Luke begins."[42] A similar heading is found in codex D at the beginning of John's Gospel. Among the epistles attributed to Paul, superscriptions with *archetai* appear frequently in codices D, E, F, and G. With only a few exceptions, these codices have headings with *archetai* for each of the books of the Pauline corpus.[43]

But one might ask whether the noun *archē*, as opposed to the verb *archetai*, occurs in such superscriptions. In other words, do we have *precise* counterparts to Mark 1:1? This is an important question in the interpretation of Mark 1:1 because an alleged lack of close parallels has been cited as evidence by those who reject the construal of that verse as an independent phrase or the construal of *archē* in the simple sense of "beginning."[44] But in fact, we have remarkably close parallels. The first group of parallels involves other New Testament books in which some manuscripts provide headings or markers similar to Mark 1:1. The following list gives the heading, its translation, and the manuscript's number. (Bracketed letters complete words that have been abbreviated in the manuscripts.)

1. *archē sun theō tou kata Matthaion euangeliou*, "The Beginning with God['s Help] of the Gospel according to Matthew," 1241[45]

2. *arch[ē] tou kat[a] Markon eua[ngeliou]*, "The Beginning of the Gospel according to Mark," 118[46]

3. *archē tou kata Loukan hagiou euangeliou*, "The Beginning of the Holy Gospel according to Luke," 1241[47]

4. *archē tou kata Iō[annēs] eua[ngeliou]*, "The Beginning of the Gospel according to John," 118[48]

Just as striking as the New Testament evidence is that of the Septuagint, or Greek Old Testament. Especially noteworthy is Hosea 1:2, a comparative text that has been cited frequently. This verse offers a close parallel to the opening words of Mark: *archē logou kuriou pros Ōsēe*, "The Beginning of the Word of the Lord to Hosea." The relevance of this parallel has sometimes been disputed, but this Septuagint translation is, in fact, quite analogous to Mark 1:1.[49]

Several Septuagint manuscripts also employ *archē* in the inscriptions of various books. This practice seems to be especially common in the Pentateuch, where more than twenty different manuscripts contain *archē* in the inscriptions of one or more books. These inscriptions invariably refer to the books in their entirety (or in some cases to the collection in its entirety), not to a beginning section. Here are some examples together with translations and the numbers by which the manuscripts are designated.

1. *archē sun th[e]ō tēs palaias hagias graphēs; biblion a; hē genesis*, "The Beginning with God['s Help] of the Ancient Holy Scripture: Book 1: Genesis," 131

2. *archē tou b bibliou; exodos*, "The Beginning of the second Book; Exodus," 75

3. *archē tou leuitikou*, "The Beginning of Leviticus," 246, et al.

4. *archē tōn arithmōn*, "The Beginning of Numbers," 246, et al.

5. *archē tou deuteronomiou*, "The Beginning of Deuteronomy," 53, et al.[50]

Finally, manuscript markers with *archē* are also found in patristic and Greco-Roman writings. Below is a sampling, again with translations, authors, and names of the works. The dates shown are for the authors.[51]

1. *archē tōn ēthikōn*, "The Beginning of the Ethics," Basil (4th cent. C.E.), *Regulae Morales*

2. *archē tōn diēgēseōn*, "The Beginning of the Narratives," John Moschus (5th–6th cent. C.E.), Prologue to *Pratum Spirituale*

3. *archē tōn oktō merōn tou logou*, "The Beginning of the Eight Parts of Speech," Dionysius Thrax (2nd cent. B.C.E.), *Art of Grammar*

4. *archē tou A*, "The Beginning of the Alpha [List]," Erotianus (1st cent. C.E.), *Sayings of Hippocrates*

5. *Hērōnos archē tōn geōmetroumenōn*, "The Beginning of Heron's Geometry," Heron of Alexandria (1st cent. C.E.), *Geometrica*

6. *archē tou A*, "The Beginning of the Alpha [List]," Diogenianus (2nd cent. C.E.), *Paroemiae*

7. *archē tou A*, "The Beginning of the Alpha [List]," Herennius Philon (1st–2nd cent. C.E.), *On the Different Meanings of Words*

A few observations can be made regarding these biblical, patristic, and Greco-Roman parallels. First and most obviously, *archē* is quite common *as the very first word* of a heading of a literary work or a division thereof.[52] Strictly speaking, these headings are manuscript markers, not titles, even though they may vaguely allude to the following contents. If they were titles, they would be more descriptive and would probably not contain the word *beginning*. Their function is to mark the starting point of the writing in the sense of "Here begins the book/the section." Second, in many of the above examples the *archē* markers were probably added by later editors. We do not always know this for sure, but it is certainly the case in those instances when we have an abundance of manuscripts and *earlier* ones lack these headings. Third, most *archē* markers refer to an entire writing rather than to a prologue or opening section. An important exception to this rule, however, is the multiple use of *archē* markers within a single document. A few comments are needed with regard to the date of the above evidence. While it must be granted that many of these head-ings or markers are found in late manuscripts (10th century and later), there are indications that this practice was known much ear-lier. First, we must remember that the date of a manuscript and the date of the text it transmits are two different things. These *archē* headings could very well predate the manuscripts in which they appear. (In other words, the above manuscripts may have been copied from exemplars that contained the headings but are themselves no longer extant.) More important, in some cases the *archē* markers are the work of the original authors or compilers rather than scribes writing centuries later. This is particularly so when *archē* is used several times within one manuscript, serving basically to outline the material. For example, Greco-Roman par-allels 4, 6, and 7 above all use alphabetical listings such that each contains about 24 *archē* headings dispersed throughout the docu-ment like section titles. Since these are integral to the structure of the work, they were almost certainly used by the original compiler, not by a medieval scribe. Erotianus (4) and Diogenianus (6) in particular compiled sayings from earlier authors and so were themselves the architects of the alphabetical arrangement. It seems very likely, therefore, that *archē* headings were used in the first and second centuries C.E. Altogether, the combination of intertextual references using *archē*, lectionary markers, and actual headings using *archē* strongly suggests that Mark 1:1 may be con-strued as an independent phrase marking the very beginning of the manuscript.[53]

6. CONCLUSIONS

If the proposal is correct, what should we conclude about the beginning of Mark's Gospel? First, Mark 1:1-15 would be less clearly the prologue to the gospel since the *inclusio* with the word *euangelion* would be accidental, created by the redactor's use of the word rather than Mark's design. Any conclusions about the extent and intent of Mark's introduction would necessarily be tentative. Second, *euangelion* in verse 1 could be construed in its later sense of "a book dealing with the life and teaching of Jesus." The only reason for rejecting this meaning was the first century date of Mark's Gospel, but as a second-century scribal gloss, the literary meaning becomes the most plausible one.[54] Third, the words "Jesus Christ" would then be an objective genitive since a written Gospel can only be *about* Jesus Christ, not *by* Jesus Christ. Fourth, it would not be the case that *Mark* called his work as a whole "a Gospel." Some second-century scribe has done so, but whether Mark conceived of his literary project in these terms is unknown. In fact, it is unlikely since every other use of the word *euangelion* in Mark's Gospel can be understood wholly in terms of the first-century meaning of "oral proclamation of good news." Fifth, the punctuation of the passage could be changed to reflect the defective state of the text. Mark 1:1 could be printed as a superscription, and 1:2 could be printed with preceding dots to indicate the loss of the beginning. Finally, while it is certainly true that Mark's Gospel (as we have it) *says* nothing about the birth of Jesus, it would be presumptuous to say that he *knew* nothing about it.[55] A writer always knows more than what he or she commits to writing in a given work, and if the beginning of Mark is defective, it would be especially unwise to deny the possibility that Mark may have had some knowledge of Jesus' birth. This caveat leads to a final thought.

If Mark's Gospel is, in fact, defective, the question naturally arises: What is missing? From what has already been said above, the material most obviously lacking in Mark's beginning is introductory information about John the Baptist, that is, some event or description that would constitute the "fulfillment" of the "prophecy" in verses 2-3. There probably was some reference to the temporal setting of John's ministry (cf. Matt 3:1*a*; Luke 3:1-3; and Mark 1:9*a* in regard to Jesus). Presumably, the lost beginning did not duplicate information Mark has given in 1:4-8 about John's activity, dress, diet, and message, but there might very well have been some information about John's origin or call. The lost portion may have been no more than a few verses or a few paragraphs. Greater precision in stating its content or extent is not possible.

The big question is, What about some sort of genealogy or birth narrative of Jesus? N. T. Wright hints at this tantalizing possibility, but it remains no more than a possibility, and I think that it is a rather slim one.[56] The introduction of Jesus in Mark 1:9, the only other nonarticular use of Jesus' name other than in 1:1, strikes me as the first mention of Jesus in the narrative.[57] But in such cases certainty is unattainable and overconfidence is unwise. It is perhaps sufficiently provocative and paradoxical to suggest that we lack the beginning of the gospel that begins with the words, "The beginning of the Gospel."

So it appears that in the Gospel of Mark we have a document that is truncated at both ends. Both the beginning and the conclusion are jagged; both are grammatically peculiar and stylistically abrupt; both have been the object of scribal repairs. Two questions remain: What circumstances in the writing, preservation, and transmission of Mark's Gospel might have brought about the mutilation of the manuscript? And how plausible is the double mutilation of the Gospel of Mark?

NOTES

An earlier version of this chapter was published in *Novum Testamentum*. See Croy (2001).

1. Aristotle, *Poet.* 50b.

2. Dionysius of Halicarnassus, *Thuc.* 10.

3. Manson (1944, 121-22); also in (1962, 30-31).

4. Meier (1994, 43). For Meier's elaboration of these difficulties, see (1994, 85 n. 112).

5. In addition to the commentaries, see C. Turner (1927), Slomp (1977), Globe (1982), Head (1991), and Ehrman (1993, 72-75).

6. I have simplified the manuscript evidence. For full details see The United Bible Societies Greek New Testament, 4th ed. or Croy (2001, 106-10). I omit here the evidence from the early versions that for syntactical reasons does not distinguish between alternatives 4 and 5. Globe (1982, 214-15) offers this information as well as detailed patristic evidence.

7. Legg (1935, *ad versum*). See also Tischendorf (1869–1872, 1:215).

8. For details on the Palestinian Syriac, see Nestle (1894, 458-60); Aland and Aland (1987, 195); and Croy (2001, 107-8 n. 6).

9. The text in question is a preface to the Arabic translation of Tatian's *Diatessaron*. For further details, see Head (1991, 622 n. 9) and Croy (2001, 108 n. 7).

10. Head (1991, 628). On the *nomina sacra*, see C. H. Roberts (1979, 26-48) and the literature he cites.

11. Ehrman (1993, 73). See also Head (1991, 629). Slomp (1977, 148) also recognizes the improbability of scribal error here: "Omission on the basis of *homoioteleuton* [similar line endings] is very unlikely in the beginning of a manuscript."

12. Both Henry Barclay Swete and Vincent Taylor mention this possibility. Swete (1927, 2) suggests "Possibly the heading existed almost from the first in two forms." Taylor (1961, 82) remarks, "It is possible that both readings may have appeared from the beginning."

13. Bratcher and Nida (1961, 2). This grammatical usage is called a nominative absolute.

14. Spitta (1904, 306, AT). See also Spitta (1893–1907, III.2.115-22).

15. Kilpatrick (1960, 340). So also J. K. Elliott (1991, 55-58).

16. Kilpatrick (1960, 340-41); my emphasis. The problem of *kathōs gegraptai* beginning a sentence has been noted by others. See Arnold (1977, 123-27), Guelich (1982, 5-15), Guelich (1989, 7), and Tolbert (1989, 242-43).

17. Heinrich Baarlink (1977, 293) notes that it is unusual even in *elevated* Greek for a sentence beginning with *kathōs*, "as," to continue without *houtōs*, "so," and Mark's diction is far from elevated. Moreover, a backwards reference from *kathōs* to a substantive like *archē* is even more unusual.

18. See Smyth (1956, 944-45); Blass and Debrunner (1961, §§ 127-28); and the exceptionally full treatment of N. Turner (1963, 294-310).

19. Doudna (1961, 4-5) makes no mention of Mark 1:1-2 in what appears to be a comprehensive list of verbless sentences in Mark. See also Elliott (2000, 585-86).

20. Blass and Debrunner (1961, § 128.3) note that the Greek word for "was" is always omitted in the phrase "whose name [was]," but "otherwise almost never." N. Turner (1963, 307) notes that some would assume an ellipsis in 1:1, but he judges that "Mark's fondness for the verb *to be* is against this interpretation."

21. See Strecker (1972, 91-104) and Gundry (1996, 321-25) and the literature they cite.

22. The 2nd edition of Bauer's lexicon describes Mark 1:1 as perhaps transitional to the meaning of *book*. See Bauer (1979, 318, 1b and 3). The new 3rd edition offers the special transitional rendering: "details relating to the life and ministry of Jesus." Although the 3rd edition still alerts the reader to the third meaning ("a book . . ."), it does not list Mark 1:1 there. See BDAG (2000, 402-3).

23. Guelich (1989, 9, 12); original emphasis.

24. Taylor (1953, 19), Blass and Debrunner (1961, 260.1, though not citing Mark 1:1 specifically), Sabourin (1967, 31), Grundmann (1974, 9:537), Bauer (1979, 887), Goppelt (1981, 1:169), DeJonge (1991, 105-6), and BDAG (2000, 1091).

25. The articular uses are 8:29, 12:35, 13:21, 14:61, and 15:32. The only nonarticular instance is 9:41. The latter is most likely titular despite the lack of the article. Moreover, the text of 9:41 is in question. See the discussions of Taylor (1966, 408) and Lane (1974, 342 n. 66).

26. For other non-Markan features, see Elliott (2000, 584-86), although Elliott proposes that not just 1:1, but 1:1-3 are a later addition.

27. In addition to those cited above, see Keck (1965–1966), Gibbs (1973), Feneberg (1974), Dormeyer (1987, 452-68), Boring (1990, 43-81), France (1990), Coote (1992, 86-90), Walter (1992), and Hooker (1997, 1-22).

28. Feneberg (1974, 186-90) helpfully correlates the grammatical options, the various interpretations, and their advocates in modern scholarship. For a thorough discussion of pre-twentieth-century scholarly opinion, including patristic commentary, see Schanz (1881, 59-64).

29. See Guelich (1989, 4) for lists of supporters of each view. France (1990, 11, 17-19) notes that Lightfoot pioneered the demarcation of the prologue of Mark as 1:1-13, but that Keck's influential article inspired the view that the prologue extends to v. 15. France himself, however, argues for 1:1-13 on the basis of shifts in geography and narrational perspective. See also Hooker (1997, 8), who asks, regarding the alleged *inclusio* with *euangelion* in vv. 1 and 14-15, "is it not just as likely that the two references to the gospel are meant to stand in parallel, marking the openings of two sections, rather than the beginning and ending of one?"

30. So Friedrich (1964, 2:719). The construal of John's preaching as "the beginning of the gospel" finds ancient support in Basil *Adversum Eunomius* 2.15. See the text in Sesboüé (1983, 58) or Croy (2001, 117 n. 32).

31. There is perhaps another difficulty for this solution. Nikolaus Walter (1992, 473) finds it odd that both Matthew and Luke would have excised Mark 1:1 from their accounts: "To me . . . it would be incomprehensible, if Mt and Lk had found this 'superscription' . . . in their exemplars of Mk, but had unanimously ignored it and for their part had gone in completely different directions." This might argue in favor of Matthew and Luke's possession of Markan exemplars that lacked 1:1. I think the latter is likely, but not for Walter's reason. If Mark 1:1 was in fact present in their exemplars, Matthew and Luke could have chosen to omit this verse because they understood their respective birth narratives as the beginning of their Gospels.

32. C. H. Turner (1925, 146); and Elliott (1993, 23-24). See also the advocates listed by Wikgren (1942, 12 n. 4) and Feneberg (1974, 186 n. 292).

33. In addition, codices Sinaiticus and W, and certain Coptic, Syriac, and Georgian manuscripts have (or presuppose) a conjunction (*kai* or *de*) with *egeneto* in v. 4, clearly construing it as a new sentence. See Legg (1935, *ad versum*).

34. For each of these interpretations, see, respectively, Coote (1992, 90), Wikgren (1942, 17), Boring (1990, 53), and Kleist (1932, 19).

35. See Moule (1982, 131-32 n. 1), Neill (1976, 76-78), and Wright (1992a, 390, n. 67). Others include Craigie (1922, 303-5), Elliott (2000, but see note 26 above), and Way-Rider (1982, 553-56). North (1977, 502-3 n. 7) notes that in the mid–sixteenth century G. Postel held the view that the apocryphal work, *The Protevangelium of James*, was the lost beginning of Mark's Gospel. Smid (1965, 3) remarks that this theory was "much discussed at that time." While the theory is wildly improbable for reasons of style, dating, and so forth, it demonstrates that even in the precritical era some readers found the beginning of Mark to be abrupt and possibly truncated.

36. Swete (1913, 1-2), Feine (1936, 55), Friedrich (1964, 2:727 n. 52), Schmithals (1979, 73-74), Koester (1990, 13-14), and Walter (1992, 473-74).

37. Ancient lectionaries were collections of scripture passages arranged for use in early Christian worship. The practice was borrowed from the synagogue, whose readings from the Law and the Prophets were supplemented with the Christian Gospels and Epistles.

38. On this subject, see the excellent treatment by Nachmanson (1941, 31-52).

39. In Porphyry's *Life of Plotinus*, the writings of Plotinus are identified both

by title and their opening words. The formula *hou hē archē* is used more than one hundred times. A similar list of the beginning lines of biblical books, each introduced with the *hou hē archē* formula, can be found in Athanasius's *Synopsis Scripturae Sacrae*. For bibliographical details, see Croy (2001, 121 n. 40).

40. See Gregory (1884, 162-63), Metzger (1992, 30-31), and Aland and Aland (1987, 163-64).

41. One of the Freer manuscripts (codex W) contains such a notation. This manuscript is dated to the fifth century; the editorial hand which added *archē* is dated to the late sixth or early seventh century. See Metzger (1981, 84-85).

42. Obviously the order of NT books in ancient manuscripts did not always follow the modern order.

43. All of data in this paragraph can be found in the rich apparatus of Tischendorf (1869–1884).

44. Guelich (1982, 8), for example, says "we have no comparable literary example of this noun used to introduce a complete literary work." Similarly, Boring (1990, 52) has said that "there are no exact, or even very close, parallels to Mark's own opening words." This is true of the parallels cited by Arnold (1977, 124-26), but the texts adduced above are without question close parallels. On the weakness of Arnold's parallels, see Baarlink (1977, 293 n. 32).

45. Barbara Aland, et al. (1993, 1).

46. Swanson (1995–1998, *Mark*, 7). It is remarkable that the scribe of manuscript 118 has added a heading to *Mark*, whose first verse, in effect, is already a heading! This scribe apparently misunderstood the function of Mark 1:1 as a manuscript marker or simply added the inscription as a matter of course without regard for first verse. Moreover, the addition was not entirely redundant since it specified the evangelist as Mark.

47. Barbara Aland, et al. (1993, 150). A similar heading appears in manuscript 118. See Swanson (1995–1998, *Luke*, 13).

48. Swanson (1995–1998, *John*, 5).

49. Guelich (1989, 7) says "the analogy breaks down when one recognizes that Hos 1:1 rather than 1:2 is the title of the book. Indeed, Hos 1:2 provides the heading for the following section." I would argue that the analogy holds up well since the superscription to Mark *(Kata Markon)* is a title parallel to Hosea 1:1, and Mark 1:1 is a textual marker parallel to Hosea 1:2. Boring (1990, 71 n. 18) likewise insists that Hosea 1:2 is "not . . . the title, but the opening line of the first section, the translator's effort to render into Greek [the Hebrew of Hosea 1:2-3]." But the sense of Hosea 1:2 and its punctuation in the Septuagint suggest that it (like Mark 1:1) is a freestanding introductory phrase, not a complete sentence whose thought continues in the next verse. The implication that the Septuagint does a clumsy job of translating the Masoretic Text is correct but irrelevant. The value of Hosea 1:2 as a semantic parallel to Mark 1:1 depends solely on the Septuagint translation.

50. These superscriptions can be found in the full apparatus of the respective volumes of the Göttingen Septuagint. See *Septuaginta* (1931–). The five volumes of the Pentateuch were edited by John William Wevers (1974–1991).

51. Full bibliographical details can be found in Croy (2000, 124-25 nn. 51-

58). On the fifth example (Heron of Alexandria), see also Elliott (2000, 588 n. 9).

52. The reader should bear in mind that the examples given above are only a small selection. *Archē* markers are found in dozens of authors' works dating from the first century to the Middle Ages, and some individual authors supply dozens of examples, particularly when such headings mark alphabetical divisions.

53. I might also point out that the *archē* markers in medieval manuscripts reflect a highly developed usage. This is evidenced by the variety of forms the headings assume, their repetitive use for multiple books or sections within a single writing, and the presence of pious flourishes such as "with God's help." The simplest usage, such as occurs in Mark 1:1, would surely have been intelligible in the early second century.

54. The second century was probably when Mark 1:1 in some form was first added to Mark. The literary meaning of *euangelion* makes a date in the late first century unlikely. Also, there is no indication in Matthew or Luke that their copies of Mark included v. 1. On the other hand, varied quotations of v. 1 in the *Diatessaron* and Irenaeus preclude a date later than the second century. It is clearly *not* the case, however, that Mark 1:1 had a *stable* form in the second century, or at any time since!

55. It would likewise be presumptuous to say that Mark *did* know about the birth of Jesus, and it cannot be said that the present study *increases* the likelihood that Mark knew of this tradition. I simply wish to underscore the distinction between "*betrays* no knowledge of" and "*has* no knowledge of."

56. See Wright (1992b, 85).

57. Of 75 other instances of Jesus' name in Mark, *all* have the definite article except 1:9 (excluding three vocative forms which could not be articular). See Elliott (1993, 137).

Seven

WAS THE CODEX THE CAUSE?

"[T]he tear at [Mark 16] verse 8 recalls the fate that many an ancient book suffered; its last page was especially at risk and was very easily lost."[1]

At the end of chapter 5 I laid out the alternatives for the means of the truncation of Mark's Gospel: (1) deliberate suppression of the ending, (2) failure to finish the gospel, or (3) accidental loss of the ending. The last of these was proposed as the simplest and most likely explanation. That explanation might now seem to be complicated by chapter 6 in which I argued for the loss of the beginning of the gospel as well. Does this corollary of the thesis have the effect of compounding the improbabilities? Not necessarily. The social circumstances and literary practices of early Christians may, in fact, have been conducive to the kind of damage that seems to have befallen the Second Gospel. In this chapter we will consider the following questions: What were the conditions to which ancient manuscripts were subject, and how common was textual damage? What form(s) of manuscripts did the early Christians use? How do these matters relate to the mutilation of Mark's Gospel?

1. THE FRAGILITY OF ANCIENT MANUSCRIPTS

Antiquity was not a good time to be a manuscript. Writing materials were not always durable, and conditions of storage and use were often less than favorable. Some libraries were tended by caring professionals, but all were subject to plunder, fire, and relocation, and none was climate controlled. In addition, the libraries of early Christians were in some times and places subject to the ravages of persecution. There were, then, many factors contributing to the deterioration, damage, and demise of writings. Moreover, we should not assume that in the earliest decades Christians had any notion of the status that their writings would eventually attain. Letters and even Gospels may originally have been written with much less pretense to permanence than we would think. Papyrologist Roger Bagnall reminds us that ancient texts "might or might not have been thought of by their authors as possessions for all time; we may imagine that most authors of what we call literature shared Thucydides' hopes [of creating an enduring work]. But the particular embodiment of a text on a physical medium was endowed with no such expectations."[2]

Accordingly, the survival of ancient writings from antiquity to the present is radically uneven. Kurt Aland laments that "the losses from normal wear and tear, persecution, war, fire, and other causes must be estimated as considerable" (1999, 2:546). We have today only a small fraction of the total literary production of ancient times. This is true even of the works of the most prominent authors. Martin Hengel comments on the extent of the loss:

> Hardly any of the great historical works of the Hellenistic and Roman period have come down to us unabbreviated. Extensive gaps in the text and abbreviation in the form of summaries are the rule here. I need mention only the three most important Greek historians of the Hellenistic and Roman period in this connection. These were Polybius and Diodore, each of whom wrote a history of the world in forty volumes . . . , and Dio Cassius, . . . whose *History of Rome* extended to eighty books. We have only about a third of Polybius' work, with the first five books in their entirety; sixteen books of Diodore, and some very fragmentary excerpts; while from Dio Cassius we have books 36-40, fragments of books 78 and 79, and some very abbreviated summaries from the Byzantine period. (1980, 6-7)

Hengel's examples can easily be multiplied. Thucydides' famous *History of the Peloponnesian War* has come down to us incomplete, the eighth book stopping abruptly in the middle of a narrative.[3] The *Roman Antiquities* of Dionysius of Halicarnassus are only partially extant: the first ten of twenty books total. Suetonius's famous *Lives of the Caesars* lacks the first chapters of the first biography (Julius Caesar). Livy wrote a massive *History of Rome*, of which only thirty-five books of the original 142 survive. The major works of Tacitus, the *Histories* and the *Annals*, together comprised thirty books, of which about half survive. Of special interest is the fact that the end of the *Annals* appears to break off shortly before the death of Nero. Nepos, author of the earliest surviving Latin biographies, wrote at least sixteen books of *Lives*. One book and parts of a second are extant. Varro, the greatest Roman scholar and polymath of his day, reportedly edited hundreds of works. We know the titles of fifty-five of them. We possess two, one of them only partially. Petronius's *Satyricon* survives only in fragments: part of book 14, most of 15, and part of 16. The original total is estimated at twenty books. Finally, even Plutarch, upon whom the Fates seem to have smiled in preserving fifty biographies and seventy-eight other essays, was credited in antiquity with the authorship of nearly one hundred works which are not extant.[4] In particular, Plutarch's biography on Alexander the Great lacks its ending, and his biography on Caesar lacks its beginning, probably the result of a single instance of damage.[5]

New Testament documents have suffered similar ravages. Virtually all biblical manuscripts contain lacunae and other defects.[6] As one might guess, the beginnings and ends of works were particularly vulnerable. Papyrus 46, for example, originally contained 104 leaves. Only eighty-six leaves survive today, seven having been lost from both the beginning and the end.[7] The celebrated parchment manuscript, Codex Sinaiticus, originally comprised perhaps 730 leaves, of which a little over half survive.

One of the reasons some New Testament scholars may be reluctant to accept the hypothesis that Mark was mutilated is our inexperience with major disruptions in the transmission of New Testament literature, at least with disruptions that cause significant portions of texts to be permanently irretrievable.[8] Of course, well-trained New Testament scholars are quite able to do textual criticism, and some of them are experts at it. But I am speaking here of direct acquaintance with textual damage on a larger scale, damage that leaves texts incomplete, truncated, or indecipherable. We rarely encounter this in New Testament studies. The chief reason for this is our fortuitous possession of thousands of manuscripts, translations, and patristic quotations. There are scores, if not hundreds, of witnesses for most verses in the New Testament. Lacunae in one manuscript are compensated for by sound texts in other manuscripts. Not a single New Testament writing (with the exception of Mark, of course!) appears to have suffered major, irreparable loss. As a result, those of us who are not paleographical experts with experience outside the New Testament canon have rarely had to deal with writings represented by a hodgepodge of deteriorating papyrus fragments. In those situations when New Testament scholars have to sift through deteriorating papyri, they have the luxury of other intact manuscripts to guide them. But outside the domain of our twenty-seven well-preserved documents, the world of paleography is much more chaotic. Classicists regularly have to deal with fragmentary writings, expansive multi-volume works of which only a fraction survives. Qumran experts are familiar with decrepit and sometimes indecipherable documents like the Thanksgiving Hymns.[9] Such phenomena are commonplace and yet not fully appreciated by those whose work seldom takes them into such areas.

Textual loss is obviously to be expected in the case of centuries-old manuscripts that have survived to the present day. But damage also could occur to manuscripts *in* antiquity, that is, *prior to* aging and extensive use. Through some simple accident of mishandling, reckless transportation, or improper storage, a manuscript might suffer loss in the first few years or decades of its existence. When such damage occurred to an autograph or to one of a small number of copies, the loss was potentially permanent.

A particular example of such a loss has come to light, and because of fortuitous circumstances, we know with some precision the chronology of the loss. Julius Africanus, a Christian philosopher of the second and third centuries, wrote a work entitled *Kestoi* ("Embroiderings") which was published about 225–230 C.E. In the early twentieth century a papyrus was discovered which had on its front side the conclusion of the eighteenth book of Africanus's

Kestoi. The significance of this manuscript is explained by Walter Bauer.

> What makes the papyrus so important . . . is the reverse side, on which there is a document dated from the reign of the emperor Claudius Tacitus, i.e., in 275-76. This use of the verso for different purposes presupposes that the final leaf of Africanus' work had been previously detached from the body of the original manuscript, thus making it available for reuse. From this we deduce that it was possible for a manuscript to be separated into its component parts within a generation of its original production, and so disappear. The process of disintegration also could have taken place much more quickly. Nothing compels us to accept the maximal limits [225 C.E. to 276 C.E.] . . . as representing the actual span of time. (1971, 159)

The relevance of this discovery for the thesis of this book is apparent. It confirms the commonsense observation that writings do not have to be aged to come apart. Just as modern magazines may lose their covers through mishandling when they are no more than a few years old, so ancient manuscripts might lose outer portions within some years of their composition.

Mishaps resulting in permanent losses have befallen a number of ancient Jewish and Christian writings. Third Maccabees, the Apocalypse of Abraham, the Gospel According to Mary, and the Acts of John have lost their beginnings.[10] First Esdras, the extra-canonical Psalm 155, and Pseudo-Philo's *Biblical Antiquities* have lost their endings.[11] The Testament (or Assumption) of Moses, Psalm 154, the Gospel of Peter, and the Muratorian Canon lack both beginning and ending.[12] Philo's *On Rewards and Punishments* has a large lacuna in the middle of the work.[13] The judgment that these writings are mutilated is shared by most scholars who have studied them and is, needless to say, quite independent of the present study.

Some scholars would grant that damage occasionally occurred to manuscripts in antiquity but would still object to the "mutilation theory" of the Gospel of Mark on the grounds that such damage would surely have been repaired by Mark or someone in his community. It is manifestly the case, however, that similar damage occurred to other Jewish, Greco-Roman, and Christian writings *without* being repaired. Take, for example, the Gospel of Peter, which clearly lacks both its beginning and ending. Why, we might ask, did its author not repair this loss? Perhaps the loss occurred after the author's death. Why, then, did those in possession of this Gospel not restore the loss from memory or from other copies? Perhaps the damage occurred prior to transcription and dissemination of the writing when neither acquaintance with the document nor copies could supply the lack. The ultimate answer to all such questions is: We do not know. We know little about the transmission of early Christian literature in the first few generations and virtually nothing about the fate of the autographs.[14] All we can say about the transmission of the Gospel of Peter is that *somehow* it suffered damage, and the author or the persons in possession of it *could not* or *cared not to* supply what was missing. Our ignorance of the precise means of its mutilation does not change the fact that it happened.

D. C. Parker implies that our inability to answer such questions with certainty constitutes a major obstacle to the theory of mutilation: "The difficulty is that if an early copy had been damaged, it could have been made good from either the autograph or another copy. If it was the autograph, then why did not the evangelist repair it?" (1997, 143). Kurt Aland, one of the most prominent textual critics of the twentieth century, has argued similarly.[15] Aland vigorously rejects the theory of mutilation: "The theory of the accidental loss of the last leaf of the Gospel of Mark containing the text coming after 16:8 has from the outset all probability against it" (1988, 456). Aland speaks almost derisively of such an idea: "The theory . . . is thought up at the writer's desk and has no setting in life."[16] "How is one actually supposed to imagine the *accidental* loss of the last page of the original: Was Mark or the circle of persons surrounding him so reduced in their powers of perception that they did not notice the end was missing from the text given by them for further copying? To pose the question is, in my opinion, to answer it" (1988, 463). Thus Aland and Parker reject the theory of mutilation on practical grounds: the supposed impossibility of a scenario in which mutilation would go unrepaired. But both Parker and Aland make assumptions that may not be warranted, namely, the continuing presence of the author or a circle of students able and ready to remedy any loss. By this assumption, however, *no* writing from antiquity should *ever* have suffered permanent loss of a beginning, ending, or medial portion, for these questions could be posed to every alleged case! But since scores of documents from antiquity have come down to us in patently mutilated form, there is no *a priori* reason it could not have happened to Mark's Gospel.

All we know with relative certainty about the early transmission history of the Gospel of Mark is that within about twenty years of its composition it was apparently known and used by two other early Christian writers, the authors of the first and third Gospels. Between the time that Mark's Gospel was written (perhaps the mid-60s) and later used by Matthew and Luke (perhaps the mid-80s), the author of the Second Gospel could very well have died.[17] First-generation Christians were doing just that in large numbers about that time![18] Given the novelty of Mark's work and the continuation and competition of oral tradition, we do not know that his Gospel was initially seen as groundbreaking or even noteworthy.[19] Fifteen or twenty years later when the authors of Matthew and Luke made use of Mark, there could very well have been only a handful of recently made copies, all stemming from a defective exemplar. Thus when D. E. Nineham objects, "in the case of a *much-copied* [manuscript] such as St Mark's, we have to ask why the missing passage, when it got lost from one copy, was not supplied from another," I must ask, where do we get the notion that Mark was "much-copied"?[20] This is sheer assumption; indeed, probably a mistaken assumption since Mark was the least popular Gospel in the early church and was probably seen as superseded by Matthew and Luke. Indeed, F. C. Burkitt argues that Mark "ran a very serious risk of being forgotten altogether" (1903–1904, 342). In sum, we should not consider it so improbable that a mutilated autograph of an ancient writing would go unrepaired. It happened frequently.[21]

Not only was the mutilation of manuscripts common, but remarkably two ancient manuscripts of Mark's Gospel were mutilated *at precisely the point of 16:8!* Bruce Metzger notes that in Greek manuscript 2386 the last page of Mark's Gospel closes with *ephobounto gar* ("for they were afraid"), but the next leaf of the manuscript is missing, and a lectionary marker implies that the missing page continued with material from Mark (presumably the Long Ending). Similarly, the original hand of an Arabic manuscript breaks off just before the end of 16:8 because of missing leaves.[22] Another interesting coincidence occurs in Horapollo's *Hieroglyphica*

(2.80). A description of a hieroglyph ends abruptly with *houtos gar* ("for this . . ."), which is obviously not a complete sentence. A lacuna in the text has left a dangling *gar* not unlike the one in Mark 16:8.[23]

If the textual remains from antiquity make it clear that damage to manuscripts was commonplace, it remains only to consider the specific nature of the damage that seems to have befallen the Gospel of Mark. I have already indicated that beginnings and endings of documents were the most vulnerable portions. That commonsense observation leads naturally to a consideration of the form of ancient manuscripts.

2. THE FORM OF ANCIENT MANUSCRIPTS

Writings in antiquity normally assumed one of two possible forms: the scroll or the codex. Literary works in the Greco-Roman world were normally published in scroll form. Scrolls were produced by gluing together, side by side, separate sheets of papyrus or parchment and then winding the resultant strip of material around a stick. A codex, on the other hand, was made by placing several sheets of papyrus or parchment in a stack. They were then folded in half and stitched down the middle to create a "leaf book."[24]

The codex is thus the forerunner of the modern book form. Although its advantages over the scroll seem obvious to us, the codex was a later development and only rather slowly replaced the scroll among Greek and Roman authors. Christians, however, preferred the codex with a zeal that to this day is not fully understood, and the disparity between Christian use of the codex and that of Greco-Roman writers is remarkable. Colin H. Roberts and T. C. Skeat, authors of the definitive work on the ancient codex, note that "[i]n contrast to the slow and piecemeal process by which the codex ousted the roll in secular literature, the Christian adoption of the codex seems to have been instant and universal" (1983, 53).

Statistics provided by Roberts and Skeat show the transition from scroll to codex among secular Greek (but not Latin) literary and scientific writings. The following graph shows successive centuries or "bridging periods" (e.g., 1-2), and the percentages of codices to the nearest half percent (Roberts and Skeat 1983, 36-37).

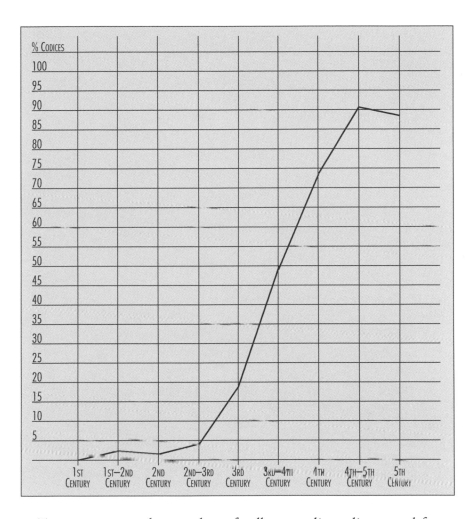

% CODICES

| | 1ST CENTURY | 1ST–2ND CENTURY | 2ND CENTURY | 2ND–3RD CENTURY | 3RD CENTURY | 3RD–4TH CENTURY | 4TH CENTURY | 4TH–5TH CENTURY | 5TH CENTURY |

To some extent the number of rolls or codices discovered from a particular century is dependent on chance factors of survival. But given that chance would not necessarily favor one form over the other, the numbers are trustworthy as a general guide. As such, they reveal an unmistakable trend and an approximate timeline. The codex only began to make modest headway among secular Greek writers in the third century, but by the fifth it was the dominant form.

The situation among Christian writings presents a stark contrast. The numbers cannot be usefully presented in a graph since a line representing "rolls" would be nearly nonexistent. Roberts and

Skeat note that "there are approximately 172 Biblical manuscripts or fragments of manuscripts written before A.D. 400 or not long thereafter (i.e., including items which have been dated fourth-fifth century)."[25] Of these 158 are from codices and fourteen are usually judged to be from scrolls. But Roberts and Skeat note that closer examination shows the disparity to be even greater. Five of the fourteen rolls are opisthographs, "back-side writings," that is, manuscripts in which biblical texts have been written on the back of reused rolls. In these cases the existing material imposed the format. Just as it would be a mistake to conclude that twentieth-century Americans normally printed maps on restaurant napkins just because a few might be discovered, so these opisthographs are exceptions that do not reveal standard practices. Of the remaining nine rolls, Roberts and Skeat judge that three are probably of Jewish origin and two more possibly so. Certain eccentricities exclude two more, leaving only two normal rolls of indisputably Christian origin. These two are both Hebrew Bible texts, one of the Psalms, the other of Isaiah. Thus Roberts and Skeat conclude that "no text of any part of the New Testament is known written on the recto of a roll."[26]

Thus the early Christian community seemed to have "not merely a preference . . . for the codex form, but an exclusive devotion to it" (Roberts and Skeat 1983, 45). If one examines the data from the *earliest* period, in particular the second century, the devotion appears to be universal. All Christian manuscripts datable to the second century (six Hebrew Bible texts and five New Testament texts) are in codex form.[27] This means that while Christians were not necessarily the inventers of the codex, they were certainly its popularizers.[28] Kurt Aland judges that "from all appearances the codex form was used by Christian writers from the very beginning."[29]

Strangely, this fact has been slow in entering the lore of New Testament scholarship. A century ago it was commonly held, probably under the influence of secular literary practice, that the codex form of a manuscript required a date later than the third century.[30] Discoveries of Christian papyri over the last hundred years have repeatedly shown that notion to be false. Nevertheless, the assumption of the priority of the scroll in early Christianity still makes an occasional appearance. W. H. P. Hatch could be excused for writing in 1939 that "The original manuscripts of the New Testament, the so-called autographs . . . were papyrus rolls."[31] Less defensible is the statement of a recent major reference work: "The form of most NT books originally was that of a roll."[32] Similarly, an entry in another authoritative work asserted: "Every manuscript of the P[astoral] E[pistles] is in codex form. Yet the Greek text of the P[astoral] E[pistles] was originally composed, in all probability, on . . . rolls" (Quinn 1992, 6:562).

It is, of course, *conceivable* that the autographs of the New Testament writings were composed on scrolls. Since the autographs are not extant and the earliest surviving copies date from a century or more later, there may have been a brief period of time during which Christian writings were in the form of scrolls, which were then *promptly* and *completely* supplanted by codices.[33] But the assumption of the priority of the scroll among Christian writings is a conjecture with scarcely any material evidence.[34] The only argument in favor of this thesis would be a supposed analogy between Christian writings and Jewish or Greco-Roman writings. Yet all the material evidence suggests that the Christian preference for the codex form was without analogy. One could say, with only slight exaggeration, that there is scarcely a *scrap* of evidence to support the priority of the scroll among New Testament writings, especially the Gospels.

On the other hand, the material evidence for the *codex* form includes all the major Christian papyrus discoveries. The eleven Chester Beatty papyri, dating from the second to fourth centuries, are all codices. The twenty-two Bodmer papyri containing biblical texts are dated to the same centuries and are without exception in codex form.[35] Most strikingly, the two earliest known fragments of any Christian writing are from codices: p[52], a small fragment of the Gospel of John, and Egerton papyrus 2, a collection of five fragments of a noncanonical, Gospel-type document. Both of these manuscripts are generally dated no later than 150.[36]

The reasons for the Christian preference for the codex seem obvious at first:

1. Compactness and Comprehensiveness. The codex format could encompass a large amount of text in a very manageable size. When the four Gospels were collected or the Pauline corpus was gathered together, the codex form could accommodate the entire

collection, something that would have been virtually impossible for a roll.

2. Convenience of Use and Reference. The codex form was easier to handle than a scroll, and it facilitated the consultation of proof texts, since turning to a given page must have been easier than rolling and unrolling a scroll, even for someone adept in the latter.

3. Economy. A codex could be inscribed on both sides, thus reducing the cost of writing material. Although little is known about ancient book prices, it has been estimated that the codex form might reduce the cost of producing a book by one quarter.[37]

But these practical explanations run up against practical questions. Why did the advantages of the codex not drive the scroll completely into extinction? Even when the codex came to dominate literature, the scroll continued to be used for administrative records. More important, why did these advantages, which swiftly and pervasively won over Christian writers, have so little effect on Greek and Roman writers until the third century and later? Would not a feature of the codex that was advantageous to a Christian author have been equally advantageous to a secular author?[38]

These questions have prompted other explanations for the Christian adoption of the codex, explanations that find some specific causation among Christians. Social class has been proposed: Christians not being members of the social elite would have been more familiar with the codices of "popular literature" than with rolls. But the two foundations of this theory are dubious: the alleged peasantry of most early Christians and the codex form of so-called popular literature.[39] Indeed, Loveday Alexander argues more persuasively that the "middle class" status of many early Christians would have predisposed them to use the codex.[40]

Alternately, it has been suggested that the geographical mobility of early Christian missionaries might have made the handy, portable codex more popular (McCormick 1985, 157-58). This again is a practical advantage that one would think would be noticed by non-Christian neighbors, given that mobility was a general characteristic of the imperial era by no means limited to Christian preachers. Indeed, the Roman poet Martial observed this very fact: the suitability of the codex for travelers. Another suggestion has involved specifically religious motivation: Perhaps early Christians used the codex as one of many ways to distinguish their worship from that of the synagogue with its scrolls.[41] But virtually the opposite argument has also been made: that early Christians were mimicking Jewish practices by writing down the sayings of Rabbi Jesus in codex notebooks, for this was the most suitable form for recording *logia*, the Christian counterpart to the oral law.[42]

It has been conjectured that some major development with particular trendsetting, religious authority must lie behind so dramatic a departure from the (secular) norm of the scroll.[43] I have already alluded to two such events in the early church: the gathering of the four Gospels in a single document and the collection of the Pauline corpus. The former has been argued by Skeat.[44] The latter has been championed by Harry Gamble.[45] Overall, I find Gamble's thesis more persuasive. The establishment of the authority of the four canonical gospels and their collection into a single manuscript probably did not occur before the latter half of the second century, but there are good grounds for the same occurring with Paul's letters several decades earlier.[46]

Thus the reasons proposed for the Christian preference for the codex format are manifold. Practical advantages and sociological distinctions probably played a role, but some major impetus such as the collection of the Epistles of Paul may have been the catalyst for the explosive spread of the codex at the end of the first century and the beginning of the second.[47] For the purposes of the present study, final resolution of this matter is not necessary, for my main concern here is with a particular writing, the Gospel of Mark. Mark's connection to the codex form and the reasons for the adoption of that form across Christendom may very well be two separate issues.[48]

3. THE GOSPEL OF MARK AND THE CODEX FORM

We must now consider the relevance of the codex form for the thesis of this book. Could Christians have adopted the codex as early as the time of Mark's composition? If so, could the codex form account for the present state of the Second Gospel? The answer to the first question appears to be yes. Again, Roberts and Skeat: "[S]o universal is the Christian use of the codex in the second century that its introduction *must date well before A.D. 100.*"[49] These same scholars also note that the earliest extant Christian codices "are all, so far as we can judge, provincial productions, and it is thus *in the highest degree unlikely* that they are the earliest codices ever produced."[50] Thus, manuscript evidence and distribution patterns together increase the possibility that Christian use of the codex could reach back to the time of Mark's autograph.[51]

A corroborating bit of evidence is the early association of the codex with Rome. Martial, who lived in Rome from about 64 C.E. until the end of the century, describes codices in several of his epigrams.[52] Roberts and Skeat identify these particular epigrams, written in 84–85 C.E., as "the first unmistakable reference to *literary* publication in codex form."[53] (The codex form had already been in use for notebooks and other unpublished writings for decades, as far back as the late Republic.[54] The distinction of Martial's remarks is the reference to *literary* works being available in codex form.) In particular, Martial refers to the works of Homer, Virgil, Cicero, Livy, and Ovid as being *in membranis* ("on parchments") or *in pugillaribus membraneis* ("on parchment writing tablets").[55] The latter description especially requires us to understand that the books were in codex form and of small size (Roberts and Skeat 1983, 25). Although this publishing venture seems not to have been immediately successful,[56] Martial's comments prove that the codex form was being employed in Rome during the last few decades of the first century C.E. Several scholars go beyond that and affirm Rome or Italy as the birthplace of the codex.[57]

Not only Martial's date (roughly contemporary with Mark) but his location (Rome) may be relevant to the composition of Mark's Gospel. Although the provenance of the Second Gospel cannot be determined with certainty, a strong tradition associates Mark with Rome.[58] If Mark composed his Gospel in Rome at any time during the 60s or 70s, he almost certainly would have been familiar with the use of codex notebooks for unofficial writings and possibly would have known of their use for literary works. The date and location of Martial's codices, then, combined with the strong penchant of early Christians for the codex form, have convinced a number of experts that Mark's Gospel was originally produced as a codex.

Mark, written in the West and for circulation privately, would almost certainly have been copied out in a vellum codex.

[I]t is not merely "a tenable hypothesis," . . . but an almost certain one, that Mark, the Roman Gospel, the simplest and least literary of all, was written first in a codex, was copied by this Christian and that into other codices as they desired to have it, and rarely or never appeared in a roll.

[A] reasonable theory to account for the probable loss of the original ending of the Gospel according to Mark is that that book was published at the outset in a codex: in a codex the last leaf is most likely to suffer damage; in a roll the destruction is most apt to be at the beginning.

That Mark's original manuscript was in codex form is independently suggested by the text of the Gospel itself. If the Gospel as we have it is incomplete, as it was clearly thought to be in the ancient world, the loss of the ending is much more intelligible if the manuscript was a codex, since the outermost leaves of a codex are the most exposed to damage, in complete contrast to the last column of a roll, which being in the interior of the manuscript when rolled up is the best protected. . . . the original manuscript [of Mark] was in all probability so neglected that it lost its final leaf.[59]

As the third and fourth quotes above indicate, the likely codex form of Mark's Gospel also provides a good explanation for the nature of its damage. Whereas the *beginning* of a scroll is exposed and therefore most vulnerable to damage (unless it is not rewound after use), the vulnerable parts of a codex are *both* the beginning *and* the ending. A single instance of damage could account for Mark's apparent losses. As C. F. D. Moule observed years ago, "if [Mark's] original autograph was on a codex and not a roll . . . , then it only requires the bottom sheet to be lost for beginning and end to go at one stroke."[60] The codex form would also make unnecessary extensive "wear and tear" or severe mishandling, inasmuch as the loss of an outer cover requires only the breakage of either a few stitches or the fold of the material.

This raises the question of the likely *material* of Mark's autograph. Here the evidence is conflicting. The paleographical evidence heavily favors papyrus since extant Christian manuscripts from the earliest period are consistently of that material.[61] Papyrus would lend itself well to the thesis of this book since it is usually considered less durable than parchment. That is *not* to say that papyrus was inherently fragile. Skeat has argued that papyrus was, in fact, rather strong *as a writing material* (1969, 59-60). While this is true, I would note that in codex form papyrus might become somewhat fragile *at the fold of the spine*. Indeed, Helmut Koester has made this very point: "Papyrus was not well suited for the production of codices, because it would tend to break at the fold."[62]

The conflicting evidence comes from Martial's statements. Although extant remains of the earliest Christian manuscripts are of papyrus, it would seem that parchment prevailed at Rome. Moreover, the prevalence of papyri among the earliest Christian manuscripts could be due in part to the place where they were discovered. The dry climate of Egypt was favorable to the survival of manuscripts. Since the Nile River was the chief source of plants for papyrus production, it should occasion no surprise that most manuscripts discovered in Egypt are of that material. So it is hard to venture more than a guess about the material of Mark's autograph. Whether papyrus or parchment, though, the codex form is probable, and damage of the sort that Mark's Gospel appears to have sustained is easily conceivable.

A final word about the form of Mark's autograph is in order. The simultaneous loss of both the first leaf and the last assumes a single-quire codex. A quire is a gathering of sheets. It would be comparable in structure to most modern magazines or stapled booklets. A codex might be made of one quire or multiple quires. Both logic and paleographic evidence suggest that single-quire codices preceded multiple-quire codices.[63] One should not think that the single-quire format would severely restrict the quantity of text that could be published. Campbell Bonner asserts that "[c]onsiderable evidence has accumulated to show that early papyrus books often consisted of surprisingly large single gatherings."[64] Bonner cites examples of single-quire papyrus codices with 21, 24, 25, 36, 41, 104, and 112 sheets. Manuscript p[75] was a single-quire codex of 144 pages! Although the single-quire format was eventually replaced by the multi-quire, in the earliest era, it was clearly not thought to be restrictive. A single-quire codex, therefore, could easily accommodate an individual gospel. It did

have certain disadvantages, however. Metzger notes that in addition to "being pudgy and somewhat clumsy to use, a single-quire
codex tends to break at the spine."[65] In sum, then, it seems more
likely that Mark's original manuscript was a single-quire codex.
The question of parchment or papyrus is a toss-up. I incline
slightly toward the latter given the greater likelihood of damage to
papyrus, but I would not wed my thesis irrevocably either to
papyrus as the material or to the single-quire as the form of Mark's
autograph.

4. THE PHYSICAL FORM AND INTERPRETATION OF ANCIENT TEXTS

Although the physical form of ancient texts would generally
seem to be a matter unrelated to the interpretation of those texts,
there are circumstances in which this is not the case. When we
engage in historical-critical interpretation, that is, the pursuit of
meaning as informed by the author's intentions and conditioned
by the author's environment, we cannot ignore the material realities of textual production and preservation. The materiality of
embodied texts sometimes affects the texts as conveyors of meaning. Losses, damage, lacunae, and rearrangement can obscure and
distort authorial intent, at times to the degree that sheer chance
becomes a kind of coauthor of the conveyed meaning.[66] Literary
scholars Parker and Binder issue a warning on this very point.

> To accept a [writing] simply impossible in its facts or lack of conti-
> nuity and to reduce it to something we can analyze is hardly defen-
> sible as "close reading"—not if we discover higher unities by
> ignoring serious disjunctions. Wishing to be objective explicators,
> we run the risk of closing our eyes to exigencies of composition and
> publication as having no possible bearing on the "work." Yet we sim-
> ply cannot read certain books unless we first study the surviving
> . . . manuscript; and we may have to face the possibility that certain
> problematical books for which such evidence does not survive may
> be ultimately unreadable, however earnestly we will, of necessity,
> continue to attempt to read them.[67]

This statement is all the more remarkable when one learns that
it was made by scholars studying nineteenth-century novels. If this

caveat is necessary for writings of that era, it is all the more necessary for writings from antiquity. Whereas ancient texts certainly
can be interpreted without reference to the physical realities of
their production and transmission, in some instances that
approach may preclude highly significant causal factors behind the
physical state of the extant manuscripts.

5. ANCIENT BOOKS AND NEW TESTAMENT TERMINOLOGY

In this chapter I have considered chiefly the paleographical evidence for the form of ancient books, especially the New Testament
writings. Another avenue to investigate the same question is the
philological evidence, that is, the terminology used by early
Christians. In other words, when Christians write about their writings, what is implied, if anything, about the physical forms of their
work? It is at least theoretically possible that such evidence could
be of decisive value. On the secular side, we saw that Martial's comments were solid proof of the existence of parchment codices in
Rome in the year 85 C.E. Are there similar comments in the New
Testament writings that reveal the forms used by early Christians?

Edgar Goodspeed thought so. Based on his understanding of
certain New Testament passages, Goodspeed asserted that "[t]o
the end of the first century at least, Christian publishers employed
the old-fashioned roll form for their books. The evidence for this is
clear and explicit" (1940, 72). Unfortunately, it is neither.
Goodspeed appeals, for example, to Acts 1:1 as evidence of the
early Christian use of scrolls. Here Luke refers to his Gospel as the
first "book" or "treatise." But the Greek word here is *logos,* from
which virtually nothing about the physical form can be inferred.

Somewhat more specific are the references in the Apocalypse of
John, which uses the word *biblion* over twenty times. First I would
note that for *biblion* the standard Greek lexicon offers "scroll,
book," suggesting that the word alone is not determinative of the
form. Context, however, may solve the dilemma. Revelation 5:1-10
is an especially important passage, for *biblion* occurs seven times in
a single, vivid scene. Here John sees "a scroll written on the inside
and on the back, sealed with seven seals" (v. 1). The description
virtually demands the roll form. But a visionary experience is not

necessarily descriptive of early Christian practice, not even of the form used by John himself. Moreover, John is clearly borrowing imagery from Ezekiel (2:9-10), a fact that suggests the details may derive from traditional apocalypticism rather than contemporary customs.[68] John's dependence on Ezekiel 2:8–3:3 is even more evident in Revelation 10:8-10 where the seer is told to take a "little scroll" (biblaridion) from the hand of an angel and eat it. Generalization from Jewish apocalyptic imagery to Christian literary customs is tenuous at best.

The scene in the Nazareth synagogue in Luke 4:16-30 is another instance in which context may favor the scroll form. Here Jesus is handed "the scroll [biblion] of the prophet Isaiah," which he "unrolled" (anaptuxas), read from, "rolled up" (ptuxas), and handed back to the attendant. The key verbs here arguably favor a scroll over a codex, but even this can be challenged since ptussō essentially means "to put something away after use by putting one part over another, fold up, roll up, close," and does not in itself require the scroll format (BDAG 2000, 895). Moreover, anoixas, meaning simply "having opened," is a strong variant reading for anaptuxas ("having unrolled") in Luke 4:17.[69] Finally, even if the scroll form is intended here, it is more likely an instance of Luke's historical accuracy, that is, reflecting the practice of the synagogue, than a subtle indication of early Christian usage.

Two final passages deserve mention. In 2 John 12 the word chartēs is usually taken to mean "a sheet of paper," with an emphasis on the material rather than the form. Although in some usages in the papyri the word means "a papyrus roll," it is not at all clear that it means that in 2 John 12 (BDAG 2000, 1081). Finally, in 2 Timothy 4:13, Paul (or a pseudonymous author) urges Timothy to bring to him "the cloak that I left with Carpus at Troas, also the books, and above all the parchments."[70] The last word is membrana. As in the case of chartēs, this word chiefly denotes the material, not the form of the writing, and both scrolls and codices have been suggested for the latter. There is also some ambiguity in the grammar, whether the "parchments" are a subset of the writings, as the above translation implies, or are appositional, meaning "the books, that is, the parchments."[71] In any event, there is no sure evidence here for early Christian usage of scrolls. If anything, Martial's use of the word, membrana, to denote parchment codices in Rome suggests that this is the more likely meaning of the word in 2 Timothy 4:13. At best, then, the philological evidence in the New Testament is inconclusive, and we must rely chiefly on paleographical evidence for early Christian customs.[72]

6. WHEN DID MARK'S GOSPEL SUSTAIN DAMAGE?

A final matter of interest is the question, when did this damage occur to Mark's Gospel? Most scholars who are sympathetic to the thesis of a lost ending would say that the window of opportunity is small. The chief reason for this assertion comes from comparisons with Matthew and Luke. Austin Farrer sums up the matter: "[I]t is the common agreement of scholars that, for all we can discern, the two synoptic evangelists had the same short text of St Mark before them which our best Egyptian [manuscripts] put before us. If there was a longer text, it must have vanished within about ten years of being written."[73] (I would be a bit more generous in estimating the window at potentially as great as fifteen to twenty years.) Synoptic comparison shows that Matthew and Luke are following Mark's general outline in their empty tomb narratives, with the exception of obvious redactional elements (e.g., Matthew's earthquake; Luke's alteration of the Galilee reference in Mark 16:7, etc.). At precisely the point of Mark 16:8, Matthew and Luke diverge significantly. Matthew tells of a meeting between the women and the risen Jesus; Luke tells of the women's report and Peter's visit to the tomb.

Robert Gundry is of the opinion that "the original ending of Mark has survived in redacted form outside Mark," namely in Matthew and Luke.[74] I am doubtful about this. The stark divergence of Matthew and Luke at this point calls into question any continued use of Mark as a common source. Matthew 28:8 and Luke 24:8-9 also seem to be quite intentional redactions of the disturbing ending at Mark 16:8, changes that would probably not have been necessary if their versions of Mark had continued. Moreover, although Gundry's view extends the window of opportunity during which the mutilation might have occurred, in other ways it makes the lost ending theory more difficult. If Matthew and Luke both had intact copies of Mark, that is, copies containing the original conclusion, then we have a scenario in which Mark was copied *at least* once, and probably twice (for both Matthew and Luke to have copies), and these copies were transported from the place of origin (Rome?) to new locations (Syria for Matthew? Greece for Luke?). Then *after* this copying and disseminating, all the existing copies of Mark but one disappeared, and the remaining one became damaged. Surely the longer the existence that one posits for intact copies of Mark and the greater their geographical dissemination, the less likely is the permanent loss of the ending. It seems more likely to me that Mark's Gospel was mutilated *before* Matthew and Luke obtained their copies and probably before transcription from the autograph. Thus, the damage would be dated somewhere between the time of composition and the use of Mark by Matthew and Luke, perhaps 65–85 C.E.

It is also evident that Matthew and Luke had nothing preceding Mark 1:1 in their copies of the Second Gospel, and may not even have had that verse. If, as I think, Mark's autograph was a codex, then the loss of the beginning occurred simultaneously with the loss of the ending and, therefore, would be dated to the same time period.

In the final chapter I will summarize the conclusions of this study, most of which are already apparent. I will attempt to do so in a way that respects the nature of historical study, particularly the fact that varying degrees of probability attach to any conclusions that one might draw. Finally, I will address the question, what theological difference does it make? In particular, what significance does the mutilation of Mark's Gospel have in relationship to the last few decades of its interpretation, and how should we proceed in reading and interpreting Mark if this thesis is correct?

NOTES

1. Schlatter (1984, 279).
2. Bagnall (1995, 10). The allusion is to Thucydides' *History* 1.22.
3. The last event narrated occurred in the winter of 411 B.C.E. Since Thucydides had earlier expressed his intent to narrate the conflict down to the year 404 (5.26.1), it appears that either manuscript damage or, more likely, the historian's death intervened.
4. I have focused in this paragraph primarily on historians and biographers. Similar data could be cited from every other genre of writing in antiquity. Early Christian writings also have suffered many losses. Hippolytus's most important

work, *The Refutation of All Heresies*, lacks its second and third books. Entire works by Origen, Clement of Alexandria, Eusebius, Methodius, and many others have not survived.

5. See Hamilton (1969, 217, also xxxiv n. 6).

6. One need only browse the manuscript lists in Aland and Aland (1987, 106-25, 128-35) to see how ubiquitous is the obelus (†) that indicates lacunae. See also Barbara Aland, et al. (1993, 684-718).

7. Metzger (1981, 64). Although I have not examined this manuscript, I would assume that an additional four medial leaves are missing.

8. It may not be coincidental that textual critics and paleographers are particularly well represented among those past and present scholars who doubt that 16:8 is Mark's intended conclusion. Note, in approximate chronological order: Griesbach, Lachmann, Kenyon, Lake, Westcott and Hort, Gregory, J. Harris, McCown, Roberts and Skeat, Metzger, Comfort, Greenlee, and J. Elliott. Such scholars are particularly in touch with the physicality and fragility of ancient texts.

9. Vermes (1999, 45) speaks of the "bad state of preservation" of the hymns and the difficulty of even determining how many hymns are contained in the document.

10. For 3 Maccabees and the Apocalypse of Abraham, see Charlesworth (2:513 and 1:689 n. 1a); for the Gospel According to Mary and the Acts of John, see Hennecke and Schneemelcher (1:340 and 2:215).

11. For 1 Esdras, see Meeks (1993, 1745); for Psalm 155 and Pseudo-Philo, see Charlesworth (2:622-23 and 2:298).

12. For the Testament of Moses and Psalm 154, see Charlesworth (1:927-34 and 2:618-19); for the Gospel of Peter and the Muratorian Canon, see Hennecke and Schneemelcher (1:179 and 1:42).

13. See Schürer (3.2.853).

14. Although our knowledge of early Christian literary collections is limited, Metzger (1992, 201 n. 1) rightly observes that the heresy debates of the early second century imply the disappearance of the autographs by that time, "otherwise an appeal would have been made directly to them. Their early loss is not surprising, for during persecutions the toll taken by imperial edicts aiming to destroy all copies of the sacred books of Christians must have been heavy."

15. See Kurt Aland (1969, 1970, and 1988). The last of these, a reprint of an article first published in 1979, is the most extensive. For other thorough treatments of the textual problem, see Hug (1978) and C. Williams (1915).

16. Aland (1988, 457): "Die Theorie . . . ist am Schreibtisch erdacht und hat keinen 'Sitz im Leben'." By the latter statement Aland means that, in his opinion, no real-life scenario would produce such mutilation.

17. Needless to say, these dates are approximate. There is no compelling reason why Mark could not have been written as early as the 50s or as late as the 70s. Exactness about the time span is immaterial to my argument.

18. One need not appeal to the possibility of violent persecution and martyrdom, Neronic or otherwise (although such a scenario should not be ruled out; see Streeter 1925, 338; and note 14 above). Christians of Mark's generation would be dying during the 70s of natural causes.

19. The preference for oral tradition is reflected in the remark of Papias preserved by Eusebius (*Hist. eccl.* 3.39.4). See Hengel (2000, 253 n. 275).

20. Nineham (1963, 441); my emphasis.

21. See Gundry (1993, 1021). One potential scenario for the mutilation of the Second Gospel is as intriguing to me as it is conjectural. The traditions about the origin of Mark's Gospel are basically twofold: a strong tradition connects the gospel with Rome; a weaker tradition locates its origin in Alexandria. Suppose that the Gospel of Mark was composed in Rome, as seems likely, and was later transported by its author to Alexandria. Then in Alexandria, the document suffered damage. About the same time the evangelist himself suffered damage, i.e., died. This would explain both the dual tradition about its origin as well as the inability of the church in Alexandria to supply the missing portions. I sketch this scenario fully aware of its speculative nature. I think it is plausible, but my thesis does not depend on it.

22. Metzger (1994, 102 n. 1 and 103 n. 3). The Arabic manuscript in question is Rom. Vat. Arab. 13.

23. Leemans (1835, 94 and 367) and Bauer (1979, 151).

24. E. Turner (1968, 7-8) and Metzger (1992, 5-6).

25. Roberts and Skeat (1983, 38). All the data in this paragraph come from Roberts and Skeat (1983, 38-44).

26. Roberts and Skeat (1983, 40). The recto is the preferred writing side of papyrus where the fibers run horizontally.

27. Roberts and Skeat (1983, 40). See also Epp (1992, 6:417).

28. See Ehrman and Holmes (1995, 374): "The discovery of the papyri has made it virtually certain that even if Christians did not invent the physical form of the codex, they exploited its possibilities and popularized its use."

29. Aland and Aland (1987, 101-2). H. Sanders (1938, 109) reached the same conclusion many years earlier: "For the Christian literature, codices were probably used from the first." See also Trobisch (2000, 19).

30. See Pietersma (1992b, 1:901, 3a) and F. Turner (1968, 10).

31. Hatch (1939, 3). Hatch acknowledges (1939, 12) that the codex was in use among Christians in Egypt "as early as the first half of the second century after Christ, and it may have made its appearance somewhat earlier." Two years earlier than Hatch, H. I. Bell (1937, 25) opined, "It looks as if Christians were the most potent influence in the substitution . . . of the codex, whether vellum or papyrus, for the roll."

32. Achtemeier (1996, 1119). The quote comes from an article entitled "Texts, Versions, Manuscripts, Editions," written by David Ewert and Bruce M. Metzger.

33. See Beare (1945, 164-66) for the argument favoring the priority of the scroll among early Christians.

34. Kümmel (1975, 513) rightly infers this from the evidence: "No NT writing has been preserved in the original, yet on the basis of the oldest papyrus manuscripts of the NT it can be conjectured that the originals of the NT writings were written on both sides of papyrus sheets ("notebook form")." I find it especially odd that Skeat, an expert paleographer, would write, "We must assume, in the absence of any evidence to the contrary, that the Gospels originally circulated in

the usual way, on papyrus *rolls*" (1994, 266; my emphasis). Three pages earlier in the same article, Skeat observed that "in the case of the Gospels, representation of the codex is not a matter of degree—it is total, 100%." Since, in fact, *all* the extant manuscript evidence is to the contrary, it is not apparent why we "must assume" the priority of the roll form, particularly with the Gospel of Mark.

35. On the Chester Beatty papyri and the Bodmer papyri, see Pietersma (1992a and b).

36. On p[52], see Metzger (1981, 62). On Egerton papyrus 2, see Gamble (1992b, 2:317-18). Welles (1964) claimed that another papyrus (P. Yale 1) was actually the earliest Christian manuscript, dated between 80 and 100 C.E. See also Oates, Samuel, and Welles (1967, 3-8 and plate 1). This discovery was at first received with much interest (see C. Roberts 1966; and Skeat 1969, 2:71), but closer examination has led to a later dating (see C. Roberts 1979, 4, 13, and 55; Metzger 1981, 62).

37. On the general advantages of the codex, see Roberts and Skeat (1983, 45-53), Gamble (1990, 266-68), Metzger (1992, 6), and Trobisch (2000, 69-77). On the cost advantage of the codex, see Skeat (1982, 169-75).

38. Richards (1998, 153) points out the failure of scholars "to explain adequately why *Christians* noticed this practicality [of the codex] and others did not—that is, why the preference for the codex was a *Christian* phenomenon." See also L. Alexander (1998, 77).

39. William V. Harris (1991, 75) rightly criticizes this theory of G. Cavallo. See also Llewelyn (1994, 252-53).

40. L. Alexander (1998, 82): "Urban Christians tended to belong precisely to the socially ambiguous groups associated with the codex in iconography: prosperous artisans, small businesspeople and clerks, clients and dependents of the educated elite, but not, for the most part, fully participant in the restricted social world of the dominant literary elite." The dominant literary elite would have chiefly used the scroll until the fourth century and later.

41. This was suggested in a short note by Peter Katz (1945, 63-65) and argued more fully by Irven M. Resnick (1992).

42. Lieberman (1962, 203-08). Lieberman's theory is weakened by the late and sketchy quality of the evidence for the use of codices in Judaism. Moreover, the suggestion that Jesus' sayings were written down in notebooks by his disciples is at best speculative. Roberts and Skeat (1983, 59) regard it as possible; Gamble (1990, 269-70) finds it unpersuasive. Equally intriguing and speculative is the suggestion of Sato, who has argued that Q, the "sayings source," took the form of a loose-leaf notebook, which facilitated the gradual collection of sayings (1988, 62-65; part of which has been translated into English in Sato 1994, 178-79).

43. Llewelyn (1994, 251-56) has an excellent summary of four hypotheses concerning the Christian adoption of the codex.

44. Skeat (1994 and 1997, 31-33).

45. Gamble (1990, esp. 271-80) and (1995, esp. 58-63). Several decades earlier Finegan (1956, esp. 88) had argued for the original collection of Paul's letters in a codex. Richards (1998) offers a variation on Gamble's thesis.

46. Gamble (1990, 278). On the recognition of the authority of Paul's letters even within the New Testament canon, see 2 Peter 3:15-16.

47. Hengel (2000, 119-21) favors a combination of theological, sociological, and practical reasons for the Christian adoption of the codex.

48. C. Roberts (1954, 187-89) originally put forward the hypothesis that (1) Mark adopted the codex form for his Gospel, that (2) he traveled to Alexandria where his Gospel was copied from the original parchment over to papyrus, and that (3) the authority of Mark's Gospel was the catalyst for the adoption of the codex form across the church. Later Roberts himself, along with Skeat (1983, 54-57) abandoned this hypothesis as too problematic. It has also been criticized by Llewelyn (1994, 251-52) and Gamble (1995, 56-57). Lest I appear here to be advocating a theory that has been forsaken by its own author, I want to emphasize that Mark's adoption of the codex is on much surer ground than parts two and three of Roberts's early hypothesis. A careful reading of Roberts and Skeat (1983, 56-57) reveals that the objections they acknowledge against the thesis *all pertain to parts two and three*. Roberts did *not* abandon the view that Mark was originally written in codex form. Indeed, one of the objections to part three of the thesis is that Mark was so ignored and neglected, particularly in Alexandria, that it could not have exerted such influence on the wider church. In acknowledging this, Roberts says that "the original manuscript was in all probability so neglected that *it lost its final leaf*" (Roberts and Skeat, 1983, 57; my emphasis). This statement clearly shows that part one of the thesis is still assumed. Llewelyn (1994, 254) makes a helpful distinction: "The earliest attestations for the use of codex format suggest that it was a Roman innovation. However, it does not follow that one should look to Rome and the Roman church in particular to account for subsequent Christian practice."

49. Roberts and Skeat (1983, 45); my emphasis. Burton Throckmorton (1992, xi) agrees: "The codex was introduced into Christian usage well before 100 A.D."

50. Roberts and Skeat (1983, 61); my emphasis

51. About fifty years ago Souter (1954, 7) observed that "[in]any New Testament papyri are in codex (book) form, which Christians favoured *(perhaps as early as St. Mark himself)* for ease of reference" (my emphasis).

52. For the Latin text, see Friedlaender (1961). For commentary, see Howell (1980), Roberts and Skeat (1983, 24-29), Leary (1996), Trobisch (2000, 69-70), and the important article by D. Fowler (1995).

53. Roberts and Skeat (1983, 24); my emphasis.

54. See McCown (1941, 221-22); Howell (1980, 105); Reynolds and Wilson (1991, 34); Horace, *Sat.* 2.3.2; and Quintilian, *Inst.* 10.3.31. On the reference to parchment notebooks in 2 Timothy 4:13, see Skeat (1979), Donfried (1989), and Richards (1998, 160-62).

55. The relevant passages in Martial are Epigrams I.2, and in the *Apophoreta*: XIV.184, 186, 188, 190, and 192.

56. See Roberts and Skeat (1983, 27-28), L. Alexander (1998, 75), and Howell (1980, 105-6).

57. Roberts and Skeat (1983, 15), McCormick (1985, 151), Llewelyn (1994, 254), Skeat (1994, 267-68), Maehler (1996, 252); and, less explicitly,

L. Alexander (1998, 74). Trobisch (2000, 21) observes: "There is plenty of evidence, especially of Roman provenance, that the codex form was popular in pre-Christian times."

58. Eusebius preserves testimony by Papias (*Hist. eccl.* 2.15.2; 3.39.15), Irenaeus (*Hist. eccl.* 5.8.2-3), and Clement of Alexandria (*Hist. eccl.* 6.14.6) that makes a connection between Mark's Gospel and Rome. Latin loanwords in Mark are sometimes thought to corroborate a Roman provenance. See Hengel (1985, 28-30), Guthrie (1990, 71-75), and Brown (1997, 161-62). Gamble's remark (1995, 57) that the Roman origin of Mark's Gospel is one of several "tenuous notions with little or no support in modern scholarship" is surprising. In fact, it claims many adherents and may even be the majority view. See Kümmel (1975, 97), Brown (1997, 161), Ellis (1999, 357), and Hengel (2000, 67-68, 78, 259 n. 318). For a serious, but I think unsuccessful, argument for Syria as the place of origin, see Marcus (2000b, 33-37).

59. These quotes come from, respectively, Sanders (1938, 110-11), McCown (1941, 239; see also 1943, 30), Finegan (1956, 88), and Roberts and Skeat (1983, 55, 57). So also P. Parker (1953, 120-21), Comfort (1992a, 49), and Hengel (2000, 122). McCown (1941, 240-41) thinks that lost leaves from a Markan codex might also account for the "great omission" in Luke's Gospel where he skips over the narrative of Mark 6:44–8:26. Luke's copy of Mark may have lacked these pages.

60. Moule (1982, 131 n. 1). See also Bonner (1934, 9).

61. Lemaire (1992, 6:1004): "Most of the NT books . . . were probably first written on papyrus." E. Turner (1977, 35-42) has argued that the supposed priority of the parchment codex over papyrus is questionable.

62. Koester (1982, 1:81). E. Turner (1968, 13) notes that the single-quire papyrus codex, "even if stiffened internally with bands of parchment, is liable to tear or break at the spine."

63. See Ibscher (1937). E. Turner (1977, 98-100) has challenged Ibscher's "law" of the priority of single-quire codex, but Turner's own evidence largely establishes Ibscher's view as a strong tendency, though perhaps not as an absolute rule. Turner is able to cite only two early multi-quire codices. His own "Table 6" (1977, 58-59), on the other hand, lists as many as forty-nine early single-quire codices, the great majority of which are dated to the third or fourth century. See also McCown (1941, 232), Gamble (1992, 1.1067), and Hengel (2000, 122).

64. Bonner (1934, 10). See also E. Turner (1977, 58).

65. Metzger (1981, 16). E. Turner (1977, 57-58) makes the same observation: a single-quire codex of the playright Menander made up of 16 sheets (32 leaves, 64 pages) is of a size that "makes it tend to break at the spine." Indeed, this particular manuscript had been restitched twice!

66. Brown (1994, 6-9) has a helpful discussion of "intended" meaning vs. "conveyed" meaning.

67. Parker and Binder (1978, 142-43). I have made two minor editorial changes in the quote to show its relevance to ancient writings as well as modern. In the first line I substituted the word "writing" for the original "chapter." In the third sentence the three dots indicate an omission of the words "draft pages or."

Shillingsburg (1997, 3) makes a similar point about texts in general: If one is concerned about the ability of authors and/or texts to communicate meaning, then "it . . . matters if the text one uses has been accidentally, rather than consciously or deliberately, altered so as to create another kind of text." Shillingsburg, like Parker and Binder, argues that even modern writings often do not have a determinate text, and editors of critical editions must decide what text to present to readers. For several fascinating examples of textual problems in modern writers, see Thorpe (1972, 3-49).

68. On Revelation 5:1, see Aune (1997, 322, 338-46).

69. On this passage generally, see Bagnall (2000).

70. On this passage, see Skeat (1979), Donfried (1989), Richards (1998, 160-62), and Hengel (2000, 281-82 n. 484).

71. Skeat (1979) argues for the appositional meaning and adduces both biblical and nonbiblical examples.

72. A number of other Greek terms denoting book forms (*deltos, kōdix, pinax,* and *sōmatikon*) do not occur in the New Testament in this sense. On terminology, see Trobisch (2000, 72).

73. Farrer (1952, 172). See also C. Williams (1951, 43-44).

74. Gundry (1993, 1011). On the question of the possible preservation of Mark's lost ending in Matthew, Luke, or John, see also Rawlinson (1925, 268-70), Streeter (1925, 342-44), Cadoux (1935, 187-92), Linnemann (1969), Trompf (1972), Osborne (1984, 63-65), and E. Powell (1994, 89-125).

EIGHT

CONCLUSIONS

"[T]he debate as to the ending of Mark is far from settled."

Here in the closing chapter of this book the relevance of the above quote by Robert H. Stein (1992, 5:648) is twofold. First, I hope that this book will reinvigorate the debate about the ending of Mark, a debate which some regard as concluded. Second, I am not so optimistic as to expect that this book will cause such a swift and massive shift toward the view of a lost ending that the debate will be concluded in the opposite direction. For the present, it would be a step in the right direction if more persons began to regard the debate as "far from settled."

Most of the conclusions of this study have been stated along the way, but it may be helpful to summarize them here, arranged according to topic and degree of probability. Inherent in this arrangement are two acknowledgments. First, the thesis really has three parts: the loss of Mark's ending, the loss of Mark's beginning, and the codex form as the mechanical means of the damage. These parts, though related, do not necessarily stand or fall together. For example, in my opinion, the evidence of damage to Mark's ending is somewhat stronger than the evidence of damage to its beginning. Either or both of these instances of damage could have happened apart from the third element, the codex form. I am not here backing away from the thesis for which I have argued in this book. I believe all three parts are true, but if one should somehow be shown false, the others would not necessarily be invalidated.

Second, as I said at the end of chapter 7, all historical theories are inherently statements of probability. Categorical proof exists in a very limited number of venues: logic and algebra, for example. Proof in biblical studies, and elsewhere in the humanities, is of a different order and depends on persuasive power and consensus. So in stating my conclusions, I acknowledge that varying degrees of probability attach to the different parts of the thesis, and that other minds may assess the evidence differently.

1. REGARDING THE ENDING OF MARK

Very probable—The conclusion of Mark's Gospel has been lost. Originally his narrative went on to relate the action of the women, who reported the news to the other disciples. The lost ending contained at least one resurrection appearance story. The appearance would have been located in Galilee and would have featured Peter prominently (14:28, 16:7).[1]

Probable—The lost conclusion in some way rehabilitated the disciples. Their disobedience and denials were forgiven; their fellowship with Jesus was restored.

Possible—Jesus may have given the disciples some sort of commission. This commissioning may have involved the conferring of the Holy Spirit on them for their task of proclaiming the gospel.

2. REGARDING THE BEGINNING OF MARK

Probable—The beginning of Mark's Gospel has been lost. Mark 1:1 is the addition of a later scribe, serving to mark the starting point of the document. The lost portion probably contained additional information about John the Baptist, although it may have been very brief.

Possible—The lost beginning may have also contained information about Jesus' parentage or birth, but this is far from certain.
On the one hand, there are virtually no statements in the extant
part of Mark, that presuppose such material. On the other hand,
given the independence of the infancy material in Matthew and
Luke from the remainder of those Gospels, it is by no means clear
that there would be intimations of a lost infancy story in the body
of Mark.[2] Thus the lack of these in Mark does not argue persuasively against the thesis. The *positive* evidence for a lost infancy narrative is, however, negligible. The case for a missing beginning
rests on the textual, grammatical, stylistic, and interpretive problems discussed in chapter 6, not on any specific lack felt in the
body of the gospel. By the very nature of the case, a lost beginning
is less perceptible than a lost ending. A narrative creates a forward
trajectory of anticipation, much less so a backward trajectory of
presuppositions.[3]

3. REGARDING THE MECHANICAL MEANS OF THE LOSS

Probable—Given the paleographical practices of the early
Christians, it is more likely than not that Mark existed in codex
form at a very early stage, perhaps even in the autograph, and that
damage to the autograph (or *perhaps* to an early copy from which
all extant manuscripts derive) resulted in the simultaneous loss of
the first and last leaves. It is possible (although I think less likely)
that Mark was originally composed on a scroll and that it lost both
beginning and ending in separate accidents. But the scroll scenario
seems to me, first of all, to complicate the thesis unnecessarily by
requiring two accidents rather than one (indeed, two accidents
involving *torn papyrus*, rather than a single accident involving a
detached page), and second, to have meager paleographical
support.[4]

Can we speak of these conclusions as "proved"? Proof in biblical studies may find a helpful analogy in the court system.
Celebrated courtroom dramas in recent American jurisprudence
have reminded us that criminal cases and civil cases have different
standards of proof. Criminal cases must be proved "beyond a reasonable doubt." Civil cases, on the other hand, must be proved "by

a preponderance of the evidence." Applying these standards to the discipline of biblical studies, I would say that the in authenticity of Mark 16:9-20 has been proved by textual and literary critics beyond a reasonable doubt. Perhaps this could be said of a small number of other scholarly conclusions about the Bible in which the evidence is plentiful, fairly objective, and one-sided. But many "assured results" of modern, scientific study of the Bible would correspond to proof in a civil case. Even a viewpoint so widely held as Markan priority among the Synoptics has not been proved beyond a reasonable doubt, although, with most others in the field, I regard it as quite likely the case and the best working assumption. Similarly, many questions of authorship fall into this category. I am not prepared, for example, to assert that Colossians or Ephesians is deutero-Pauline beyond a reasonable doubt. So perhaps the analogy of a civil case is useful for evaluating the thesis presented in this book. My claim, then, is that a preponderance of the evidence points to the twofold truncation of Mark's Gospel, a gospel originally composed in codex form. I believe that this thesis, while not proved beyond a reasonable doubt, is more likely than the alternative explanations of the peculiarities of Mark's beginning and ending.

4. WHAT DIFFERENCE DOES IT MAKE THEOLOGICALLY?

Many modern readers will continue to interpret the Gospel of Mark based on the extant form of the text (1:1–16:8), assuming its literary integrity and disregarding the historical question of its mutilation (although even here we are allowing a historical judgment about the inauthenticity of 16:9-20 to modify a strict narrative or reader response approach). As I acknowledged in chapter 5, such approaches have yielded provocative interpretations. Readers who regard the locus of meaning as the text alone or the text in the hands of a specific interpretive community are unhampered by the historical quirks of a text's transmission and may proceed freely, especially given the unlikelihood that the lost ending or beginning of Mark will be discovered any time soon, and the probability that we have, in fact, the great majority of what Mark wrote. But for interpreters who consider authorial intent

THE MUTILATION OF MARK'S GOSPEL

important, the probability that we lack both the beginning and the ending of Mark's Gospel should temper any historical interpretations of Mark.

If in fact Mark has been truncated, it is almost certain that the author's intended ending would significantly alter our view of two of the most bedeviling problems in Markan studies: the Markan portrayal of the disciples and the so-called messianic secret. Regarding these very issues, Grant Osborne has suggested that "the whole 'messianic misunderstanding' and discipleship failure themes look to the resurrection for the time of victorious reversal" (1984, 60). It is likely that the repeated efforts by Jesus to suppress testimony about himself in Mark are meant to come to an end with the resurrection. This is stated explicitly in Mark 9:9, which places a temporal limit on the restraint of the disciples' witness. The announcement and command of the young man at the tomb (16:6-7) would thus signal the lifting of the ban. James Dunn has, therefore, rightly observed that "in Mark [the resurrection] resolves 'the messianic secret' " (1992, 982). Only after the passion *and* the resurrection can God's revelation in Jesus be fully understood and thus communicated to others.[5] The lost ending of Mark would likely have made this clear.

As for the "discipleship failure" theme, there are indications in Mark that ultimately the disciples will "get it."[6] In particular, I suspect that the original Markan ending showed that the women did, in fact, fulfill their commission to tell the others and turned out to be among the best examples of discipleship in the gospel. This would corroborate certain studies that have argued that women are model disciples in Mark and would counter the charge that in Mark 16:8 the evangelist is presenting women as "inadequate male surrogates."[7] In all likelihood both male and female disciples were rehabilitated by the ending of Mark. Interpreters should, therefore, be very cautious about ascribing to the evangelist views of discipleship that depend too heavily on 16:8 as the intended conclusion.

The most important theological difference implied by the thesis of mutilation would be the high probability that the Second Gospel had an utterly fitting conclusion to the narrative trajectory created by the evangelist. The suggestion that the evangelist was indifferent to resurrection appearances is belied by 14:28 and

16:7.[8] The suggestion that Mark only knew of the *fact* of appearances, but no narratives, is quite unlikely.[9] Paul was able at least a decade earlier to list several appearances as accomplished events (1 Cor 15:3-8). If Mark ends at 16:8, he has given us considerably less than Paul: an unfulfilled prediction of a single appearance, not even a summary statement of an event, let alone of multiple events. It is "utterly improbable that about forty years after the origin of the primitive community still no appearance narratives should have existed, that is to say, that such a tradition would have remained completely unknown to the earliest evangelist" (Lindemann 1980, 301). Mark has prepared his readers for an appearance narrative, and the lost ending surely contained one. A resurrection appearance would not undercut Mark's call to cruciform discipleship. A "theology of glory" or vindication is not utterly incompatible with a "theology of the cross."[10] Just as the resurrection vindicates Jesus' message, so the hope of resurrection energizes and empowers discipleship. If Mark intentionally ended at 16:8, he leaves us less certain of Jesus' vindication and of the basis of Christian hope.

5. HOW SHOULD THE READING AND INTERPRETATION OF MARK PROCEED?

Those favorably disposed toward the thesis of this book should resist the urge to reconstruct *in any detail* the lost beginning and ending, and should simply note that whatever we say about the evangelist's overall intent is necessarily contingent on a truncated text. The credibility of some "lost ending theorists" has been eroded by a failure to exercise restraint in this regard.[11] As papyrologist Roger Bagnall has said, "Editors and critics often succumb to the temptation to rewrite the lost [portion of a] text, but that must be viewed as an exercise in prose composition, not as restoration."[12]

I do not expect that this book will bring to a halt attempts to interpret Mark's Gospel in its extant form, nor should it. Unless the manuscript discovery of the millennium occurs and the lost ending or beginning surfaces in some European monastery, we will have to work with Mark as we have it: 1:1–16:8. There should be neither a halt to macrointerpretations of the extant Mark nor a rush to new and tenuous interpretations based on detailed restorations. But the probability that Mark is mutilated should certainly temper *historical-critical* interpretations of the extant text, that is, those interpretations which analyze the text in terms of the author's intentions. It should also sound a cautionary note for narrative, reader-response, and other text- or reader-centered interpreters. Scholars who bracket historical questions about the text's transmission and preservation should not then turn around and attribute interpretations of a likely truncated text to the historical author. At the very least, those who interpret Mark based on 1:1–16:8 should make explicit their *assumption* of the text's integrity.

All interpretive methods have costs and benefits. Most newer methods of reading biblical texts do not purport to deal with the history of the text. Critics who employ these methods are obviously capable of considering a text's history, but their methodologies predispose them to bracket it. A text whose integrity is assumed can often be interpreted in creative and meaningful ways. If, however, one chooses to do historically oriented interpretation, one must take into account the *physicality* of ancient texts and the potential for loss, damage, deterioration, and other quirks of transmission. We must acknowledge that bad things happened to good manuscripts.

We need not and should not cease to be active, responsive readers who construct meaning in interaction with texts, even if some of those texts may be extant in a form other than the one that their authors intended. If I were writing a commentary on the Gospel of Mark I would probably offer a brief summary of the arguments in this book in favor of Mark's Gospel having been truncated, along with some tentative suggestions about where the evangelist may have been heading. But I might very well go on to suggest how the text could be interpreted in its extant form: Readers can "complete the story" in their own experience, break the women's silence by proclaiming the resurrection, and reverse the men's abandonment by going to Galilee to meet Jesus. This is an appealing way to read or preach the ending of Mark, but it is surely a reading that arises from the accidental state of the text, not from the mind of Mark.

Is our appreciation of the Gospel of Mark then seriously impaired by its textual damage? Not necessarily. In the book,

Poetic Closure, Barbara Herrnstein Smith judges that a failure of closure by no means deprives a poem of its value.

> An inadequately closed poem is not necessarily a bad poem, although it may be bad in that respect. . . . The sixty-sixth is, I think, among Shakespeare's best sonnets, and although one's experience of it is ultimately defective, one's sense of its greatness is not thereby annihilated; we may always say, "A great poem . . . with a weak conclusion." Since our experience of a poem is not instantaneous but extensive, there is no reason why we cannot read (and reread) with pleasure a poem that concludes badly. (1968, 220)

Replace the word *poem* in the foregoing paragraph with *gospel,* and one sees how Mark can simultaneously be experienced as truncated and yet evaluated positively. Indeed, some interpreters would argue that Mark is *more* powerful, *more* poignant, and *more* able to speak to modern readers precisely because of its lack of closure. A friend of mine once described the powerful effect of Mark 16:8 as "a punch in the stomach" of the unsuspecting reader.[13] That, of course, could be true along with the thesis of this book, although I'm not convinced that it is true for most readers of Mark.

In this book, I have attempted to show that Mark's Gospel lacks its original beginning and ending. I would not be so bold as to claim that I have proved this beyond a reasonable doubt. Some readers will think I am sufficiently brazen to suggest that a preponderance of the evidence favors this thesis. But the cumulative force of the arguments presented here is significant. If we reject the thesis of mutilation, we are forced to believe that Mark has committed grammatical and/or stylistic gaffes at the outset and conclusion of his Gospel, passages that one would think would be the focus of particularly careful attention. We are forced to believe that Mark was either inept, perverse, or astonishingly modernistic as a narrator. We must come up with explanations for the widespread perception in antiquity that the Second Gospel needed repair or augmentation, and the widespread judgment up through the first half of the twentieth century that the text was truncated. We must explain how Mark hit on a narrative technique that was unknown in antiquity but appeals to the modern literary mind, why he fails to narrate events that he has predicted, and why he pulls the rug out from under the reader in the last verse. This series of improbabilities, combined with the fact that damage to texts in antiquity was commonplace, suggests that the thesis of mutilation, far from being an act of interpretive desperation, is the most plausible explanation of all the data. The chief reason for resisting this conclusion may be no more than our modern predisposition toward reading texts a certain way. We should instead reckon seriously with the probability of the mutilation of Mark's Gospel.

NOTES

1. It has been suggested that the ending of Mark may have contained an appearance to Mary Magdalene, a story recounted in Matt 28:8-10, John 20:11-18, and Mark 16:9-11. The prominence of Mary Magdalene in early Christian tradition may stem from such a Christophany. See Hengel (1963, especially 251-52). There are, however, no explicit anticipations of this story in Mark, such as we have in the case of Peter and the disciples (16:7).

2. It cannot be said that if Mark originally contained a genealogy or an infancy account, its loss would surely be evident. Consider a parallel scenario with Matthew or Luke. Raymond Brown observed: "If the first two chapters had been lost and the Matthean Gospel came down to us beginning with 3:1, no one would have ever suspected the existence of the missing chapters." Regarding Luke 3:1-2 Brown noted that "historiographical parallels in other Greek writing suggest that Luke 3:1-2 could well have served as the original opening of the Lucan Gospel. . . . As was true also with Matthew's Gospel, none of the Lucan infancy narrative has had major influence on the body of the Gospel, so that, if the first two chapters had been lost, we could never have suspected their existence." See Brown (1993, 49 and 240).

3. Paul Goodman notes that "in the beginning [of a narrative] anything is possible; in the middle things become probable; in the end everything is necessary." Quoted in Danove (1993, 14).

4. McCown (1941, 240): "While not impossible, a mechanical explanation of the truncation of Mark has always seemed to me difficult if the Gospel were in roll form. On the contrary it is quite natural if the little book were a codex."

5. Beker (1994, 76).

6. See, again, Mark 9:9-10, and many of the passages discussed in chapter 4, part 6.

7. This harshly negative judgment about Mark's Gospel comes from Liew (1999, 143). For positive interpretations of Mark's portrayal of women, see Schüssler Fiorenza (1983, 321-23), Kinukawa (1994, 96), and Myers (1988, 396-97). For helpful discussions of recent literature, see J. Williams (1994, 191-203) and Phillips (2001).

8. See the quotes from Cunningham, Crossan, and Tate in chapter 1, p. 15.

9. This has been suggested by Wilckens (1970, 50-51; ET: 33-34).

10. So Hare (1996, 223) rightly asserts: "Even if Mark's writing originally included resurrection appearances, it is clear that it would remain a passion Gospel. The Easter narratives, however powerful in themselves, would not erase the profound impression made on the reader by the persistent emphasis on Jesus' dying, which dominates the narrative from 8:31 on." See also Magness (1986, 91) and Gundry (1993, 1017).

11. Ayles (1918, 471-72), for example, offered a nine-verse reconstruction of the lost ending. Daniell (1937, 349) thinks that something on the order of four to five chapters has been lost, traces of which he finds in Acts. See also Burkitt (1924, 83), Probyn (1925), Streeter (1925, 351-60), Major, et al. (1938, 210-11), Haefner (1958), Linnemann (1969), Trompf (1971–1972, 321-25), and Osborne (1984, 64-65). More modestly, Moule (1955–1956, 58-59) suggests a sentence that might have followed Mark 16:8, and J. Harris (1908, 86) suggests that the next two words after "they feared" would have been "the Jews."

12. Bagnall (1995, 30-31). Bagnall's remark pertained to the editorial restoration of lacunae; its relevance is all the more obvious when entire textual units have been lost.

13. Austin Farrer (1952, 178), who appreciated the impact of Mark 16:8, mused that accidental loss in this case would be auspicious: "And if the mice in the bishop's house at Rome ate the appendix, what highly discriminating mice they must have been!"

CHRONOLOGICAL LIST OF SCHOLARS

For those somewhat familiar with the cast of characters in New Testament scholarship, I offer the following chronological list of persons inclined in various degrees *not* to accept Mark 16:8 as the intended ending of the gospel. The theses favored by these scholars take three basic forms: an unfinished gospel (through death or arrest of the evangelist), a deliberately suppressed ending, or an ending lost through accidental damage to the manuscript. The last of these has been by far the most popular view. The degree of support varies from emphatic advocacy to a general affirmation of probability. Details can be found in the references cited.

J. J. Griesbach (1789–1790; in Orchard and Longstaff 1978, 127) Lost ending
Karl Lachmann (1830, 841) Unfinished
Henry Alford (1863, 1:431) Lost ending

August Klostermann (1867, 309) Unfinished

B. F. Westcott and F. J. A. Hort (1882, Appendix, 47) Lost ending or unfinished

H. A. W. Meyer (1884, 197) Lost ending or unfinished

Theodor Zahn (1977, 2:479; orig. German, 1897–1899) Lost ending or unfinished

F. C. Burkitt (1901, 28) Lost ending

Allan Menzies (1901, 290) Lost ending

Adolf Jülicher (1904, 329) Lost ending

Casper Rene Gregory (1907, 512) Lost ending

Kirsopp Lake (1907, 73) Lost ending

Friedrich Spitta (1893–1907, 3:2, 111) Lost ending

J. Rendel Harris (1908, 87) Lost ending

Benjamin Wisner Bacon (1909, xvii, xix) Lost ending

Maurice Goguel (1909, 301) Suppression

J. Armitage Robinson (1911, 5) Lost ending

Arthur S. Peake (1912, 121) Lost ending

George Milligan (1913, 182) Lost ending

James Moffatt (1914, 238) Lost ending, unfinished, or suppression

Rudolf Bultmann (1963, 285 n. 2; orig. German, 1921) Suppression

B. H. Streeter (1925, 337) Lost ending

Henry Barclay Swete (1927, 399) Lost ending

A. H. McNeile (1927, 57) Lost ending

A. W. F. Blunt (1929, 268) Unfinished?

Walter Lowrie (1929, 553) Lost ending

Arthur Temple Cadoux (1935, 187) Lost ending

Adolf Schlatter (1984, 279; 1st ed. 1935) Lost ending

Ernest Findlay Scott (1936, 60-61) Lost ending

Edgar J. Goodspeed (1937, 156) Lost ending

Floyd V. Filson (1938, 158) Lost ending

H. A. Sanders (1938, 110-11) Lost ending

C. C. McCown (1941, 240) Lost ending

W. L. Knox (1942, 22-23) Lost ending or unfinished

Ethelbert Stauffer (1943–1944, 13) Lost ending

A. M. Hunter (1949, 149) Lost ending

Oscar Cullmann (1962, 61; orig. German, 1952, 67) Lost ending

C. H. Dodd (1953, 440 n. 1) Lost ending or unfinished

G. Bornkamm (1975, 213 n. 2; orig. German, 1956) Lost ending
Jack Finegan (1956, 88) Lost ending
C. C. Martindale (1956, 174) Unfinished
C. Leslie Mitton (1957, 138) Lost ending
Albert E. Barnett (1958, 142) Lost ending
K. Bornhäuser (1958, 211) Lost ending
F. G. Kenyon (1958, 214) Lost ending or unfinished
Alfred Wikenhauser (1958, 172-73) Lost ending or unfinished
C. E. B. Cranfield (1959, 471) Unfinished
Julius Schniewind (1960, 172) Lost ending or suppression
Vincent Taylor (1961, 90) Lost ending
T. W. Manson (1962, 30) Lost ending
Robert M. Grant (1963, 120) Lost ending
Martin Hengel (1963, 252 and n. 2) Lost ending
Hans Grass (1964, 86) Lost ending
Everett F. Harrison (1964, 92) Lost ending or unfinished
C. F. D. Moule (1965, 133) Lost ending
Horst Balz (1969, 633) Lost ending
W. D. Davies (1969, 207) Lost ending
Eta Linnemann (1969, 286-87) Lost ending (but preserved in
    Matt 28 and the long ending of Mark)
Herschel H. Hobbs (1970, 259) Lost ending
Eduard Schweizer (1970, 373) Lost ending
George Eldon Ladd (1975, 83-84) Lost ending
Philipp Vielhauer (1975, 348) Suppression
Stephen Neill (1976, 76-77) Lost ending
Karl Martin Fischer (1980, 52) Lost ending
Charles W. Hedrick (1983, 263) Lost ending
C. H. Roberts and T. C. Skeat (1983, 55) Lost ending
F. F. Bruce (1984, 74, n. 16) Lost ending?
Grant R. Osborne (1984, 65) Lost ending
Walter Schmithals (1985, 322) Lost ending
Peter Carnley (1987, 216) Lost ending
I. Howard Marshall (1991, 276) Lost ending or unfinished
Robert H. Stein (1991, 65) Lost ending
Philip Wesley Comfort (1992a, 138) Lost ending
Bruce M. Metzger (1992, 228) Lost ending
N. T. Wright (1992a, 390, n. 67) Lost ending
Robert H. Gundry (1993, 1009) Lost ending

Julio Trebolle Barrera (1998, 413) Lost ending
Udo Schnelle (1998, 207) Lost ending
Georg Strecker (2000, 266 n. 7) Lost ending
J. K. Elliott (2000, 586) Lost ending
Lee Martin McDonald and Stanley E. Porter (2000, 290) Lost ending
Craig A. Evans (2001, 539) Lost ending or unfinished
Ben Witherington III (2001, 49) Lost ending
James R. Edwards (2002, 503) Lost ending
R. T. France (2002, 673) Lost ending, unfinished, or suppression
Jane Schaberg (2002, 293) Suppression

APPENDIX B

TEXTUAL VARIANTS AT THE END OF MARK'S GOSPEL

1. Concluding at 16:8. Three Greek witnesses; Codex Sinaiticus (ℵ), Codex Vaticanus (B), and manuscript 304 (11th cent.), and certain Latin, Syriac, Armenian, and Georgian manuscripts conclude the gospel at 16:8. No further ending was known to Clement of Alexandria and Origen. Most Greek manuscripts known to Eusebius and Jerome had nothing further.

Mark 16:8 "for they were afraid."

2. Plus Short Ending. The short ending (with nothing following) is found in a single Latin manuscript (it^k). The short ending does not have verse numbers. It begins: "And all that had been commanded them they told briefly to those around Peter."

Mark 16:8 "for they were afraid."	Short Ending

3. Plus Short Ending and Long Ending. Found in four Greek manuscripts (L, Ψ, 099, 0112), and certain Syriac, Coptic, and Ethiopic manuscripts.

Mark 16:8 "for they were afraid."	Short Ending	Long Ending Mark 16:9-20

4. Plus Long Ending. Found in the vast majority of manuscripts, including several uncials (A, C, D, K, etc.)

Mark 16:8 "for they were afraid."	Long Ending—Mark 16:9-20

5. Plus Long Ending Marked with *Asterisks*, †Obeli†, or with a Note After Verse 8. Such indications that the scribes regarded the additional verses as spurious are found in several manuscripts: 1, 20, 22, 137, 138, 209, 1582.

Mark 16:8 "for they were afraid."	Long Ending—†*Mark 16:9-20*†

6. Plus Long Ending with "Freer Logion." The long ending with an insertion after verse 14 is found in Codex Washingtonianus, a fifth-century Greek manuscript located in the Smithsonian Institute (Freer Gallery of Art). Since this manuscript was acquired by Charles L. Freer, the insertion is sometimes called the "Freer Logion."

Mark 16:8 "for they were afraid."	First Half of Long Ending—Mark 16:9-14	Freer Logion	Remainder of Long Ending—Mark 16:15-20

HIGH FREQUENCY FINAL GAR

Listed in descending order of final γάρ (γάρ.) frequency

Name of Author	Occurrences of γάρ	γάρ.	Notes on Genre and/or the γάρ sentences	γάρ;
All Authors on TLG CD ROM-E	Over 763,000	1884	One fourth of one percent of all instances	786
Plato (Phil.)	5491	158	All end sentences in dialogue.	182
Scholia in Homerum	8191	148	Marginal notes and glosses	2
Eustathius (Philol.)	8780	144	Commentaries on Iliad and Odyssey	1
Aristotle (Phil.)	19,479	67	Dialogues, Essays	1
Herodianus, Aelius &	4873	67	Works on Grammar, Orthography,	2

Pseudo-Herodianus		Rhetoric	
Scholia in Aeschylum	3161	Marginal notes and glosses	0
Scholia in Aristophanem	4917	Marginal notes and glosses	0
Scholia in Pindarum	3209	Marginal notes and glosses	1
Stobaeus, Joannes (Anthologus)	4095	An anthology of literary excerpts	21
Lucianus	2905	Speeches, Letters All in dialogue	8
Alexander of Aphrodisias (Phil.)	17,240	Commentaries on Aristotle's Works	3
Athenaeus (Soph.)	2862	*The Deipnosophists*, a symposium (dialogue)	0

Name of Author	Occurrences of γάρ	γάρ.	Notes on Genre and/or the γάρ sentences	γάρ;
Libanius (Rhet.)	7848	19	2 end epistles; 4 end a ¶; Others end sentences.	8
Proclus (Phil.)	14,445	19	Commentaries on Plato	9
Suda	4105	17	A historical and literary encyclopedia	3
Menander	1078	16	New comedy; all in dialogue	17
Thomas Magister (Philol.)	300	15	Scholia, orations, and letters	0
Zonaras, Pseudo- (Lexicogr.)	1640	14	Lexicographical works	0
Theognostus (Gramm.)	392	12	Grammatical works	0
Aristophanes (Comic)	1372	10	Comedy, dialogue	5
Demosthenes	2900	10	Orations	18

APPENDIX D

LOW FREQUENCY FINAL GAR

Listed in ascending order of final γάρ (γἀρ.) frequency

Name of Author	Occurrences of γάρ	γάρ.	Notes on Author, Genre, or γάρ sentences	γάρ;
Appianus	736	0	Historian 2nd century C.E.	0
Diodorus Siculus	3046	0	Historian 1st century B.C.E.	1
Herodotus	1479	0	Historian 5th century B.C.E.	0
Josephus, Flavius	3678	0	Historian 1st century C.E.	1
Procopius (Hist.)	2081	0	Historian 6th century C.E.	0
Thucydides	1116	0	Historian 5th century B.C.E.	0
Philo	6065	1	Ends a sentence mid-paragraph. *Agr.* 73, line 5	1

Name of Author	Occurrences of γάρ	γάρ.	Notes on Author, Genre, or γάρ sentences	γάρ;
Polybius (Hist.)	2189	1	Middle of paragraph; *Histories* 2.60.1	2
Dio Cassius	5776	2	Both end sentences in the middle of a paragraph.	1
Dionysius of Halicarnassus	2642	2	Both midparagraph; one in dialogue	4
New Testament	1039	2	Mark 16:8; John 13:13, the latter is in dialogue.	1
Plutarch	8973	2	*Mor.* 88c (an excerpt from Euripides); *Mor.* 1100d (midparagraph, dialogue)	6
Xenophon (Hist.)	2664	2	Both midparagraph; one in dialogue	8
Septuagint	1547	5	Genesis 18:15; 45:3 Isaiah 8:1; 16:10; 29:11	7

| Diogenes Laertius | 797 | 7 | None ends a paragraph; 3 in maxims; 1 in dialogue | 2 |
| Philostratus, Flavius (Soph.) | 2017 | 9 | Vit. Apoll. 2.15.1; 2.40.26; 3.26.19; 6.9.37; 6.11.4; 6.22.12; 6.27.35; 7.14.83; Vit. soph. 2. page 583, line 5. All in dialogue | 1 |

The following examples are especially significant in that γάρ clauses come at the end of a work or section.

| Musonius Rufus, Gaius | 157 | 1 | End of a philosophical essay; Discourse 12 | 0 |
| Plotinus (Phil.) | 2797 | 11 | Ten in middle of a paragraph; one at end of Enn. 5, chapter 5. But work was edited and rearranged in antiquity. | 9 |

GLOSSARY OF TECHNICAL TERMS

Affective Fallacy—A principle of New Criticism that asserts that the meaning of a text is independent of its effect on readers. Meaning is internal to the text. It is, therefore, a fallacy to think that meaning depends on how the text affects readers.

Aposiopesis—A technique of oratory in which some brief background matter is alluded to or assumed but not fully related, usually for reasons of modesty or passion.

Autograph—The original manuscript of an ancient writing, as opposed to copies that are made by transcription.

Closure—The sense that a literary work has reached its proper conclusion; "a confirmation of expectations that have been established by the structure of the sequence. . . . the sense of stable conclusiveness, finality, or 'clinch' which we experience" (Smith 1968, 2); "a sense of completeness, integrity, and coherence, both formal and thematic, that the reader experiences at the end of the work" (Fusillo 1997, 210).

Codex—An ancient book form akin to the modern book, consisting of sheets of papyrus or parchment laid on top of each other and stitched down the middle forming a spine. The codex seems to have been used from the outset by Christians and eventually replaced the scroll in Greco-Roman writings.

Conveyed Meaning—The meaning transmitted by the words of a text, usually close to the meaning intended by the author, but not always identical to it.

Extant Form—Generally equivalent to "canonical form," the extant form of an ancient writing is the form in which it has survived in the manuscript tradition to modern times. Extant form may, therefore, be affected by damage, deletion, addition, or alteration, when such changes occurred early enough in the transmission of the writing to be permanent and irremediable.

Final Form—the form of an ancient writing in which it left the author's hand. Final form is not concerned with sources or editing, that is, with stages prior to the final composition. Final form may differ from extant form, if irremediable damage, deletion, addition, or alteration has occurred in the transmission of the text.

Formal Closure—Formal closure refers to language that appropriately rounds off the narrative, as in the fairy tale conclusion, "And they all lived happily ever after."

Formalism—See New Criticism.

Implied Reader—A theoretical construct of narrative criticism referring to a reader who is informed and shaped purely by the text. The implied reader accepts the assumptions of the text and knows only what the text communicates. In contrast, an actual reader may share or resist the assumptions of the text and will often have knowledge from many other sources.

Inclusio—The use of the same or similar words at both the beginning and ending of a unit so as to enclose or bracket the material and provide thematic unity.

Intended Meaning—The meaning that the author wanted to communicate. If the author is skillful and the message is well crafted, the intended meaning is close to the conveyed meaning.

Intentional Fallacy—A principle of New Criticism that asserts that an author's intentions and life circumstances are inessential in the interpretation of that author's writings. The meaning of a text can be found through a close analysis of the text itself, without investigating the psychology of the author or questions of social, historical, and literary contexts.

Lacuna—A missing portion in an ancient manuscript, usually caused by deterioration or damage to the writing material.

Narrative Commentary—Explanatory comments by which the narrator interrupts the reporting of events in order to clarify something.

New Criticism—A method of literary analysis that stressed the derivation of meaning primarily from close examination of the text itself. A text's meaning does not depend on the psychology and historical circumstances of the author (the intentional fallacy) nor on the impact of the text on readers (the affective fallacy). New Criticism came into vogue in the 1940s and 1950s, and it began to influence biblical scholarship a decade or two later. Also known as "Formalism."

Nomina Sacra—Literally "sacred words," these are common contractions in ancient Christian manuscripts. Words such as "God," "Lord," "Jesus," "Christ," and "Son" were abbreviated by writing only the first and last letters. Certain other words were contracted by writing more than one letter from the beginning and/or ending of the word. In addition, a horizontal line was drawn above the letters to distinguish the contraction from adjacent letters.

Nominative Absolute—Introductory words of a text that stand in the nominative case but are grammatically independent of what follows.

Opisthograph—Literally "written on the back," this is a manuscript in which an older scroll is reused by inscribing a new text on its blank, reverse side.

Paleography—the study of ancient writings.

Papyrus—an ancient writing material made from dried strips of the papyrus plant.

Parchment—an ancient writing material made from animal skins, usually of cattle, sheep, or goats. Also called "vellum."

Quire—A single gathering of folded sheets in a codex. A quire might contain a small or a very large number of sheets. The earliest codices were probably single-quire.

Reader-Response Criticism—A theory of literary analysis that emphasizes the contribution of readers in the creation of meaning. All reader-response critics regard the reader's contribution as significant. More radical reader-response critics would say that the reading community is largely determinative of a text's meaning.

Recto—The "front" side of a sheet of papyrus. The strips of papyrus on the recto side normally run horizontally, making it the easier side for writing. The side opposite the recto is the verso.

Sociology of Knowledge—"The study of the way in which the production of knowledge is shaped by the social context of thinkers" (Hess, Markson, and Stein 1991, 621); more pejoratively, "group think," or the tendency of people to decide what constitutes reliable knowledge in the context of social groups.

Textual Criticism—The science and art of determining the original (or oldest recoverable) text of an ancient document, through comparing manuscripts and deciding which variant reading is primary (closest to the original) and which is secondary (changes introduced in transcription). Textual criticism of the Gospel of Mark tries to determine, as closely as possible, what the evangelist originally wrote.

Textus Receptus—Literally the "Received Text," this term refers to a form of the Greek New Testament that came to be highly revered in the sixteenth and seventeenth centuries. It was based on late Greek manuscripts that in some cases contained errors and interpolations. Although most of the Textus Receptus corresponds to superior manuscripts discovered in later centuries, it remains a somewhat less reliable, less original textual base for the New Testament. The Textus Receptus lies behind the King James Version.

Thematic Closure—The fulfillment of the expectations that the work has generated, sometimes recapitulating motifs from the narrative, sometimes providing an inclusio with the beginning of the work.

Vellum—See Parchment.

Verso—The "back" side of a sheet of papyrus. The strips of papyrus on the verso side normally run vertically, making it the more difficult side for writing. The side opposite the verso is the recto.

Zeitgeist—the mood or intellectual trend of a particular era.

BIBLIOGRAPHY

Abbott, Lyman. 1877. *An Illustrated Commentary on the Gospels according to Mark and Luke*. New York: A. S. Barnes.

Achtemeier, Paul J. 1975. *Mark*. Proclamation Commentaries. Philadelphia: Fortress.

———. 1986. *Mark*. 2d ed., rev. and enl. Proclamation Commentaries. Philadelphia: Fortress.

———, ed. 1996. *HarperCollins Bible Dictionary*. Rev. ed. San Francisco: HarperSanFrancisco.

Achtemeier, Paul J., Joel B. Green, and Marianne Meye Thompson. 2001. *Introducing the New Testament: Its Literature and Theology*. Grand Rapids: Eerdmans.

Adam, A. K. M. 1995. *What Is Postmodern Biblical Criticism?* GBS. Minneapolis: Fortress.

Aichele, George. 1996. *Jesus Framed*. London and New York: Routledge.

Aland, Barbara, Kurt Aland, Johannes Karavidopoulos, Carlo M. Martini, and Bruce M. Metzger. 1993. *Novum Testamentum Graece*. 27th ed. Stuttgart: Deutsche Bibelgesellschaft.

Aland, Barbara, Kurt Aland, Gerd Mink, and Klaus Wachtel. 1997. *Novum Testamentum Graecum. Editio Critica Maior. IV. Die Katholischen Briefe. 1. Der Jakobusbrief.* Stuttgart: Deutsche Bibelgesellschaft.

Aland, Kurt. 1969. "Bemerkungen zum Schluss des Markusevangeliums." Pages 157-80 in *Neotestamentica et Semitica: Studies in Honour of Matthew Black.* Edited by E. E. Ellis and M. Wilcox. Edinburgh: T. & T. Clark.

———. 1970. "Der wiedergefundene Markusschluss? Eine methodologische Bermerkung zur textkritischen Arbeit." *ZTK* 67:3-13.

———. 1988. "Der Schluß des Markusevangeliums." Pages 435-70 in *L'Évangile selon Marc: Tradition et Rédaction.* Edited by M. Sabbe. BETL 34. Rev. Ed. Gembloux, Belgium: Leuven University Press, 1988; see also pages 573-75. (First published in 1979 as "Der Schluß des Markusevangeliums." Pages 246-83 in *Neutestamentliche Entwürfe.* Munich: Chr. Kaiser.)

———. 1999. "Textual Criticism, New Testament." Revised by B. Köster. Pages 546-51 in vol. 1 of *Dictionary of Biblical Interpretation.* Edited by John H. Hayes. 2 vols. Nashville: Abingdon.

Aland, Kurt and Barbara Aland. 1987. *The Text of the New Testament: An Introduction to the Critical Editions and to the Theory and Practice of Modern Textual Criticism.* Translated by Erroll F. Rhodes. Grand Rapids: Eerdmans; Leiden, Netherlands: E. J. Brill.

Albertz, Martin. 1922. "Zur Formengeschichte der Auferstehungsberichte." *ZNW* 21:259-69.

Albright, W. F., and C. S. Mann. 1972. *Matthew.* AB. Garden City, N.Y.: Doubleday.

Alexander, David and Pat Alexander. 1999. *Zondervan Handbook to the Bible.* Grand Rapids: Zondervan.

Alexander, Loveday. 1998. "Ancient Book Production and the Circulation of the Gospels." Pages 71-105 in *The Gospels for All Christians: Rethinking the Gospel Audiences.* Edited by Richard Bauckham. Grand Rapids: Eerdmans.

Alford, Henry. 1863. *The Greek Testament.* 5th ed. London: Deighton, Bell, & Co.

Allen, Willoughby C. 1907. *A Critical and Exegetical Commentary on the Gospel according to Matthew.* ICC. New York: Charles Scribner's Sons.

———. 1915. *The Gospel according to Saint Mark.* London: Rivingtons.

———. 1946. "St. Mark xvi.8. 'They were afraid.' Why?" *JTS* 47:46-49.

———. 1947. "Fear in St. Mark." *JTS* 48:201-3.

Alsup, John E. 1975. *The Post-resurrection Appearance Stories of the Gospel Tradition.* Stuttgart: Calwer.

———. 1976. "John Dominic Crossan, 'Empty Tomb and Absent Lord,' A Response." Pages 263-67 in *Society of Biblical Literature 1976 Seminar Papers.* Edited by George MacRae. Missoula, Mont.: Scholars Press.

Amann, Émile. 1910. *Le Protévangile de Jacques et ses remaniements latins.* Paris: Letouzey et Ané.

Anderson, Hugh. 1964. *Jesus and Christian Origins: A Commentary on Modern Viewpoints.* New York: Oxford University Press.

———. 1965. "The Easter Witness of the Evangelists." Pages 35-55 in *The New Testament in Historical and Contemporary Perspective: Essays in Memory of G. H. C. Macgregor.* Edited by Hugh Anderson and William Barclay. Oxford: Basil Blackwell.

———. 1977. *The Gospel of Mark.* Greenwood, S.C.: Attic Press.

Anderson, Janice Capel, and Stephen D. Moore, eds. 1992. *Mark & Method: New Approaches in Biblical Studies.* Minneapolis: Fortress.

Arndt, W. 1955. *Does the Bible Contradict Itself?* St. Louis: Concordia.

Arnold, Gerhard. 1977. "Mk 1:1 und Eröffnungswendungen in griechischen und lateinischen Schriften." *ZNW* 68:123-27.

Augustine, John H. 1993. "Mark." Pages 387-97 in *A Complete Literary Guide to the Bible.* Edited by Leland Ryken and Tremper Longman III. Grand Rapids: Zondervan.

Aune, David E. 1987. *The New Testament and Its Literary Environment.* LEC 8. Philadelphia: Westminster.

———. 1997. *Revelation 1–5.* WBC. Dallas: Word.

Ayles, H. H. B. 1918. "The Lost Conclusion of St. Mark's Gospel." *Expositor,* 8th series, 15:466-72.

Baarlink, Heinrich. 1977. *Anfängliches Evangelium: Ein Beitrag zur näheren Bestimmung der theologischen Motive im Markusevangelium.* Kampen: J. H. Kok.

Bacon, Benjamin W. 1905. "Against the Authorship of the Last Verses of Mark." *Expositor,* 6th series, 12:401-12.

———. 1907. "The Prologue of Mark: A Study of Sources and Structure." *JBL* 26:84-106.

———. 1909. *The Beginnings of Gospel Story.* New Haven: Yale University Press.

———. 1925. *The Gospel of Mark: Its Composition and Date.* New Haven: Yale University Press.

Badham, Paul and Linda Badham. 1982. *Immortality or Extinction?* Totowa, N.J.: Barnes & Noble Books.

Bagnall, Roger S. 1995. *Reading Papyri, Writing Ancient History.* Approaching the Ancient World. London and New York: Routledge.

———. 2000. "Jesus Reads a Book." *JTS* n.s. 51:577-88.

Bailey, James L., and Lyle D. Vander Broek. 1992. *Literary Forms in the New Testament: A Handbook.* Louisville: Westminster John Knox.

Balz, Horst Robert. 1969. "Furcht vor Gott?" *EvT* 29:626-44.

Balz, Horst, and Günther Wanke. 1974. "φοβέω, φοβέομαι, φόβος, δέος." Pages 189-219 in vol. 9 of *TDNT.*

Barclay, William. 1975. *Introduction to the First Three Gospels.* A Revised Edition of *The First Three Gospels.* Philadelphia: Westminster.

Barnett, Albert E. 1957. *Disciples to Such a Lord: The Gospel according to St. Mark*. New York: Woman's Division of Christian Service Board of Missions, the Methodist Church.

———. 1958. *The New Testament: Its Making and Meaning*. Nashville: Abingdon.

Barr, David L. 1995. *New Testament Story: An Introduction*. 2d ed. Belmont, Calif.: Wadsworth.

Bartlet, Vernon. 1904–1905. "Mark the 'Curt-fingered' Evangelist." *JTS* 6:121-24.

Bartsch, Hans Werner. 1971. "Der Schluss des Markus-Evangeliums." *TZ* 27:241-54.

———. 1988 "Der ursprüngliche Schluß der Leidensgeschichte. Überlieferungsgeschichtliche Studien zum Markus-Schluß." Pages 411-33 in *L'Évangile selon Marc: Tradition et Rédaction*. Edited by M. Sabbe. BETL 34. Rev. ed. Leuven, Belgium: Leuven University Press.

Bauer, Adolf. 1912. "Der Schluß des Markusevangeliums." Wiener Studien 34:301-17.

Bauer, Walter. 1971. *Orthodoxy and Heresy in Earliest Christianity*. Edited by Robert Kraft and Gerhard Krodel. Philadelphia: Fortress.

———. 1979. *A Greek-English Lexicon of the New Testament and Other Early Christian Literature*. 2d ed. Revised and augmented by F. Wilbur Gingrich and Frederick W. Danker. Chicago: Chicago University Press.

———. 2000. *A Greek-English Lexicon of the New Testament and Other Early Christian Literature*. 3d ed. Edited and revised by Frederick William Danker. Chicago: University of Chicago Press.

Beal, T. K., K. A. Keefer, and T. Linafelt. 1999. "Literary Theory, Literary Criticism, and the Bible." Pages 79-85 in vol. 2 of *Dictionary of Biblical Interpretation*. Edited by John H. Hayes. 2 vols. Nashville: Abingdon, 1999.

Beare, Frank W. 1945. "Books and Publication in the Ancient World." University of Toronto Quarterly 14:150-67.

———. 1962. *The Earliest Records of Jesus*. Oxford: Basil Blackwell.

Beavis, Mary Ann. 1989. *Mark's Audience: The Literary and Social Setting of Mark 4.11-12*. JSNTSup 33. Sheffield: JSOT Press.

Beck, Robert R. 1996. *Nonviolent Story: Narrative Conflict Resolution in the Gospel of Mark*. Maryknoll, N.Y.: Orbis.

Beker, J. Christiaan. 1994. *The New Testament: A Thematic Introduction*. Minneapolis: Fortress.

Bell, H. I. 1937. *Recent Discoveries of Biblical Papyri*. Oxford: Clarendon.

Bennett, W. H. 1907. *The Life of Christ according to St. Mark*. London: Hodder & Stoughton.

Benoit, Pierre. 1969. *The Passion and Resurrection of Jesus Christ*. New York: Herder & Herder.

Berger, Klaus. 1976. *Die Griechische Daniel-Diegese. Eine Altkirchliche Apokalypse*. Leiden, Netherlands: Brill.

Best, Ernest. 1981. *Following Jesus: Discipleship in the Gospel of Mark*. JSNTSup 4. Sheffield: JSOT Press.

———. 1983. *Mark: The Gospel as Story*. Edinburgh: T. & T. Clark.

Betz, H. D., ed. 1971. *Christology and a Modern Pilgrimage: A Discussion with Norman Perrin*. Missoula, Mont.: Society of Biblical Literature.

Bickermann, E. 1924. "Das leere Grab." *ZNW* 23:281-92.

Bilezikian, Gilbert. 1977. *The Liberated Gospel: A Comparison of the Gospel of Mark and Greek Tragedy*. Grand Rapids: Baker.

Bird, C. H. 1953. "Some γάρ Clauses in St. Mark's Gospel." *JTS* n.s. 4:171-87.

Bischoff, Bernhard. 1990. *Roman Palaeography: Antiquity and the Middle Ages*. Cambridge: Cambridge University Press.

Black, C. Clifton. 1989. *The Disciples according to Mark: Markan Redaction in Current Debate*. JSNTSup 27. Sheffield: JSOT Press.

———. 2001. *Mark: Images of an Apostolic Interpreter*. Minneapolis: Fortress.

Blackwell, John. 1986. *The Passion as Story: The Plot of Mark*. Philadelphia: Fortress.

Blaiklock, E. M. 1965. *The Young Man Mark: Studies in Some Aspects of Mark and His Gospel*. Exeter: Paternoster.

Blair, J. Fulton. 1896. *The Apostolic Gospel*. London: Smith, Elder, & Co.

Blanck, Horst. 1992. *Das Buch in der Antike*. Munich: C. H. Beck.

Blass, F., and A. Debrunner. 1961. *A Greek Grammar of the New Testament and Other Early Christian Literature*. Translated and revised by Robert W. Funk. Chicago: University of Chicago Press.

Bleek, Friedrich. 1869. *An Introduction to the New Testament*. Translated by William Urwick. Edinburgh: T. & T. Clark.

Blount, Brian K. 1998. *Go Preach! Mark's Kingdom Message and the Black Church Today*. Maryknoll, N.Y.: Orbis.

Blunt, A. W. F. 1929. *The Gospel according to Saint Mark*. The Clarendon Bible. Oxford: Clarendon.

Bode, Edward L. 1970a. *The First Easter Morning: The Gospel Accounts of the Women's Visit to the Tomb of Jesus*. AnBib 45. Rome: Pontifical Biblical Institute.

———. 1970b. "A Liturgical *Sitz im Leben* for the Gospel Tradition of the Women's Easter Visit to the Tomb of Jesus?" *CBQ* 32:237-42.

Bolt, Peter G. 1996. "Mark 16:1-8: the Empty Tomb of a Hero?" *TynBul* 47.1:27-37.

Bonner, Campbell. 1934. *A Papyrus Codex of the Shepherd of Hermas*. Vol. 22 of University of Michigan Studies *Humanistic Series*. Ann Arbor: University of Michigan Press.

Boomershine, Thomas E. 1981. "Mark 16:8 and the Apostolic Commission." *JBL* 100:225-39.

———. 1988. *Story Journey: An Invitation to the Gospel as Storytelling*. Nashville: Abingdon.

Boomershine, Thomas E., and G. L. Bartholomew. 1981. "The Narrative Technique of Mark 16:8." *JBL* 100:213-23.

Borg, Marcus J., and N. T. Wright. 1999. *The Meaning of Jesus: Two Visions*. San Francisco: HarperSanFrancisco.

Boring, M. Eugene. 1990. "Mark 1:1-15 and the Beginning of the Gospel." *Semeia* 52:43-81.

Bornhäuser, K. 1958. *The Death and Resurrection of Jesus Christ*. Bangalore, India: CLS Press.

Bornkamm, G. 1975. *Jesus of Nazareth*. San Francisco: Harper & Row. (German original 1956.)

Borret, Marcel, ed. 1967. *Origène. Contra Celse*. Paris: Cerf.

Bousset, Wilhelm. 1970. *Kyrios Christos: A History of the Belief in Christ from the Beginnings of Christianity to Irenaeus*. Nashville: Abingdon.

Bover, J. M. 1944. "El final de San Marcos." *EstBib* 3:561-62.

Bowie, Ewen Lyall. 1996. "Novel, Greek." Pages 1049-50 in *OCD*.

Bowman, John. 1965. *The Gospel of Mark: The New Christian Jewish Passover Haggadah*. Leiden, Netherlands: Brill.

Brändle, Max. 1967. "Die synoptischen Grabeserzählungen," *Orientierung* 31:179-84 (ET, "Narratives of the Synoptics about the Tomb." *TD* 16 [1968]: 22-26).

Branscomb, B. Harvie. 1937. *The Gospel of Mark*. New York and London: Harper.

Bratcher, Robert G., and Eugene A. Nida. 1961. *A Translator's Handbook on the Gospel of Mark*. Vol. 2 of *Helps for Translators* by United Bible Societies. Leiden, Netherlands: Brill.

Briggs, R. C. 1973. *Interpreting the New Testament Today*. Nashville: Abingdon.

Broadhead, Edwin K. 1995. "In Search of the Gospel: Research Trends in Mark 14–16." *ABR* 43:20-49.

Brooks, James A. 1991. *Mark*. NAC 23. Nashville: Broadman.

Brown, Raymond E. 1973. *The Virginal Conception and Bodily Resurrection of Jesus*. New York: Paulist.

———. 1993. *The Birth of the Messiah*. New updated edition. ABRL. New York: Doubleday.

———. 1994. *The Death of the Messiah: From Gethsemane to the Grave*. Vol. 1. ABRL. New York: Doubleday.

———. 1997. *Introduction to the New Testament*. New York: Doubleday.

Bruce, Alexander Balmain. 1961. *The Synoptic Gospels*. Pages 1-651 in *The Expositor's Greek Testament*. Edited by W. R. Nicoll. London: n.p., 1897. Repr., Grand Rapids: Eerdmans.

Bruce, F. F. 1945. "The End of the Second Gospel." *EvQ* 17:169-81.

———. 1984. "The Date and Character of Mark." Pages 69-89 in *Jesus and the Politics of His Day*. Edited by Ernst Bammel and C. F. D. Moule. Cambridge: Cambridge University Press.

Brun, Lyder. 1911. "Bemerkungen zum Markusschluss." *TSK* 84:157-80.

————. 1914. "Die Auferstehungsbericht des Markusevangeliums," *TSK* 87:346-88.

————. 1925. *Die Auferstehung Christi in der urchristlichen Ueberlieferung.* Giessen: Töpelmann.

Bruns, J. Edgar. 1947. "A Note on Mark 16:9-10." *CBQ* 9:358-59.

Bultmann, Rudolf. 1994. *The History of the Synoptic Tradition.* Rev. ed. New York: Harper & Row, 1963. Repr., Peabody, Mass.: Hendrickson. [German original 1921.]

Bundy, Walter E. 1955. *Jesus and the First Three Gospels: An Introduction to the Synoptic Tradition.* Cambridge: Harvard University Press.

Burgon, John. 1871. *The Last Twelve Verses of the Gospel according to Saint Mark.* Oxford: James Parker.

Burkill, T. A. 1963. *Mysterious Revelation: An Examination of the Philosophy of St. Mark's Gospel.* Ithaca, N.Y.: Cornell University Press.

Burkitt, F. C. 1901. *Two Lectures on the Gospels.* London: Macmillan.

————. 1903–1904. "The Early Church and the Synoptic Gospels." *JTS* 5:330-42.

————. 1911. "The Historical Character of the Gospel of Mark." *AJT* 15:169-93.

————. 1922. *The Earliest Sources for the Life of Jesus.* London: Constable & Company.

————. 1924. *Christian Beginnings: Three Lectures.* London: University of London.

Burridge, Richard A. 1992. *What Are the Gospels? A Comparison with Graeco-Roman Biography.* Cambridge: Cambridge University Press.

Burton, Ernest De Witt. 1904. *Studies in the Gospel According to Mark.* Chicago: University of Chicago.

Bush, Roger Anthony. 1986. "Mark's Call to Action: a Rhetorical Analysis of Mark 16:8." Pages 22-30 in *Church Divinity 1986.* Edited by John H. Morgan. Notre Dame, Ind.: J. H. Morgan.

Butts, James R. 1986. "The Progymnasmata of Theon: A New Text with Translation and Commentary." Ph.D. diss., Claremont Graduate School.

Cadbury, H. J. 1927. "Mark 16.8." *JBL* 46:344-45.

Cadoux, Arthur Temple. 1935. *The Sources of the Second Gospel.* London: James Clarke & Company.

Camery-Hoggatt, Jerry. 1992. *Irony in Mark's Gospel: Text and subtext.* SNTSMS 72. Cambridge: Cambridge University Press.

Campenhausen, H. von. 1968. "The Events of Easter and the Empty Tomb." Pages 42-89 in *Tradition and Life in the Church.* Philadelphia: Fortress.

Carnley, Peter. 1987. *The Structure of Resurrection Belief.* Oxford: Oxford University Press.

Carrington, Philip. 1960. *According to Mark: A Running Commentary on the Oldest Gospel.* Cambridge: Cambridge University Press.

Carson, D. A., Douglas J. Moo, and Leon Morris. 1992. *An Introduction to the New Testament.* Grand Rapids: Zondervan.

Catchpole, David. 1977. "The Fearful Silence of the Women at the Tomb: A Study in Markan Theology." JTSA 18:3-10.

Charlesworth, James H., ed. 1983–1985. *Old Testament Pseudepigrapha.* 2 Vols. Garden City, N.Y.: Doubleday.

Childs, Brevard S. 1984. *The New Testament as Canon: An Introduction.* Philadelphia: Fortress.

Clarke, W. K. Lowther. 1934. "The Ending of St. Mark." *Theology* 29:106-7.

Clarke, W. N. 1881. *Commentary on the Gospel of Mark.* Philadelphia: American Baptist Publication Society.

Cole, R. A. 1989. *The Gospel according to Mark: An Introduction and Commentary.* 2d ed. Leicester, England: InterVarsity; Grand Rapids: Eerdmans.

Collins, Adela Yarbro. 1992. *The Beginning of the Gospel: Probings of Mark in Context.* Minneapolis: Fortress.

———. 1993. "The Empty Tomb in the Gospel according to Mark." Pages 107-40 in *Hermes and Athena: Biblical Exegesis and Philosophical Theology.* Edited by Eleonore Stump and Thomas P. Flint. Notre Dame, Ind.: University of Notre Dame Press.

———. 1995a. "Establishing the Text: Mark 1:1." Pages 111-27 in *Texts and Contexts: Biblical Texts in Their Textual and Situational Contexts: Essays in Honor of Lars Hartman.* Edited by Tord Fornberg and David Hellholm. Oslo, Norway: Scandinavian University Press.

———. 1995b. "Mysteries in the Gospel of Mark." *ST* 49/1:11-23. Also pages 11-23 in *Mighty Minorities? Minorities in Early Christianity, Positions, and Strategies: Essays in Honour of Jacob Jervell on his 70th Birthday, 21 May 1995.* Edited by David Hellholm, Halvor Moxness, and Turid Karlsen Seim. Oslo, Norway: Scandinavian University Press.

Colwell, Ernest C. 1937. "Mark 16:9-20 in the Armenian Version." *JBL* 56:369-86.

Comfort, Philip Wesley. 1992a. *The Quest for the Original Text of the New Testament.* Grand Rapids: Baker.

———. 1992b. "Texts and Manuscripts of the New Testament." Pages 179-207 in *The Origin of the Bible.* Edited by Philip Wesley Comfort. Wheaton, Ill.: Tyndale.

Conybeare, F. C. 1893. "Aristion, the Author of the Last Twelve Verses of Mark." *Expositor,* 4th series, 8:241-54.

———. 1895. "On the Last Twelve Verses of St. Mark's Gospel." *Expositor,* 5th series, 2:401-21.

Conzelmann, Hans, and Andreas Lindemann. 1988. *Interpreting the New Testament.* Peabody, Mass.: Hendrickson.

Cook, F. C., ed. 1878. *The Holy Bible according to the Authorized Version with an Explanatory and Critical Commentary. Speaker's Commentary on the New Testament.* London: John Murray.

Cook, Guillermo, and Ricardo Foulkes. 1990. *Marcos: Comentario Biblico Hispanoamericano.* Miami: Editorial Caribe.

Coote, Robert B. 1992. "Mark 1.1: arche, 'Scriptural Lemma.' " Pages 86-90 in

Text as Pretext: Essays in Honour of Robert Davidson. JSOTSup 138. Edited by Robert P. Carroll. Sheffield: JSOT Press.

Cotes, Mary. 1992. "Women, Silence, and Fear." Pages 150-66 in *Women in the Biblical Tradition*. Edited by George J. Brooke. Lewiston, N.Y.: Edwin Mellen.

Cowles, Henry. 1882. *Matthew and Mark, with Notes, Critical, Explanatory, and Practical*. New York: Appleton.

Cox, Steven Lynn. 1993. *A History and Critique of Scholarship Concerning the Markan Endings*. Lewiston, N.Y.: Edwin Mellen.

Craddock, Fred B. 1981. *The Gospels*. Nashville: Abingdon.

Craigie, W. A. 1922. "The Beginning of St Mark's Gospel." *Expositor*, 8th series, 24:303-5.

Cranfield, C. E. B. 1952. "St. Mark 16.1-8." *SJT* 5:282-98, 398-414.

———. 1959. *The Gospel according to Saint Mark*. CGTC. Cambridge: Cambridge University Press.

———. 1962. "Mark, Gospel of." Pages 267-77 in vol. 3 of *The Interpreter's Dictionary of the Bible*. Edited by George A. Buttrick, et al. 4 vols. Nashville: Abingdon, 1962.

Creed, J. M. 1929–1930. "The Conclusion of the Gospel according to Saint Mark." *JTS* 31:175-80.

Crossan, John Dominic. 1976. "Empty Tomb and Absent Lord." Pages 135-52 in *The Passion in Mark: Studies on Mark 14–16*. Edited by Werner H. Kelber. Philadelphia: Fortress.

———. 1978. "A Form for Absence: The Markan Creation of Gospel." *Semeia* 11:41-55.

———. 1991. *The Historical Jesus: The Life of a Mediterranean Jewish Peasant*. San Francisco: HarperSanFrancisco.

———. 1995. *Who Killed Jesus? Exposing the Roots of Anti-Semitism in the Gospel Story of the Death of Jesus*. San Francisco: HarperSanFrancisco.

Crouch, Walter B. 1994. "To Question an End, to End a Question: Opening the Closure of the Book of Jonah." *JSOT* 62:101-12.

———. 2000. *Death and Closure in Biblical Narrative*. Studies in Biblical Literature 7. New York: Peter Lang.

Croy, N. Clayton. 2001. "Where the Gospel Text Begins: A Non-theological Interpretation of Mark 1:1." *NovT* 43:105-27.

Cullmann, Oscar. 1952. *Petrus: Jünger—Apostel—Märtyrer*. 2d ed. Zürich: Zwingli Verein. (ET, *Peter: Disciple, Apostle, Martyr*. Philadelphia: Westminster, 1962.)

Culpepper, Alan. 1978. "The Passion and Resurrection in Mark." *RevExp* 75:583-600.

Cunningham, Phillip J. 1995. *Mark: The Good News Preached to the Romans*. New York and Mahwah, N.J.: Paulist.

Daniell, E. H. 1937. "The Lost Ending of St. Mark's Gospel." *Baptist Quarterly* 8:346-52.

Danker, Frederick W. 1963–1964. "Menander and the New Testament." *NTS* 10:365-68.

———. 1967. "Postscript to the Markan Secrecy Motif." *CTM* 38:24-27.

Danove, Paul L. 1993. *The End of Mark's Story: A Methodological Story*. Biblical Interpretation Series 3. Leiden, Netherlands: E. J. Brill.

———. 1996. "The Characterization and Narrative Function of the Women at the Tomb (Mark 15,40-41. 47; 16,1-8)." *Bib* 77:375-97.

Daubanton, F. E. 1919. " 'Αρχη του εὐαγγελιου 'Ιησου Χριστου (Mk.I:1)." Nieuwe Theologische Studiën 2:168-70.

Dautzenberg, Gerhard. 1977. "Die Zeit des Evangeliums. Mk 1,1-15 und die Konzeption des Markusevangeliums." *BZ* 21:219-34.

Davies, W. D. 1969. *Invitation to the New Testament*. Garden City, N.Y.: Doubleday.

Davis, Stephen, Daniel Kendall, and Gerald O'Collins, eds. 1997. *The Resurrection: An Interdisciplinary Symposium on the Resurrection of Jesus*. New York: Oxford University Press.

Davison, Samuel. 1894. *An Introduction to the Study of the New Testament*. 3d ed. Vol. 1. London: Kegan Paul, Trench, Trübner & Co.

De la Mare, Albinia A., and Nigel Guy Wilson. 1996. "Palaeography." Pages 1094-99 in OCD.

Deibert, Richard I. 1999. *Mark*. Interpretation Bible Studies. Louisville: Geneva.

DeJonge, Marinus. 1991. *Jewish Eschatology, Early Christian Christology and the Testaments of the Twelve Patriarchs*. NovTSup 63. Leiden, Netherlands: Brill.

Delorme, Jean. 1969. "Résurrection et Tombeau de Jesus: Marc 16, 1-8 dans la tradition evangélique." Pages 105-53 in *La Résurrection du Christ et l'exégèse moderne*. Edited by P. de Surgy, et al. Paris: Cerf. (ET, "The Resurrection and Jesus' Tomb: Mark 16,1-8 in the Gospel Tradition," Pages 74-106 in *The Resurrection and Modern Biblical Thought*. Edited by P. de Surgy, et al. New York and Cleveland: Corpus Books, 1970.)

Denniston, J. D. 1934. *The Greek Particles*. 2d ed. Oxford: Clarendon.

Depasse-Livet, J. 1970. "Le problème de la finale de Marc: Mc 16.8, Etat de la question." Diss., Louvain.

Descamps, Albert. 1959. "La Structure des Récits Évangéliques de la Résurrection." *Bib* 40:726-41.

Dewey, Joanna. 1994. "The Gospel of Mark as an Oral-Aural Event: Implications for Interpretation." Pages 145-63 in *The New Literary Criticism and the New Testament*. Edited by Edgar V. McKnight and Elizabeth Struthers Malbon. Valley Forge, Pa.: Trinity.

Dhanis, Édouard. 1958. "L'ensevelissement de Jésus et la visite au tombeau dans l'évangile de saint Marc." *Greg* 39:367-410.

Dibelius, Martin. 1934. *From Tradition to Gospel*. London: Ivor Nicholson & Watson.

Dionysius of Halicarnassus. 1974. *The Critical Essays*. 2 vols. LCL. Cambridge: Harvard University Press.

Dodd, C. H. 1953. *The Interpretation of the Fourth Gospel*. Cambridge: Cambridge University Press.

Dodds, E. R. 1970. "Plotinus." Pages 847-48 in *Oxford Classical Dictionary*. 2d ed. Edited by N. G. L. Hammond and H. H. Scullard. Oxford: Oxford University Press, 1970.

Donahue, John R., and Daniel J. Harrington. 2002. *The Gospel of Mark*. SP 2. Collegeville, Minn.: Liturgical.

Donfried, Karl Paul. 1989. "Paul as Σκηνοποιός and the use of the Codex in Early Christianity." Pages 249-56 in *Christus Bezeugen: Festschrift für Wolfgang Trilling zum 65. Geburtstag*. Edited by Karl Kertelge, Traugott Holtz, and Claus-Peter März. Leipzig: St. Benno.

Dormeyer, Detlev. 1987. "Die Kompositionsmetapher 'Evangelium Jesu Christi, Des Sohnes Gottes' Mk 1.1. Ihre theologische und literarische Aufgabe in der Jesus-Biographie des Markus." *NTS* 33:452-68.

Dormeyer, Detlev, and Hubert Frankemölle. 1984. "Evangelium als literarische Gattung und als theologischer Begriff." *ANRW Principat* 2.25.2, 1543-1704.

Doudna, John Charles. 1961. *The Greek of the Gospel of Mark*. SBLMS 12. Philadelphia: Society of Biblical Literature and Exegesis.

Dowd, Sharyn. 2000. *Reading Mark: A Literary and Theological Commentary on the Second Gospel*. Reading the New Testament Series. Macon, Ga.: Smyth & Helwys.

Drewermann, Eugen. 1990. *Das Markusevangelium*. Vol. 2: Mk 9:14 to 16:20. Olten and Freiburg: Walter-Verlag.

Drury, John. 1985. "Mark 1.1-15: An Interpretation." Pages 25-36 in *Alternative Approaches to New Testament Study*. Edited by A. E. Harvey. London: SPCK.

———. 1987. "Mark." Pages 402-17 in *The Literary Guide to the Bible*. Edited by Robert Alter and Frank Kermode. Cambridge: Harvard University Press.

DuBuisson, J. C. 1906. *The Gospel According to St Mark*. London: Methuen.

Dunn, James D. G. 1975. *Jesus and the Spirit*. London: SCM.

———. 1985. *The Evidence for Jesus*. Louisville: Westminster.

———. 1992. "Christology (NT)." Pages 979-91 in vol. 1 of *ABD*.

Dwyer, Timothy. 1996. *The Motif of Wonder in the Gospel of Mark*. JSNTSup 128. Sheffield: Sheffield Academic Press.

Eagleton, Terry. 1983. *Literary Theory: An Introduction*. Minneapolis: University of Minnesota Press.

Earle, Ralph. 1957. *The Gospel according to Mark*. Grand Rapids: Zondervan.

Edmunds, Albert J. 1917. "The Text of the Resurrection in Mark, and Its Testimony to the Apparitional Theory: With a Preface on Luke's Mutilation of Mark." *The Monist* 27:161-78.

Edwards, James R. 2002. *The Gospel according to Mark*. The Pillar New Testament Commentary. Edited by D. A. Carson. Grand Rapids: Eerdmans.

Efird, James M. 1980. *The New Testament Writings: History, Literature and Interpretation*. Atlanta: John Knox.

Ehrman, Bart D. 1991. "The Text of Mark in the Hands of the Orthodox." Pages 19-31 in *Biblical Hermeneutics in Historical Perspective: Studies in Honor of Karlfried Froehlich on His Sixtieth Birthday*. Edited by Mark S. Burrows and Paul Rorem. Grand Rapids: Eerdmans. Also in *LQ* 5 (Summer 1991) 143-56.

―――. 1993. *The Orthodox Corruption of Scripture: The Effect of Early Christological Controversies on the Text of the New Testament*. New York: Oxford University Press.

Ehrman, Bart D., and Michael W. Holmes, eds. 1995. *The Text of the New Testament in Contemporary Research: Essays on the* Status Quaestionis. Vol. 46 of *Studies and Documents*. Grand Rapids: Eerdmans.

Eidem, Erling. 1925. "Ingressen till Markusevangeliet." Pages 35-49 in *Studier tilegnede Frants Buhl*. Edited by Johannes Jacobsen. Copenhagen: V. Pios Boghandel.

Elliott, J. K. 1971. "The Text and Language of the Ending to Mark's Gospel." *TZ* 27:255-62.

―――. 1991. "ΚΑΘΩΣ and ΩΣΠΕΡ in the New Testament." *Filologia Neotestamentaria* 7:55-58.

―――. 1993. *The Language and Style of the Gospel of Mark*. NovTSup 71. Leiden, Netherlands: Brill.

―――. 2000. "Mark 1.1-3—A Later Addition to the Gospel?" *NTS* 46:584-88.

Elliott, Keith, and Ian Moir. 1995. *Manuscripts and the Text of the New Testament: An Introduction for English Readers*. Edinburgh: T. & T. Clark.

Ellis, E. Earle. 1999. *The Making of the New Testament Documents*. Biblical Interpretation Series 39. Leiden, Netherlands: Brill.

Else, Gerald F. 1963. *Aristotle's Poetics: The Argument*. Cambridge: Harvard University Press.

Enslin, Morton S. 1927. "ἐφοβοῦντο γάρ, Mark 16.8." *JBL* 46:62-68.

―――. 1938. *Christian Beginnings*. New York: Harper.

Epp, Eldon Jay. 1992. "Textual Criticism (NT)." Pages 412-35 in vol. 6 of *ABD*.

Erdmann, Gottfried. 1932. *Die Vorgeschichten des Lukas- und Matthaus- Evangeliums*. Göttingen: Vandenhoeck & Ruprecht.

Ernst, Josef. 1981. *Das Evangelium nach Markus*. Regensburg: Friedrich Pustet.

Evans, C. F. 1954. "I Will Go before You into Galilee." *JTS* n.s. 5:3-18.

―――. 1970. *Resurrection and the New Testament*. London: SCM.

Evans, Craig A. 1978. "Mark's Use of the Empty Tomb Tradition." *Studia Biblica et Theologica* 8.2:50-55.

―――. 2000. "Mark's Incipit and the Priene Calendar Inscription: From Jewish Gospel to Greco-Roman Gospel." *Journal of Greco-Roman Christianity and Judaism* 1:67-81.

―――. 2001. *Mark 8:27–16:20*. WBC. Nashville: Thomas Nelson.

Farmer, William R. 1974. *The Last Twelve Verses of Mark*. SNTSMS 25. Cambridge: Cambridge University Press.

Farrer, Austin. 1948. *The Glass of Vision*. Westminster: Dacre Press.

———. 1952. *A Study in St Mark*. New York: Oxford University Press.

———. 1954. *St Matthew and St Mark*. Westminster: Dacre Press.

Feine, Paul. 1936. *Einleitung in das Neuen Testament*. 8th ed., rev. by Johannes Behm. Leipzig: Quelle & Meyer.

Feneberg, Wolfgang. 1974. *Der Markusprolog: Studien zur Formbestimmung des Evangeliums*. SANT 36. Munich: Kösel-Verlag.

Fenton, J. C. 1990. "Resurrection Narratives." Pages 589-91 in *A Dictionary of Biblical Interpretation*. Edited by R. J. Coggins and J. L. Houlden. London: SCM; Philadelphia: Trinity.

Fenton, John. 1994. "The Ending of Mark's Gospel." Pages 1-7 in *Resurrection: Essays in Honour of Leslie Houlden*. Edited by S. Barton and G. Stanton. London: SPCK.

Feuillet, A. 1978. "Le 'Commencement' de l'Économie Chrétienne d'après He II.3-4; Mc I.1 et Ac I.1-2." *NTS* 24:163-74.

Filson, Floyd V. 1938. *Origins of the Gospels*. New York: Abingdon.

———. 1964. *A New Testament History*. Philadelphia: Westminster.

Finegan, Jack. 1956. "The Original Form of the Pauline Collection." *HTR* 49:85-103.

———. 1974. *Encountering New Testament Manuscripts: A Working Introduction to Textual Criticism*. Grand Rapids: Eerdmans.

Fischer, Karl Martin. 1980. *Das Ostergeschehen*. 2d ed. Göttingen: Vandenhoeck & Ruprecht.

Fitzmyer, Joseph A. 1998. *The Acts of the Apostles*. AB. New York: Doubleday.

Fowler, D. P. 1995. "Martial and the Book." *Ramus* 24:31-58.

Fowler, Robert M. 1986. "Reading Matthew Reading Mark: Observing the First Steps toward Meaning-as-Reference in the Synoptic Gospels." Pages 1-16 in the *SBL Seminar Papers, 1986*. Edited by Kent Harold Richards. Society of Biblical Literature Seminar Papers vol. 25. Atlanta: Scholars Press.

———. 1991. *Let the Reader Understand: Reader-Response Criticism and the Gospel of Mark*. Minneapolis: Fortress.

France, R. T. 1990. "The Beginning of Mark." *RTR* 49:11-19.

———. 1998. *The Gospel of Mark*. New York: Doubleday.

———. 2002. *The Gospel of Mark: A Commentary on the Greek Text*. NIGTC. Grand Rapids: Eerdmans; Carlisle, England: Paternoster.

Frankemölle, Hubert. 1988. *Evangelium—Begriff und Gattung*. Stuttgart: Katholisches Bibelwerk.

Freese, N. F. 1932. "Der Anfang des Markusevangeliums." *TSK* 104:429-38.

Freyne, Seán. 1980. *Galilee from Alexander the Great to Hadrian 323 B.C.E. to 135 C.E.: A Study of Second Temple Judaism*. University of Notre Dame Center for the Study of Judaism and Christianity in Antiquity 5. Wilmington, Del.: Michael Glazier; Notre Dame, Ind.: University of Notre Dame Press.

Freyne, Seán, and Henry Wansbrough. 1971. *Mark and Matthew*. Scripture Discussion Commentary. Chicago: ACTA Foundation.

Friedlaender, Ludwig. 1961. *M. Valerii Martialis: Epigrammaton Libri*. Amsterdam: Hakkert.

Friedrich, Gerhard. 1964. "εὐαγγελίζομαι, εὐαγγέλιον, προευαγγελίζομαι, εὐαγγελιστής." Pages 707-37 in vol. 2 of *TDNT*.

Fuller, Daniel P. 1965. *Easter Faith and History*. Grand Rapids: Eerdmans.

Fuller, Reginald H. 1971. *The Formation of the Resurrection Narratives*. Philadelphia: Fortress.

Fusillo, Massimo. 1997. "How Novels End: Some Patterns of Closure in Ancient Narrative." Pages 209-27 in *Classical Closure: Reading the End in Greek and Latin Literature*. Edited by Deborah H. Roberts, Francis M. Dunn, and Don Fowler. Princeton: Princeton University Press.

Gamble, Harry Y. 1990. "The Pauline Corpus and the Early Christian Book." Pages 265-80, 392-98 in *Paul and the Legacies of Paul*. Edited by William S. Babcock. Dallas: SMU Press.

———. 1992a. "Codex." Pages 1067-69 in vol. 1 of *ABD*.

———. 1992b. "Egerton Papyrus 2." Pages 317-18 in vol. 2 of *ABD*.

———. 1995. *Books and Readers in the Early Church: A History of Early Christian Texts*. New Haven and London: Yale University Press.

———. 2000. "Literacy and Book Culture." Pages 644-48 in *Dictionary of New Testament Background*. Edited by Craig A. Evans and Stanley E. Porter. Downers Grove, Ill.: InterVarsity.

Garland, David E. 1996. *Mark*. The NIV Application Commentary. Grand Rapids: Zondervan.

Garrett, Susan R. 1998. *The Temptations of Jesus in Mark's Gospel*. Grand Rapids: Eerdmans.

Geddert, Timothy J. 2001. *Mark*. Believers Church Bible Commentary. Scottdale, Pa.: Herald.

Giangrande, Giuseppe. 1970. "Novel, Greek." Pages 739-40 in *The Oxford Classical Dictionary*. 2d ed. Edited by N. G. L. Hammond and H. H. Scullard. Oxford: Oxford University Press.

Gibbs, J. M. 1973. "Mark 1, 1-15, Matthew 1, 1-4, 16, Luke 1, 1-4, 30, John 1, 1-51. The Gospel Prologues and their Function." Pages 154-88 in *Studia Evangelica VI*. Edited by Elizabeth A. Livingstone. Berlin: Akademie-Verlag.

Giblin, Charles Homer. 1992. "The Beginning of the Ongoing Gospel (Mk 1,2–16,8)." Pages 975-85 in *The Four Gospels, 1992 Festschrift Frans Neirynck*. BETL 100. Edited by F. Van Segbroeck, et al. Leuven, Belgium: Leuven University Press; Uitgeverij Peeters.

Gideon, Virtus E. 1975. "The Longer Ending of Mark in Recent Study." Pages 3-12 in *New Testament Studies: Essays in Honor of Ray Summers in his Sixty-fifth Year*. Edited by Huber L. Drumwright and Curtis Vaughan. Waco: Baylor University Press.

Glasswell, Mark E. 1974. "The Beginning of the Gospel. A Study of St Mark's Gospel with regard to its First Verse." Pages 36-43 in *New Testament Christianity for Africa and the World: Essays in honour of Harry Sawyerr.* Edited by Mark E. Glasswell and Edward W. Fasholé-Luke. London: SPCK.

Globe, Alexander. 1982. "The Caesarean Omission of the Phrase 'son of God' in Mark 1:1." *HTR* 75:209-18.

Gnilka, Joachim. 1979. *Das Evangelium nach Markus.* EKKNT 2. Cologne: Benziger.

Godwin, Johnnie C. 1979. *Mark.* Vol. 16 of Layman's Bible Book Commentary. Nashville: Broadman.

Goetz, Karl Gerold. 1927. *Petrus als Gründer und Oberhaupt der Kirche und Schauer von Gesichten nach den altchristlichen Berichten und Legenden.* Leipzig: J. C. Hinrichs.

Goguel, Maurice. 1909. *L'Evangile de Marc et ses Rapports avec ceux de Mathieu et de Luc.* Paris: Ernest Leroux.

———. 1923. *Introduction au Nouveau Testament.* Paris: Ernest Leroux.

———. 1933. *La Foi à la Résurrection de Jésus dans le Christianisme Primitif.* Paris: Ernest Leroux.

Goodspeed, Edgar J. 1905. "The Original Conclusion of the Gospel of Mark." *AJT* 9:484-90.

———. 1919. "The Original Conclusion of Mark." *Expositor,* 8th series, 18:155-60.

———. 1927. *New Solutions of New Testament Problems.* Chicago: University of Chicago Press.

———. 1937. *An Introduction to the New Testament.* Chicago: University of Chicago.

———. 1940. *Christianity Goes to Press.* New York: Macmillan.

Goppelt, Leonhard. 1981. *Theology of the New Testament.* Vol. 1. Grand Rapids: Eerdmans.

Gould, Ezra P. 1907. *A Critical and Exegetical Commentary on the Gospel according to St. Mark.* New York: Charles Scribner's Sons.

Goulder, Michael D. 1978. "Mark XVI. 1-8 and Parallels." *NTS* 24:235-40.

Grant, Robert M. 1963. *A Historical Introduction to the New Testament.* New York: Harper & Row.

Grass, Hans. 1964. *Ostergeschehen und Osterberichte.* 3d ed. Göttingen: Vandenhoeck & Ruprecht.

Green, S. Walter. 1908. *The Gospel According to St. Mark.* New York: Fleming H. Revell.

Green, Thomas Sheldon. n.d. *A Course of Developed Criticism on Passages of the New Testament Materially Affected by Various Readings.* London: Samuel Bagster & Sons.

Greenlee, J. Harold. 1985. *Scribes, Scrolls, and Scripture: A Student's Guide to New Testament Textual Criticism.* Grand Rapids: Eerdmans.

Gregory, Casper Rene. 1884. *Novum Testamentum Graece: Prolegomena*. Vol. 3. Leipzig: J. C. Hinrichs.

———. 1907. *Canon and Text of the New Testament*. New York: Scribner's.

Griesbach, J. J. 1774–1775. *Commentarius Criticus in Textum Graecum Novi Testamenti*. Ienae [Jena], Germany: J. C. G. Goepferdt.

Grimme, Hubert. 1946. "Harmonie zwischen Anfang und Schluß des Markusevangeliums." *TQ* 126:276-89.

Grobel, K. 1962. "Gospels." Page 449 in vol. 2 of *IDB*.

Grundmann, Walter. 1989. *Das Evangelium nach Markus*. 10th ed. THKNT 2. Berlin: Evangelische Verlagsanstalt.

Grundmann, Walter, et al. 1974. "χρίω, χριστός, ἀντίχριστος, χρίσμα, χριστιανός." Pages 493-580 in vol. 9 of *TDNT*.

Guelich, Robert A. 1982. " 'The Beginning of the Gospel,' Mark 1:1-15." *BR* 27:5-15.

———. 1989. *Mark 1–8:26*. WBC. Dallas: Word.

———. 1992. "Mark, Gospel of." Pages 512-25 in *The Dictionary of Jesus and the Gospels*. Edited by Joel B. Green, et al. Downers Grove, Ill.: InterVarsity.

Gundry, Robert H. 1993. *Mark: A Commentary on his Apology for the Cross*. Grand Rapids: Eerdmans.

———. 1996. "ΕΥΑΓΓΕΛΙΟΝ: How Soon a Book?" *JBL* 115:321-25.

Guthrie, Donald. 1990. *New Testament Introduction*. Leicester, England: Apollos; Downers Grove, Ill.: InterVarsity.

Güttgemanns, Erhardt. 1972. "Linguistische Analyse von Mk 16,1-8," *LB* 11/12:13-53.

Guy, Harold A. 1955. *A Critical Introduction to the Gospels*. London: Macmillan.

———. 1957. *The Origin of the Gospel of Mark*. London: Hodder & Stoughton.

———. 1968. *The Gospel of Mark*. London: Macmillan; New York: St Martin's.

Haefner, Alfred E. 1958. "The Bridge between Mark and Acts." *JBL* 77:67-71.

Haenchen, E. 1966. *Der Weg Jesu: Eine Erklärung des Markus-Evangeliums und der kanonischen Parallelen*. Berlin: Töpelmann.

Hägg, Tomas. 1983. *The Novel in Antiquity*. Berkeley and Los Angeles: University of California.

Haines-Eitzen, Kim. 2000. *Guardians of Letters: Literacy, Power, and the Transmitters of Early Christian Literature*. Oxford: Oxford University Press.

Hall, David R. 1990. *The Seven Pillories of Wisdom*. Macon, Ga.: Mercer University Press.

Halliwell, Stephen. 1987. *The Poetics of Aristotle*. Chapel Hill: University of North Carolina Press.

Hamerton-Kelly, Robert G. 1994. *The Gospel and the Sacred: Poetics of Violence in Mark*. Minneapolis: Fortress.

Hamilton, J. R. 1969. *Plutarch, Alexander: A Commentary*. Oxford: Clarendon.

Hamilton, Neill. Q. 1965. "Resurrection Tradition and the Composition of Mark." *JBL* 84:415-21.

Hanhart, Karel. 1995. *The Open Tomb: A New Approach, Mark's Passover Haggadah (ca. 72 C.E.)*. Collegeville, Minn.: Liturgical.

Hansen, William, ed. 1998. *Anthology of Ancient Greek Popular Literature*. Bloomington and Indianapolis: Indiana University Press.

Hanson, James S. 2000. *The Endangered Promises: Conflict in Mark*. Atlanta: Society of Biblical Literature.

Hanson, R. P. C. 1962. *Tradition in the Early Church*. London: SCM.

———. 1970. *Biblical Criticism*. The Pelican Guide to Modern Theology. Baltimore: Penguin.

Hare, Douglas R. A. 1996. *Mark*. Westminster Bible Companion. Louisville: Westminster John Knox.

Hargreaves, John. 1965. *A Guide to St Mark's Gospel*. London: SPCK.

Harnack, Adolf von. 1893. "Conybeare, Aristion, the Author of the Last Twelve Verses of Mark." *TLZ* 18:561-64.

———. 1908. "Neues zum unechten Markusschluss." *TLZ* 33:168-70.

Harrington, Daniel J. 1990. "The Gospel According to Mark." Pages 596-629 in *The New Jerome Biblical Commentary*. Edited by Raymond E. Brown, et al. Englewood Cliffs, N.J.: Prentice Hall.

Harrington, Wilfrid J. 1968. *Record of the Fulfillment: The New Testament*. London: Geoffrey Chapman.

———. 1979. *Mark: New Testament Message*. Wilmington, Del.: Michael Glazier.

Harris, J. Rendel. 1893. "On the Alternative Ending of St. Mark's Gospel." *JBL* 12:96-103.

———. 1908. *Side-Lights on New Testament Research*. London: Kingsgate.

Harris, Murray J. 1983. *Raised Immortal: Resurrection and Immortality in the New Testament*. Grand Rapids: Eerdmans.

Harris, William V. 1991. "Why Did the Codex Supplant the Book-Roll?" Pages 71-85 in *Renaissance Society and Culture: Essays in Honor of Eugene F. Rice, Jr.* Edited by John Monfasani and Ronald G. Musto. New York: Italica.

Harrison, Everett F. 1964. *Introduction to the New Testament*. Grand Rapids: Eerdmans.

Hartmann, Gerhard. 1936. *Der Aufbau des Markusevangeliums mit einem Anhang: Untersuchungen zur Echtheit des Markusschlusses*. Münster: Aschendorff.

Hartstock, Reinhold. 1920. "Visionsberichte in den synoptischen Evangelien." Pages 130-45 in *Festgabe für D. Dr. Julius Kaftan*. Tübingen: J. C. B. Mohr.

Harvey, A. E. 1977. *Something Overheard: An Invitation to the New Testament*. Atlanta: John Knox.

Hatch, William Henry Paine. 1939. *The Principal Uncial Manuscripts of the New Testament*. Chicago: University of Chicago Press.

Hauck, D. Friedrich. 1931. *Das Evangelium des Markus*. THKNT 2. Leipzig: Deichert.

Hawkins, John C. 1909. *Horae Synopticae: Contributions to the Study of the Synoptic Problem*. Oxford: Clarendon.

Hays, Richard B. 1996. *The Moral Vision of the New Testament: Community, Cross, New Creation.* San Francisco: HarperSanFrancisco.

Head, Peter M. 1991. "A Text-critical Study of Mark 1.1 'The Beginning of the Gospel of Jesus Christ.' " *NTS* 37:621-29.

————. 1995. "The Date of the Magdalen Papyrus of Matthew (P. MAGD. GR. 17 = P64): A Response to C. P. Thiede." *TynBul* 46.2:251-85.

Headley, P. L. 1934. "The Egyptian Texts of the Gospels and Acts." *CQR* 118 (April): 23-39, and (July): 188-230.

Hebert, Gabriel. 1962. "The Resurrection-Narrative in St. Mark's Gospel." *SJT* 15:66-73. [= *ABR* 7 (1959): 58-65.]

Heckel, Theo K. 1999. *Vom Evangelium des Markus zum viergestaltigen Evangelium.* Tübingen: Mohr Siebeck.

Hedrick, Charles W. 1983. "What is a Gospel? Geography, Time and Narrative Structure." PRSt 10:255-68.

Heil, John Paul. 1992. *The Gospel of Mark as Model for Action: A Reader-Response Commentary.* New York: Paulist.

Helton, Stanley N. 1994. "Churches of Christ and Mark 16:9-20." *ResQ* 36.1:33-52.

Helzle, Eugen. 1959. *Der Schluß des Markusevangelium (Mk 16.9-20) und das Freer-Logion (Mk 16,14 W), ihre Tendenzen und ihr gegenseitiges Verhältnis: Eine wortexegetische Untersuchung.* Phil. Diss. Tübingen. Summary in *TLZ* 85 (1960): 470-72.

Henaut, Barry W. 1986. "Empty tomb or empty argument: A failure of nerve in recent studies of Mark 16?" *SR* 15:177-90.

Hendrickx, Herman. 1994. *The Resurrection Narratives of the Synoptic Gospels.* London: Geoffrey Chapman.

Hendriksen, William. 1975. *New Testament Commentary: Exposition of the Gospel according to Mark.* Grand Rapids: Baker.

Hengel, Martin. 1963. "Maria Magdalena und die Frauen als Zeugen." Pages 243-56 in *Abraham unser Vater: Juden und Christen im Gespräch über die Bibel.* AGSU 5. Edited by Otto Betz, et al. Leiden, Netherlands: Brill.

————. 1980. *Acts and the History of Earliest Christianity.* Philadelphia: Fortress.

————. 1985. *Studies in the Gospel of Mark.* Philadelphia: Fortress.

————. 2000. *The Four Gospels and the One Gospel of Jesus Christ.* Harrisburg, Pa.: Trinity.

Hennecke, Edgar, and Wilhelm Schneemelcher. 1963–1965. *New Testament Apocrypha.* 2 Vols. Philadelphia: Westminster.

Herklotz, F. 1921. "Zu Mk 16, 9-20." *BZ* 15:149-50.

Hermann, Ingo. 1967. *Das Markusevangelium.* Dusseldorf: Patmos.

Hess, Beth B., Elizabeth W. Markson, and Peter J. Stein. 1991. *Sociology.* New York: Macmillan.

Hester, J. David. 1995. "Dramatic Inconclusion: Irony and the Narrative Rhetoric of the Ending of Mark." *JSNT* 57:61-86.

Hobbs, Herschel H. 1970. *An Exposition of the Gospel of Mark.* Grand Rapids: Baker.

Hobbs, Jack A., and Robert L. Duncan. 1992. *Arts, Ideas and Civilization.* 2d ed. Englewood Cliffs, N.J.: Prentice Hall.

Hoffmann, Richard A. 1904. *Das Marcusevangelium und seine Quellen: Ein Beitrag zur Lösing der Urmarcusfrage.* Königsberg: Thomas und Oppermann.

Holmes, Michael W. 2001. "To Be Continued . . . The Many Endings of the Gospel of Mark." *BRev* 17 (August): 12-23, 48-50.

Holmes, Mike. 1976. "The Ending of Mark 16:8, Intentional or Accidental?" *TJ* 5:102-8.

Holtzmann, H. J. 1901. *Hand-Commentar zum Neuen Testament: Die Synoptiker.* Tübingen and Leipzig: J. C. B. Mohr.

Hooker, Morna D. 1991a. *The Gospel according to Saint Mark.* Peabody, Mass.: Hendrickson.

———. 1991b. "Beginning of the Gospel." Pages 18-28 in *The Future of Christology: Essays in Honor of Leander E. Keck.* Edited by Abraham J. Malherbe and Wayne A. Meeks. Minneapolis: Fortress.

———. 1997. *Beginnings: Keys That Open the Gospels.* Harrisburg, Pa.: Trinity.

———. 1999. "Mark, Gospel of." Pages 124-31 in vol. 2 of *Dictionary of Biblical Interpretation.* Edited by John H. Hayes. 2 vols. Nashville: Abingdon, 1999.

Horsley, G. H. R. 1995. "Classical Manuscripts in Australia and New Zealand, and the Early History of the Codex." *Antichthon* 27:60-83.

Horvath, Tibor. 1973. "The Early Markan Tradition on the Resurrection." *RUO* 43, 3:445-48.

Houlden, J. L. 1987. *Backward into Light: The Passion and Resurrection of Jesus according to Matthew and Mark.* London: SCM Press.

Howell, Peter. 1980. *A Commentary on Book One of the Epigrams of Martial.* London: Athlone.

Huby, Joseph. 1948. *Evangile selon Saint Marc: Traduction et Commentaire.* Paris: Beauchesne.

Huffmann, Norman. 1945. "Emmaus Among the Resurrection Narratives." *JBL* 64:205-26.

Hug, Joh. Leonhard. 1826. *Einleitung in die Schriften des Neuen Testaments.* 3d ed. 2 vols. Stuttgart and Tübingen: J. G. Cotta. (ET, *Hug's Introduction to the New Testament.* Andover: Gould & Newman, 1836.)

Hug, Joseph. 1978. *La Finale de l'Évangile de Marc (Mc 16,9-20).* Paris: Gabalda.

Humphrey, Hugh M. 1992. *"He is Risen!" A New Reading of Mark's Gospel.* New York: Paulist.

Hunt, B. P. W. Stather. 1923. "Is Our Second Gospel Complete?" *Expositor,* 8th series, 26:284-97.

Hunter, A. M. 1946. *Introducing the New Testament.* Philadelphia: Westminster.

———. 1949. *The Gospel according to Saint Mark.* London: SCM.

———. 1951. *Interpreting the New Testament 1900–1950.* London: SCM.

Hurtado, Larry W. 1983. *Mark.* Good News Commentary. San Francisco: Harper & Row.

Ibscher, Hugo. 1937. "Der Kodex." *Jahrbuch der Einbandkunst* 4:3-15.

Iser, Wolfgang. 1978. *The Act of Reading: A Theory of Aesthetic Response.* Baltimore and London: Johns Hopkins University Press.

James, M. R. 1971. *The Biblical Antiquities of Philo.* New York: Ktav.

Jefford, Clayton N. 1992. "Mark, John." Pages 557-58 of vol. 4 of *ABD.*

Jeremias, Joachim. 1955. *The Eucharistic Words of Jesus.* New York: Macmillan.

Johnson, Luke Timothy. 1986. *The Writings of the New Testament: An Interpretation.* Philadelphia: Fortress.

―――. 1992. *The Acts of the Apostles. Sacra Pagina* 5. Collegeville, Minn.: Liturgical Press.

Johnson, Sherman E. 1960. *A Commentary on the Gospel According to Mark.* New York: Harper.

Judge, E. A., and S. R. Pickering. 1978. "Biblical Papyri prior to Constantine: Some Cultural Implications of their Physical Form." *Prudentia* 10:1-13.

Juel, Donald H. 1990. *Mark.* ACNT. Minneapolis: Augsburg.

―――. 1994. *A Master of Surprise: Mark Interpreted.* Minneapolis: Fortress.

―――. 1999. *The Gospel of Mark.* Interpreting Biblical Texts. Nashville: Abingdon.

Juel, Donald with James S. Ackerman and Thayer S. Warshaw. 1978. *An Introduction to New Testament Literature.* Nashville: Abingdon.

Jülicher, Adolf. 1904. *An Introduction to the New Testament.* New York: G. P. Putnam's Sons.

Kahle, P. E. 1951. "The End of St. Mark's Gospel. The Witness of the Coptic Versions." *JTS* n.s. 2:49-57.

Kasteren, J. P. van. 1902. "L'Épilogue canonique de second Évangile, Mr. 16, 9-20." *RB* 11:240-55.

Katz, Peter. 1945. "The Early Christians' Use of Codices instead of Rolls." *JTS* 46:63-65.

Kealy, Seán P. 1982. *Mark's Gospel: A History of its Interpretation.* New York: Paulist.

Keck, Leander E. 1965–1966. "The Introduction to Mark's Gospel." *NTS* 12:352-70.

Kee, Howard Clark. 1990. "Mark, Long Ending of." Page 551 in the *Mercer Dictionary of the Bible.* Edited by Watson E. Mills. Macon, Ga.: Mercer University Press.

Keenan, John P. 1995. *The Gospel of Mark: A Mahāyāna Reading.* Maryknoll, N.Y.: Orbis.

Kelber, Werner H. 1979. *Mark's Story of Jesus.* Philadelphia: Fortress.

Kelhoffer, James A. 2000. *Miracle and Mission: The Authentication of Missionaries and their Message in the Longer Ending of Mark.* WUNT, 2d ser., vol. 112. Tübingen: J. C. B. Mohr.

———. 2001. "The Witness of Eusebius' *ad Marinum* and Other Christian Writings to Text-Critical Debates Concerning the Original Conclusion to Mark's Gospel." *ZNW* 92:78-112.

Kenyon, Frederic G. 1932. *Books and Readers in Greece and Rome.* Chicago: Ares.

———. 1939. "Papyrus Rolls and the Ending of St. Mark." *JTS* 40 (1939): 56-57.

———. 1958. *Our Bible and the Ancient Manuscripts.* New York: Harper.

Kermode, Frank. 1967. *The Sense of an Ending: Studies in the Theory of Fiction.* New York: Oxford University Press.

———. 1969. "The Structures of Fiction." *Modern Language Notes* 84:891-915.

———. 1978. "Sensing Endings." *Nineteenth Century Fiction* 33:144-58.

———. 1979. *The Genesis of Secrecy: On the Interpretation of Narrative.* The Charles Eliot Norton Lectures, 1977–1978. Cambridge: Harvard University Press.

Kevin, Robert Oliver. 1926. "The Lost Ending of the Gospel according to Mark." *JBL* 45:81-103.

Kilgallen, John J. 1989. *A Brief Commentary on the Gospel of Mark.* New York: Paulist.

Kilpatrick, G. D. 1960. "The Punctuation of John vii.37-38," *JTS* n.s. 11:340-42.

Kingsbury, Jack Dean. 1989. *Conflict in Mark: Jesus, Authorities, Disciples.* Minneapolis: Fortress.

Kinukawa, Hisako. 1994. *Women and Jesus in Mark: A Japanese Feminist Perspective.* Maryknoll, N.Y.: Orbis.

Kleist, James A. 1932. *The Memoirs of St. Peter.* Milwaukee: Bruce.

Klijn, A. F. J. 1967. *An Introduction to the New Testament.* Leiden, Netherlands: Brill.

Klostermann, August. 1867. *Das Markusevangelium: nach seinem Quellenwerthe für die evangelische Geschichte.* Göttingen: Vandenhoeck & Ruprecht.

Klostermann, Erich. 1950. *Das Markusevangelium.* 4th ed. Tübingen: J. C. B. Mohr.

Knox, B. M. W., and P. E. Easterling. 1985. "Books and Readers in the Greek World." Pages 1-41 in vol. 1 of *The Cambridge History of Classical Literature.* Edited by P. E. Easterling and B. M. W. Knox. Cambridge: Cambridge University Press.

Knox, Wilfred Lawrence. 1942. "The Ending of St. Mark's Gospel." *HTR* 35:13-23.

Koch, G. 1959. *Die Auferstehung Jesu Christi.* Tübingen: J. C. B. Mohr.

Koch, H. 1908. "Der erweiterte Markusschluss und die kleinasiatischen Presbyter." *BZ* 6:266-78.

Koester, Helmut. 1982. *Introduction to the New Testament: History, Culture, and Religion of the Hellenistic Age.* Hermeneia: Foundations and Facets. Philadelphia: Fortress.

———. 1989. "From the Kerygma-Gospel to Written Gospels." *NTS* 35:361-81.

———. 1990. *Ancient Christian Gospels.* Philadelphia: Trinity.

Kraeling, Carl H. 1925. "A Philological Note on Mark 16.8." *JBL* 44:357-58.

Kremer, Jacob. 1968. *Die Osterbotschaft der vier Evangelien.* Stuttgart: Katholisches Bibelwerk.

Krentz, Edgar. 1975. *The Historical-Critical Method.* GBS. Philadelphia: Fortress.

———. 1993. "Biblical Interpretation for a New Millennium." *CurTM* 20:345-359.

Kümmel, Werner Georg. 1948–1949. "Das Urchristentum." *TRu* 17:3-50.

———. 1950. "Das Urchristentum." *TRu* 18:1-53.

———. 1973. *The Theology of the New Testament.* Nashville: Abingdon.

———. 1975. *Introduction to the New Testament.* Translated and revised by Howard Clark Kee. Nashville: Abingdon.

Kuthirakkattel, Scaria. 1990. *The Beginning of Jesus' Ministry according to Mark's Gospel (1,14-3,6): A Redaction Critical Study.* AnBib 123. Rome: Pontifical Biblical Institute.

Lachmann, Karl. 1830. "Rechenschaft über seine Ausgabe des Neuen Testaments." *TSK* 3:817-45.

Ladd, George Eldon. 1967. *The New Testament and Criticism.* Grand Rapids: Eerdmans.

———. 1975. *I Believe in the Resurrection of Jesus.* Grand Rapids: Eerdmans.

Lagrange, P. M.-J. 1947. *Évangile selon Saint Marc.* Paris: Gabalda.

Lake, Kirsopp. 1907. *The Historical Evidence for the Resurrection of Jesus Christ.* New York: Putnam's Sons.

Lake, Kirsopp and Silva. 1937. *An Introduction to the New Testament.* New York: Harper.

Lamarche, P. 1970. "Commencement de l'évangile de Jésus, Christ, Fils de Dieu (Mc I,1)," *NRTh* 92:1024-36.

Lane, William L. 1974. *The Gospel According to Mark.* Grand Rapids: Eerdmans.

Lausberg, Heinrich. 1960. *Handbuch der literarischen Rhetorik: Eine Grundlegung der Literaturwissenschaft.* 2 Vols. Munich: Max Heuber. (ET, *Handbook of Literar: Rhetoric. A Foundation for Literary Study.* Leiden, Netherlands: Brill, 1998.)

LaVerdiere, Eugene. 1996. "The Passion-Resurrection According to Mark, Act III, Scene Two, the Burial of Jesus (15:42-47) and the Women's Visit to the Tomb (16:1-8)." *Emmanuel* 102 (October): 475-79, 482-88.

———. 1999. *The Beginning of the Gospel: Introducing the Gospel according to Mark.* Vol. 2. Collegeville, Minn.: Liturgical.

Leaney, A. R. C. 1972. *The New Testament.* Knowing Christianity Series. Edited by William Neil. London: Hodder & Stoughton.

Leary, T. J. 1996. *Martial Book XIV: The Apophoreta.* London: Duckworth.

Lee, David. 1999. *Luke's Stories of Jesus: Theological Reading of Gospel Narrative and the Legacy of Hans Frei.* JSNTSup 185. Sheffield: Sheffield Academic Press.

Leemans, Conradus, ed. 1835. *Horapollinis Niloi Hieroglyphica.* Amsterdam: J. Muller et Socios.

Legg, S. C. E. 1935. *Novum Testamentum Graece: Evangelium Secundum Marcum.* Oxford: Clarendon.

———. 1940. *Novum Testamentum Graece: Evangelium Secundum Matthaeum.* Oxford: Clarendon.

Lemaire, André. 1992. "Writing and Writing Materials." Pages 999-1008 in vol. 6 of *ABD*.

Léon-Dufour, Xavier. 1974. *Resurrection and the Message of Easter.* New York: Holt, Rinehart & Winston.

Lewis, Greville P. 1954. *An Approach to the New Testament.* London: Epworth.

Lieberman, Saul. 1962. "Jewish and Christian Codices." Pages 203-8 in *Hellenism in Jewish Palestine*. 2d ed. Edited by Saul Lieberman. New York: Jewish Theological Seminary of America.

Liew, Tat-Siong Benny. 1999. *Politics of Parousia: Reading Mark Inter(con)textually.* Biblical Interpretation Series 42. Leiden, Netherlands: Brill.

Lightfoot, R. H. 1938. *Locality and Doctrine in the Gospels.* New York and London: Harper & Brothers.

———. 1945. Review of N. B. Stonehouse *The Witness of Matthew and Mark to Christ*. *JTS* 46:217-24.

———. 1950. *The Gospel Message of St. Mark.* Oxford: Clarendon.

Lincoln, Andrew T. 1989. "The Promise and the Failure: Mark 16:7, 8." *JBL* 108:283-300.

Lindemann, Andreas. 1980. "Die Osterbotschaft des Markus." *NTS* 26:298-317.

Lindton, Olof. 1929. "Der vermißte Markusschluß." *TBl* 8:229-34.

Linnemann, Eta. 1969. "Der (wiedergefundene) Markusschluß." *ZTK* 66:255-87.

Linton, Olof. 1967–1968. "Evidences of a Second-Century Revised Edition of St. Mark's Gospel." *NTS* 14:321-55.

Llewelyn, S. R. 1994. With the collaboration of R. A. Kearsley. *A Review of the Greek Inscriptions and Papyri published in 1982–83*. Vol. 7 of *New Documents Illustrating Early Christianity*. New South Wales, Australia: Macquarie University.

Lohmeyer, Ernst. 1936. *Galiläa und Jerusalem.* FRLANT 52. Göttingen: Vandenhoeck & Ruprecht.

———. 1951. *Das Evangelium des Markus.* 11th ed. KEK Göttingen: Vandenhoeck & Ruprecht.

Lohse, Eduard. 1981. *The Formation of the New Testament.* Nashville: Abingdon. (German original, 1972.)

Loisy, Alfred. 1912. *L'Évangile selon Marc.* Paris: Émile Nourry.

———. 1950. *The Origins of the New Testament.* London: George Allen.

Longstaff, Thomas R. W. 1976. "Empty Tomb and Absent Lord: Mark's Interpretation of Tradition." Pages 269-77 in *SBL Seminar Papers, 1976*. Edited by George MacRae. Missoula, Mont: Scholars Press.

Lowrie, Walter. 1929. *Jesus according to St. Mark: An Interpretation of St. Mark's Gospel.* London: Longmans, Green & Co.

Lubsczyk, Hans. 1977. "KYRIOS JESUS: Beobachtungen und Gedanken zum Schluß des Markusevangeliums." Pages 133-74 in *Die Kirche Des Anfangs: Festschrift für Heinz Schürmann zum 65. Geburtstag*. Edited by Rudolf Schnackenburg, et al. Leipzig: St. Benno-Verlag.

Luedemann, Gerd. 1994. *The Resurrection of Jesus: History, Experience, Theology*. Minneapolis: Fortress.

Lührmann, D. 1987. *Das Markusevangelium*. HNT 3.Tübingen: Mohr-Siebeck.

Luzarraga, J. 1969. "Retraducción semítica de φοβέομαι en, Mc 16,8." *Bib* 50:497-510.

MacDonald, Dennis R. 2000. *The Homeric Epics and the Gospel of Mark*. New Haven: Yale University Press.

Mack, Burton L. 1988. *A Myth of Innocence*. Philadelphia: Fortress.

MacLean, A. J. 1908. "Gospel according to Mark." Pages 120-36 in vol. 2 of *A Dictionary of Christ and the Gospels*. Edited by James Hastings. New York: Scribners.

Mader, J. 1905. "Der Markusschluss." *BZ* 3:269-72.

Maehler, Herwig. 1996. "Books, Greek and Roman." Pages 249-52 in OCD.

Magness, J. Lee. 1986. *Sense and Absence: Structure and Suspension in the Ending of Mark's Gospel*. SemeiaSt. Atlanta: Scholars Press.

Major, H. D. A., T. W. Manson, and C. J. Wright. 1938. *The Mission and Message of Jesus*. New York: Dutton.

Malbon, Elizabeth Struthers. 2000. *In the Company of Jesus: Characters in Mark's Gospel*. Louisville: Westminster John Knox.

————. 2002. *Hearing Mark: A Listener's Guide*. Harrisburg, Pa.: Trinity.

Maldfeld, Georg, and Bruce M. Metzger. 1949. "Detailed List of the Greek Papyri of the New Testament." *JBL* 68:359-70.

Mally, Edward J. 1968. "The Gospel according to Mark." Pages 21-61 in *The Jerome Biblical Commentary*. Edited by Raymond E. Brown, et al. Englewood Cliffs, N.J.: Prentice-Hall.

Mann, C. S. 1986. *Mark: A New Translation with Introduction and Commentary*. AB. Garden City, N.Y.: Doubleday.

Manson, T. W. 1944. "The Life of Jesus: A Survey of the Available Material. 2. The Foundation of the Synoptic Tradition: The Gospel of Mark." *BJRL* 28.1:119-36.

————. 1962. "The Foundation of the Synoptic Tradition: The Gospel of Mark." Pages 29-45 in *Studies in the Gospels and Epistles*. Manchester: Manchester University Press.

Marcovich, Miroslav. 1986. *Hippolytus: Refutatio Omnium Haeresium*. Berlin and New York: Walter de Gruyter.

Marcus, Joel. 2000a. "Mark, Gospel of." Pages 858-61 in *Eerdman's Dictionary of the Bible*. Edited by David Noel Freedman. Grand Rapids: Eerdmans.

————. 2000b. *Mark 1–8: A New Translation with Introduction and Commentary*. AB. New York: Doubleday.

Marin, Louis. 1976. "The Women at the Tomb: A Structural Analysis Essay of a Gospel Text." Pages 73-96 in *The New Testament and Structuralism*. PTMS 11. Edited by Alfred M. Johnson, Jr. Pittsburgh: Pickwick.

Marmardji, A.-S. 1935. *Diatessaron de Tatien*. Beirut: Imprimerie Catholique.

Marshall, I. Howard. 1991. "Luke and His 'Gospel'." Pages 273-92 in *The Gospel and the Gospels*. Edited by Peter Stuhlmacher. Grand Rapids: Eerdmans.

Martin, Ralph P. 1975. *New Testament Foundations*. Vol. 1. Grand Rapids: Eerdmans.

———. 1986. "Mark, Gospel according to." Pages 548-59 in vol. 2 of *The International Standard Bible Encyclopedia*. Edited by Geoffrey W. Bromiley, et al. Grand Rapids: Eerdmans.

Martin, Wallace. 1986. *Recent Theories of Narrative*. Ithaca, N.Y.: Cornell University Press.

Martindale, C. C. 1956. *The Gospel according to Saint Mark*. Westminster, Md.: Newman.

Marxsen, W. 1968. *Introduction to the New Testament*. Philadelphia: Fortress. (German original, 1964.)

———. 1969. *Mark the Evangelist*. Nashville: Abingdon.

———. 1970. *The Resurrection of Jesus of Nazareth*. London: SCM.

———. 1990. *Jesus and Easter: Did God Raise the Historical Jesus from the Dead?* Nashville: Abingdon.

Masson, Charles. 1944. "Le Tombeau vide: Essai sur la Formation d'une Tradition." *Revue de Théologie et de Philosophie*, n.s. 32:161-74.

Matera, Frank J. 1987. *What are They Saying about Mark?* Mahwah, N.J.: Paulist.

———. 1988. "The Prologue as the Interpretative Key to Mark's Gospel." *JSNT* 34:3-20.

McArthur, H. K. 1964. "The Earliest Divisions of the Gospels." Pages 266-72 in *Studia Evangelica*. Vol. 3. Edited by F. L. Cross. [= *TU* 88, Berlin: Academie Verlag.]

McCormick, Michael. 1985. "The Birth of the Codex and the Apostolic Life-Style." *Scriptorium* 39:150-58.

McCown, C. C. 1941. "Codex and Roll in the New Testament." *HTR* 34:219-50.

———. 1943. "The Earliest Christian Books." *BA* 6.2 (May): 21-31.

McDonald, Lee Martin, and Stanley E. Porter. 2000. *Early Christianity and Its Sacred Literature*. Peabody, Mass.: Hendrickson.

McMillan, Earle. 1973. *The Gospel according to Mark*. Austin: Sweet Publishing Company.

McNeile, A. H. 1927. *An Introduction to the Study of the New Testament*. Oxford: Clarendon.

———. 1957. *The Gospel according to St. Matthew*. London: Macmillan.

Meagher, John. 1979. *Clumsy Construction in Mark's Gospel: A Critique of Form- and Redaktionsgeschichte*. Lewiston, N.Y.: Edwin Mellen.

Meeks, Wayne A., ed. 1993. *The HarperCollins Study Bible.* New Revised Standard Version. New York: HarperCollins.

Meier, John P. 1991. *A Marginal Jew: Rethinking the Historical Jesus.* ABRL 1. New York: Doubleday.

———. 1994. *A Marginal Jew: Rethinking the Historical Jesus.* ABRL 2. New York: Doubleday.

Meltzer, Hermann. 1902. "Von Kephas gesehen—Simoni erschienen." Pages 147-56 in *Protestantische Monatshefte.* Berlin: Georg Reimer.

Menzies, Allan. 1901. *The Earliest Gospel: A Historical Study of the Gospel according to Mark.* London: Macmillan.

Merklein, Helmut. 1993. "Mk 16,1-8 als Epilog des Markusevangeliums." Pages 209-38 in *The Synoptic Gospels: Source Criticism and the New Literary Criticism.* BETL 110. Edited by Camille Focant. Leuven, Belgium: Leuven University Press.

Metzger, Bruce M. 1951–1952. "Recently Published Fragments of the Greek New Testament." *ExpTim* 63:309-11.

———. 1972. "The Ending of the Gospel According to Mark in Ethiopic Manuscripts." Pages 167-80 in *Understanding the Sacred Text: Essays in Honor of Morton S. Enslin.* Edited by John Reumann. Valley Forge, Pa.: Judson.

———. 1981. *Manuscripts of the Greek Bible: An Introduction to Greek Palaeography.* New York: Oxford University Press.

———. 1992. *The Text of the New Testament: Its Transmission, Corruption, and Restoration.* 3d ed. Enl. New York: Oxford University Press.

———. 1994. *A Textual Commentary on the Greek New Testament.* 2d ed. Stuttgart: German Bible Society.

Meye, Robert P. 1969. "Mark 16:8—The Ending of Mark's Gospel." *BR* 14:33-43.

Meyer, E. 1924. *Ursprung und Anfänge des Christentums.* 3 vols. Stuttgart and Berlin: J. G. Cotta'sche Buchhandlung.

Meyer, Heinrich August Wilhelm. 1884. *Critical and Exegetical Hand-Book to the Gospels of Mark and Luke.* Translated by Robert Ernest Wallis. New York: Funk & Wagnalls.

Michaelis, Wilhelm. 1944. *Die Erscheinungen des Auferstandenen.* Basel, Switzerland: Heinrich Majer.

———. 1946. *Einleitung in das Neue Testament.* Bern, Switzerland: BEG-Verlag.

Millard, Alan. 1994. "Ancient Abbreviations and the Nomina Sacra." Pages 221-26 in *The Unbroken Reed: Studies in the Culture and Heritage of Ancient Egypt.* Edited by Christopher Eyre, Anthony Leahy, and Lisa Montagno Leahy. London: The Egypt Exploration Society.

Milligan, George. 1913. *The New Testament Documents: Their Origin and Early History.* London: Macmillan.

———. 1932. *The New Testament and its Transmission.* London: Hodder & Stoughton.

Minear, Paul S. 1962. *The Gospel According to Mark*. Richmond: John Knox.

Minor, Mitzi. 1996. *The Spirituality of Mark: Responding to God*. Louisville: Westminster John Knox.

Mirecki, Paul Allan. 1986. "Mark 16:9-20: Composition, Tradition and Redaction." Ph.D. diss., Harvard University.

Mitton, C. Leslie. 1957. *The Gospel according to St Mark*. London: Epworth.

Moffatt, James. 1914. *An Introduction to the Literature of the New Testament*. New York: Scribner's.

Molland, Einar. 1934. *Das Paulinische Euangelion*. Oslo, Norway: Jacob Dybwad.

Moloney, Francis J. 1992. *Beginning the Good News: A Narrative Approach*. Collegeville, Minn.: Liturgical.

Moncrieff, C. E. Scott. 1926. "The Lost Ending of Mark." *Theology* 12:218-20.

Montague, George T. 1981. *Mark: Good News for Hard Times*. Ann Arbor, Mich.: Servant Books.

Moore, Stephen D. 1989. *Literary Criticism and the Gospels*. New Haven and London: Yale University Press.

Morgan, Robert with John Barton. 1988. *Biblical Interpretation*. Oxford Bible Series. Edited by P. R. Ackroyd and G. N. Stanton. Oxford: Oxford University Press.

Morison, James. 1873. *Mark's Memoirs of Jesus Christ: A Commentary on the Gospel according to Mark*. London: Hamilton, Adams, & Co.

Morton, A. Q. 1996. *The Making of Mark*. Lewiston, N.Y.: Edwin Mellen.

Moule, C. F. D. 1955–1956. "St Mark XVI.8 Once More." *NTS* 2:58-59.

———. 1965. *The Gospel according to Mark*. Cambridge: Cambridge University Press.

———. 1978. "On Defining the Messianic Secret in Mark." Pages 239-52 in *Jesus und Paulus: Festschrift für Werner Georg Kümmel zum 70. Geburtstag*. Edited by E. Earle Ellis and Erich Grässer. Göttingen: Vandenhoeck & Ruprecht.

———. 1982. *The Birth of the New Testament*. 3d ed. Harper's New Testament Commentaries. San Francisco: Harper & Row.

Moule, C. F. D., and Don Cupitt. 1972. "The Resurrection: A Disagreement." *Theology* 75:507-19.

Myers, Ched. 1988. *Binding the Strong Man: A Political Reading of Mark's Story of Jesus*. Maryknoll, N.Y.: Orbis.

Nachmanson, Ernst. 1941. *Die Griechische Buchtitel: Einige Beobachtungen*. Göteborg, Sweden: Elanders Boktryckeri Aktiebolag.

Nauck, Wolfgang. 1956. "Die Bedeutung des leeren Grabes für den Glauben an den Auferstandenen." *ZNW* 47:243-67.

Neill, Stephen. 1976. *Jesus Through Many Eyes*. Philadelphia: Fortress.

Neirynck, F. 1980. "Mark 16,1-8: tradition et rédaction." *ETl* 56:56-88.

———. 1992. *The Gospel of Mark: A Cumulative Bibliography 1950–1990*. BETL 102. Leuven, Belgium: Leuven University Press.

Nestle, E. 1894. "How does the Gospel of Mark Begin?" *Expositor,* 4th series, 10:458-60.

Nickle, Keith F. 1980. *The Synoptic Gospels: An Introduction.* Atlanta: John Knox.

Nicklin, T. 1926–1927. "St. Mark 16,8." *ExpTim* 38:429.

Nineham, D. E. 1963. *The Gospel of St Mark.* The Pelican New Testament Commentaries. New York: Seabury.

North, J. L. 1977. "Markos ho kolobodaktylos: Hippolytus Elenchus vii.30." *JTS* 28:498-507.

Norton, Andrews. 1837. *The Evidences of the Genuineness of the Gospels.* Boston: American Stationers' Company.

Nuttall, A. D. 1992. *Openings: Narrative Beginnings from the Epic to the Novel.* Oxford: Clarendon.

Oates, John F., Alan E. Samuel, and C. Bradford Welles. 1967. *Yale Papyri in the Beinecke Rare Book and Manuscript Library. ASP* 2. New Haven and Toronto: The American Society of Papyrologists.

O'Collins, Gerald. 1988. "The Fearful Silence of Three Women (Mark 16:8c)." *Greg* 69:489-503.

Olson, Richard Allan. 1993. "Mark 16:1-8." *Interpretation* 47 (October): 406-9.

Oppermann, Ralf. 1987. "Eine Beobachtung in bezug auf das Problem des Markusschlusses." *BN* 40:24-29.

Orchard, Bernard, and Thomas R. W. Longstaff, eds. 1978. *J. J. Griesbach: Synoptic and text-critical studies, 1776–1976.* SNTSMS 34. Cambridge: Cambridge University Press.

Osborne, Grant R. 1984. *The Resurrection Narratives: A Redactional Study.* Grand Rapids: Baker.

Ottley, R. R. 1926. "ἐφοβοῦντο γάρ Mark xvi 8." *JTS* 27:407-9.

Parker, D. C. 1992. *Codex Bezae: An Early Christian Manuscript and Its Text.* Cambridge: Cambridge University Press.

———. 1997. *The Living Text of the Gospels.* Cambridge: Cambridge University Press.

Parker, Hershel, and Henry Binder. 1978. "Exigencies of Composition and Publication: Billy Budd, Sailor and Pudd'nhead Wilson." *Nineteenth Century Fiction* 33:131-43.

Parker, Pierson. 1953. *The Gospel before Mark.* Chicago: University of Chicago Press.

Patzia, Arthur G. 1995. *The Making of the New Testament: Origin, Collection, Text & Canon.* Downers Grove, Ill.: InterVarsity.

Paulsen, Henning. 1980. "Mark xvi.1-8." *NovT* 22:138-75.

Peake, Arthur S. 1912. *A Critical Introduction to the New Testament.* New York: Scribners.

Perkins, Pheme. 1992. "I Have Seen the Lord (John 20:18): Women Witnesses to the Resurrection." *Int* 46 (January) 31-41.

———. 1995. "Mark." Pages 507-734 in vol. 8 of *The New Interpreter's Bible.* Edited by Leander E. Keck. 12 volumes. Nashville: Abingdon, 1994-2002.

Perrin, Norman. 1977. *The Resurrection: According to Matthew, Mark, and Luke.* Philadelphia: Fortress.

Perrin, Norman, and Dennis C. Duling. 1982. *The New Testament: An Introduction.* 2d ed. New York: Harcourt Brace Jovanovich.

Perry, Ben Edwin. 1952. *Aesopica.* Urbana, Ill.: University of Illinois Press.

Perry, Michael C. 1959. *The Easter Enigma: An Essay on the Resurrection with Special Reference to the Data of Psychical Research.* London: Faber & Faber.

Pesch, Rudolf. 1970. "Anfang des Evangeliums Jesu Christi: Eine Studie zum Prolog des Markusevangeliums (Mk 1,1-15)." Pages 108-44 in *Die Zeit Jesu: Festschrift für Heinrich Schlier.* Edited by Günther Bornkamm and Karl Rahner. Freiburg: Herder.

———. 1976. *Das Markusevangelium.* HTKNT 2. Freiburg, Basel, and Vienna: Herder.

———. 1988. "Der Schluß der vormarkinischen Passionsgeschichte und des Markusevangeliums: Mk 15,42–16,8." Pages 365-410 in *L'Évangile selon Marc: Tradition et Rédaction.* Edited by M. Sabbe. BETL 34. Leuven, Belgium: Leuven University Press.

Petersen, N. R. 1980. "When is the End not the End? Literary Reflections on the Ending of Mark's Narrative." *Int* 34:151-66.

———. 1984. "The Reader in the Gospel." *Neot* 18:38-51.

Pherigo, Lindsey P. 1971. "The Gospel according to Mark." Pages 644-71 in *The Interpreter's One Volume Commentary on the Bible.* Edited by Charles M. Laymon. Nashville: Abingdon.

Phillips, Victoria. 2001. "The Failure of the Women Who Followed Jesus in the Gospel of Mark." Pages 222-34 in *A Feminist Companion to Mark.* By Amy-Jill Levine. Vol. 2 of Feminist Companion to the New Testament and Early Christian Writings. Edited by Amy-Jill Levine and Marianne Blickenstaff. Sheffield: Sheffield University Press.

Pickering, S. R. 1992. "Papyri, Early Christian." Pages 143-46 in vol. 5 of *The Anchor Bible Dictionary.* Edited by David Noel Freedman. 6 vols. New York: Doubleday, 1992.

Pietersma, Albert. 1992a. "Bodmer Papyri." Pages 766-67 in vol. 1 of *The Anchor Bible Dictionary.* Edited by David Noel Freedman. 6 vols. New York: Doubleday, 1992.

———. 1992b. "Chester Beatty Papyri." Pages 901-3 in vol. 1 of *The Anchor Bible Dictionary.* Edited by David Noel Freedman. 6 vols. New York: Doubleday, 1992.

Plummer, A. 1938. *The Gospel according to St Mark.* Cambridge: Cambridge University Press.

Pokorny, Petr. 1977. "Anfang des Evangeliums: Zum Problem des Anfangs und des Schlusses des Markusevangeliums." Pages 115-32 in *Die Kirche Des Anfangs: Festschrift für Heinz Schürmann zum 65. Geburtstag.* Edited by Rudolf Schnackenburg, et al. Leipzig: St. Benno.

———. 1984. "Das Markusevangelium: Literarische und theologische Einleitung mit Forschungsbericht." Pages 1969-2035 in part 2, *Principat,* vol. 25.3 of the *ANRW.*

Poland, Lynn M. 1985. *Literary Criticism and Biblical Hermeneutics: A Critique of Formalist Approaches.* Chico, Calif.: Scholars Press.

Porter, J. Scott. 1848. *Principles of Textual Criticism with their Application to the Old and New Testaments.* London: Simms & McIntyre.

Porter, S. E. 2000. "Manuscripts, Greek New Testament." Pages 670-78 in *Dictionary of New Testament Background.* Edited by Craig A. Evans and Stanley E. Porter. Downers Grove, Ill., and Leicester, England: InterVarsity.

Powell, Evan. 1994. *The Unfinished Gospel: Notes on the Quest for the Historical Jesus.* Westlake Village, Calif.: Symposium Books.

Powell, Mark Allan. 1990. *What Is Narrative Criticism?* GBS. Minneapolis: Fortress.

———. 1993. "Toward a Narrative-Critical Understanding of Mark." *Int* 47:341-46.

———. 1998. *Fortress Introduction to the Gospels.* Minneapolis: Fortress.

Pregeant, Russell. 1995. *Engaging the New Testament: An Interdisciplinary Introduction.* Minneapolis: Fortress.

Price, James L. 1961. *Interpreting the New Testament.* New York: Holt, Rinehart & Winston.

———. 1971. *Interpreting the New Testament.* 2d ed. New York: Holt, Rinehart & Winston.

———. 1987. *The New Testament: Its History and Theology.* New York: Macmillan; London: Collier Macmillan.

Probyn, H. E. H. 1925. "The End of the Gospel of St. Mark." *Expositor,* 9th series, 4:120-25.

Puech, Aimé. 1928. *Histoire de la Littérature Grecque Chrétienne.* Vol. 1 of *Le Nouveau Testament.* Paris: Budé.

Puskas, Charles B. 1989. *An Introduction to the New Testament.* Peabody, Mass.: Hendrickson.

Quinn, Jerome D. 1992. "Timothy and Titus, Epistles to." Pages 560-71 in vol. 6 of *ABD.*

Ramsey, A. Michael. 1946. *The Resurrection of Christ.* Philadelphia: Westminster.

Rawlinson, A. E. J. 1925. *St. Mark.* London: Methuen.

Reardon, B. P., ed. 1989. *Collected Ancient Greek Novels.* Berkeley: University of California Press.

Reddish, Mitchell G. 1997. *An Introduction to the Gospels.* Nashville: Abingdon.

Redlich, E. Basil. 1948. *St. Mark's Gospel: A Modern Commentary.* London: Duckworth.

Reedy, Charles J. 1972. "Mk 8:31–11:10 and the Gospel Ending: A Redactional Study." *CBQ* 34:188-97.

Reiser, Marius. 1984. *Syntax und Stil des Markusevangeliums*. Tübingen: J. C. B. Mohr.

Reiser, William. 2000. *Jesus in Solidarity with His People: A Theologian Looks at Mark*. Collegeville, Minn.: Liturgical.

Resnick, Irven M. 1992. "The Codex in Early Jewish and Christian Communities." *JRH* 17:1-17.

Reynolds, L. D., and N. G. Wilson. 1974. *Scribes and Scholars*. 2d ed. Oxford: Clarendon. [3d ed. 1991.]

Rhoads, David, and Donald Michie. 1982. *Mark as Story: An Introduction to the Narrative of a Gospel*. Philadelphia: Fortress.

Richards, E. Randolph. 1998. "The Codex and the Early Collection of Paul's Letters." *BBR* 8:151-66.

Richardson, L. J. D. 1948. "St. Mark xvi.8." *JTS* 49:144-45.

Richter, David H. 1974. *Fable's End: Completeness and Closure in Rhetorical Fiction*. Chicago: University of Chicago Press.

Rigaux, Béda. 1973. *Dieu l'a Ressuscité: Exégèse et Théologie Biblique*. Gembloux, Belgium: Duculot.

Rist, Martin. 1932. "Is Mark a Complete Gospel?" *ATR* 14:143-51.

Ritt, Hubert. 1983. "Die Frauen und die Osterbotschaft: Synopse der Grabesgeschichten." Pages 117-33 in *Die Frau im Urchristentum*. QD 95. Edited by G. Dautzenberg, et al. Freiburg: Herder.

Robbins, Vernon K. 1984. *Jesus the Teacher: A Socio-Rhetorical Interpretation of Mark*. Philadelphia: Fortress.

———. 1996. *Exploring the Texture of Texts: A Guide to Socio-Rhetorical Interpretation*. Valley Forge, Pa.: Trinity.

Roberts, C. H. 1939. "The Ancient Book and the Ending of St Mark." *JTS* 40:253-57.

———. 1949. "The Christian Book and the Greek Papyri." *JTS* 50:155-68.

———. 1954 "The Codex." *Proceedings of the British Academy* 40:169-204.

———. 1966. "P. Yale 1 and the Early Christian Book." Pages 25-28 in *Essays in Honor of C. Bradford Welles*. Edited by A. E. Samuel. New Haven, Conn.: American Society of Papyrologists.

———. 1970. "Books in the Graeco-Roman World and in the New Testament." Pages 48-66 in vol. 1 of *The Cambridge History of the Bible*. Edited by P. R. Ackroyd and C. F. Evans. Cambridge: Cambridge University Press.

———. 1979. *Manuscript, Society and Belief in Early Christian Egypt*. London: Oxford University Press.

Roberts, Colin H., and T. C. Skeat. 1983. *The Birth of the Codex*. London: Oxford University Press.

Roberts, D. H. 1996. "Closure" in *OCD*.

Roberts, Deborah H., Francis M. Dunn, and Don Fowler, eds. 1997. *Classical Closure: Reading the End in Greek and Latin Literature*. Princeton: Princeton University Press.

Robertson, A. T. 1925. *An Introduction to the Textual Criticism of the New Testament.* New York: George H. Doran.

———. 1934. *A Grammar of the Greek New Testament in the Light of Historical Research.* Nashville: Broadman.

———. 1958. *Studies in Mark's Gospel.* Nashville: Broadman.

Robinson, J. A. T. 1962. "Resurrection in the NT." Pages 43-53 in vol. 4 of *The Interpreter's Dictionary of the Bible.* Edited by George Arthur Buttrick. 4 vols. Nashville: Abingdon, 1962.

Robinson, J. Armitage. 1911. *The Study of the Gospels.* London: Longmans, Green, & Co.

Robinson, James M. 1982. *The Problem of History in Mark and Other Marcan Studies.* Philadelphia: Fortress.

Rohrbach, Paul. 1894. *Der Schluss des Markusevangeliums, der Vier-Evangelien-Kanon und die Kleinasiatischen Presbyter.* Berlin: Georg Nauck.

———. 1898. *Die Berichte über die Auferstehung Jesu Christi.* Berlin: Georg Reimer.

Rördam, Torkild Skat. 1905. "What Was the Lost End of Mark's Gospel?" *HeyJ* 3:769-90.

Sabourin, Leopold. 1967. *The Names and Titles of Jesus.* New York: Macmillan.

Salmon, George. 1888. *A Historical Introduction to the Study of the Books of the New Testament.* 3d ed. London: John Murray.

Sanders, E. P., and Margaret Davies. 1989. *Studying the Synoptic Gospels.* Philadelphia: Trinity.

Sanders, H. A. 1938. "Beginnings of the Modern Book." *Michigan Alumnus Quarterly Review* 44:95-111.

Sankey, P. J. 1995. "Promise and Fulfillment: Reader-Response to Mark 1.1-15." *JSNT* 58:3-18.

Sato, Migaku. 1988. *Q und Prophetie: Studien zur Gattungs- und Traditionsgeschichte der Quelle Q.* WUNT 2/29. Tübingen: J. C. B. Mohr.

———. 1994. "The Shape of the Q-Source." Pages 156-79 in *The Shape of Q: Signal Essays on the Sayings Gospel.* Edited by John S. Kloppenborg. Minneapolis: Fortress.

Schaberg, Jane. 2002. *The Resurrection of Mary Magdalene: Legends, Apocrypha, and the Christian Testament.* New York: Continuum.

Schabert, Arnold. 1964. *Das Markus-evangelium.* Munich: Claudius Verlag.

Schaff, Philip, ed. 1879. *A Popular Commentary on the New Testament.* 3 vols. New York: Charles Scribner's Sons.

Schanz, Paul. 1881. *Commentar über das Evangelium des heiligen Marcus.* Freiburg: Herder.

Schearer, W. C. 1893. "The Last Twelve Verses of St. Mark's Gospel." *ExpTim* 5:227-28.

Schenke, Ludger. 1968. *Auferstehungsverkündigung und Leeres Grab: Eine traditions-geschichtliche Untersuchung von Mk 16,1-8.* SBS 33. Stuttgart: Verlag Katholisches Bibelwerk.

Schenkel, Daniel. 1869. *A Sketch of the Character of Jesus: A Biblical Essay*. London: Longmans, Green, & Co.

Schildgen, Brenda Deen. 1999. *Power and Prejudice: The Reception of the Gospel of Mark*. Detroit: Wayne State University Press.

Schlatter, Adolf. 1984. *Markus: Der Evangelist für die Griechen*. 2d ed. Stuttgart: Calwer.

Schmid, Josef. 1958. *Das Evangelium nach Markus*. Regensburg, Germany: Friedrich Pustet. (ET, Alba House, 1968.)

Schmidt, Hans. 1907. "Zur Frage des ursprünglichen Markusschlusses." *TSK* 80:487-513.

Schmidt, Karl Ludwig. 1944. *Kanonische und Apokryphe Evangelien und Apostelgeschichten*. Basel, Switzerland: Heinrich Majer.

Schmidt, Paul Wilhelm. 1904. *Die Geschichte Jesu*. Tübingen and Leipzig: J. C. B. Mohr (Paul Siebeck).

Schmithals, Walter. 1972. "Der Markusschluβ, die Verklärungsgeschichte und die Aussendung der Zwölf." *ZTK* 69:379-411.

———. 1979. *Das Evangelium nach Markus*. ÖTK 2. Würzburg: Echter Verlag.

———. 1985. *Einleitung in die drei ersten Evangelien*. Berlin and New York: Walter de Gruyter.

Schnackenburg, Rudolf. 1971. *Das Evangelium nach Markus*. 2 vols. Geistliche Schriftlesung. Erläuterungen zum Neuen Testament für die Geistliche Lesung; 2/1-2 Dusseldorf: Patmos. (ET, *The Gospel according to St. Mark*. 2 vols. New York: Herder & Herder, 1971.)

———. 1973. " 'Das Evangelium' im Verständnis des ältesten Evangelisten." Pages 309-24 in *Orientierung an Jesus: Zur Theologie der Synoptiker*. Edited by P. Hoffman. Freiburg: Herder.

Schnelle, Udo. 1998. *The History and Theology of the New Testament Writings*. Translated by M. Eugene Boring. Minneapolis: Fortress.

Schniewind, Julius. 1960. *Das Evangelium nach Markus*. 9th ed. NTD 1. Göttingen: Vandenhoeck & Ruprecht.

Schubart, Wilhelm. 1921. *Das Buch bei den Griechen und Römern*. 2d ed. Berlin and Leipzig: Walter de Gruyter.

Schürer, Emil. 1973–1987. *The History of the Jewish People in the Age of Jesus Christ*. 3 vols. Revised and edited by Geza Vermes, Fergus Millar, and Martin Goodman. Edinburgh: T. & T. Clark.

Schüssler Fiorenza, Elisabeth. 1983. *In Memory of Her: A Feminist Theological Reconstruction of Christian Origins*. New York: Crossroad.

Schwartz, Eduard. 1943. *Fünf Vorträge über den Griechischen Roman*. Berlin: Walter de Gruyter.

———. 1970. *The Good News according to Mark*. Richmond: John Knox.

Scott, Ernest Findlay. 1936. *The Literature of the New Testament*. Vol. 15 of *Records of Civilization, Sources and Studies*. Edited by Austin P. Evans. New York: Columbia University Press.

Seidensticker, Philip. 1967. *Die Auferstehung Jesu in der Botschaft der Evangelisten.* Stuttgart: Katholisches Bibelwerk.

Seilenberger, Michael. 1905. *Das Evangelium nach Markus.* Regensburg: G. J. Manz.

Seitz, Oscar J. F. 1963. "Praeparatio Evangelica in the Markan Prologue." *JBL* 82:201-6.

————. 1964. "Gospel Prologues: A Common Pattern?" *JBL* 83:262-68.

Selby, Donald J. 1971. *Introduction to the New Testament: "The Word Became Flesh."* New York: Macmillan.

Septuaginta. Vetus Testamentum Graecum. 1931–. Göttingen: Vandenhoeck & Ruprecht.

Sesboüé, Bernard, ed. 1983. *Basil de Césarée, Contre Eunome.* Paris: Cerf.

Sharpe, John L., III, and Kimberly Van Kampen. 1998. *The Bible as Book: The Manuscript Tradition.* London: The British Library; New Castle, Del.: Oak Knoll.

Shillingsburg, Peter L. 1997. *Resisting Texts: Authority and Submission in Constructions of Meaning.* Ann Arbor: University of Michigan Press.

Skeat, T. C. 1949. "St. Mark XVI.8: A Modern Greek Parallel." *JTS* 50:57-58.

————. 1969. "Early Christian Book-Production: Papyri and Manuscripts." Pages 54-79 in vol. 2 of *The Cambridge History of the Bible.* Edited by G. W. H. Lampe. Cambridge: Cambridge University Press.

————. 1979. " 'Especially the Parchments': A Note on 2 Timothy IV.13." *JTS* 30:173-77.

————. 1982. "The Length of the Standard Papyrus Roll and the Cost-advantage of the Codex." *ZPE* 45:169-75.

————. 1994. "The Origin of the Christian Codex." *ZPE* 102:263-68.

————. 1997. "The Oldest Manuscript of the Four Gospels?" *NTS* 43:1-34.

Sledd, Andrew. 1927. *Saint Mark's Life of Jesus.* Nashville: Cokesbury.

Slomp, Jan. 1977. "Are the Words 'son of God' in Mark 1.1 Original?" *BT* 28:143-50.

Smid, H. R. 1965. *Protevangelium Jacobi: A Commentary.* Assen: Van Gorcum.

Smith, Barbara Herrnstein. 1968. *Poetic Closure: A Study of How Poems End.* Chicago: University of Chicago Press.

Smith, Dennis E. 1990. "Narrative Beginnings in Ancient Literature and Theory." *Semeia* 52:1-9.

Smith, Marion. 1981. "The Composition of Mark 11-16." *HeyJ* 22:363-77.

Smith, Robert H. 1972. "New and Old in Mark 16:1-8." *CTM* 43:518-27.

————. 1983. *Easter Gospels: The Resurrection of Jesus According to the Four Evangelists.* Minneapolis: Augsburg.

Smyth, Herbert Weir. 1956. *Greek Grammar.* Cambridge: Harvard University Press.

Souter, Alexander. 1954. *The Text and Canon of the New Testament.* 2d ed. London: Gerald Duckworth.

Spitta, Friedrich. 1893–1907. *Zur Geschichte und Litterature des Urchristentums.* 3 vols. Göttingen: Vandenhoeck & Ruprecht.

———. 1904. "Der Anfang des Markus-Evangeliums," *ZNW* 5:305-8.

———. 1918. *Die Auferstehung Jesu.* Göttingen: Vandenhoeck & Ruprecht.

Spivey, Robert A., and D. Moody Smith. 1995. *Anatomy of the New Testament.* 5th ed. Englewood Cliffs, N.J.: Prentice Hall.

Stamm, Raymond T. 1944. "The Gospel according to Mark." Pages 238-309 in *New Testament Commentary.* Edited by Herbert C. Alleman. Philadelphia: Muhlenberg.

Standaert, Benoît. 1983. *L'Évangile selon Marc: Commentaire.* Paris: Cerf.

Stanton, Graham N. 1989. *The Gospels and Jesus.* Oxford Bible Series. Edited by P. R. Ackroyd and G. N. Stanton. Oxford: Oxford University Press.

———. 1997. "The Fourfold Gospel." *NTS* 43:317-46.

Stanton, Vincent Henry. 1909. *The Synoptic Gospels.* Vol. 2 of *The Gospels as Historical Documents.* Cambridge: Cambridge University Press.

Stauffer, Ethelbert. 1943–1944. "Zur Vor- und Frühgeschichte des Primatus Petri." *ZKG* 62:3-34.

Stein, Robert H. 1971. "The Proper Methodology for Ascertaining a Markan Redaction History." *NovT* 13 (1971): 181-98.

———. 1974. "A Short Note on Mark xiv.28 and xvi.7." *NTS* 20:445-52.

———. 1991. *Gospels and Tradition: Studies on Redaction Criticism of the Synoptic Gospels.* Grand Rapids: Baker.

———. 1992. "Redaction Criticism (NT)." Pages 644-48 in vol. 5 of *ABD.*

Steinseifer, Bernd. 1971. "Der Ort der Erscheinungen des Auferstandenen." *ZNW* 62:232-65.

Stemberger, Günter. 1974. "Galilee—Land of Salvation?" Appendix iv, Pages 409-38 in *The Gospel and the Land.* Edited by W. D. Davies. Berkeley: University of California.

Stephens, Susan A. 1988. "Book Production." Pages 421-36 in vol. 1 of *Civilization of the Ancient Mediterranean: Greece and Rome.* Edited by Michael Grant and Rachel Kitzinger. New York: Scribner.

Stock, Augustine. 1982. *Call to Discipleship: A Literary Study of Mark's Gospel.* Wilmington, Del.: Michael Glazier.

———. 1989. *The Method and Message of Mark.* Wilmington, Del.: Michael Glazier.

Stonehouse, Ned Bernard. 1944. *The Witness of Matthew and Mark to Christ.* Philadelphia: The Presbyterian Guardian.

Stott, John. 1994. *Men with a Message: An Introduction to the New Testament and Its Writers.* Rev. by Stephen Motyer. Grand Rapids: Eerdmans.

Strecker, Georg. 1968. "The Passion- and Resurrection Predictions in Mark's Gospel." *Interpretation* 22:421-42.

———. 1972. "Literarkritische Überlegungen zum εὐαγγέλιον-Begriff im Markusevangelium." Pages 91-104 in *Neues Testament und Geschichte:*

Historische Geschehen und Deutung im Neuen Testament. Oscar Cullmann zum 70. Geburtstag. Edited by Heinrich Baltensweiler and Bo Reicke. Zürich: Theologischer Verlag; Tübingen: J. C. B. Mohr (Paul Siebeck).

————. 2000. *Theology of the New Testament.* Louisville: Westminster John Knox; Berlin: de Gruyter.

Streeter, B. H. 1925. *The Four Gospels: A Study of Origins.* New York: Macmillan.

Stuhlmacher, P., ed. 1991. *The Gospel and the Gospels.* Grand Rapids: Eerdmans.

Swanson, Reuben J., ed. 1995–1998. *New Testament Greek Manuscripts: Variant Readings Arranged in Horizontal Lines Against Codex Vaticanus.* 5 vols. Matt.–Acts. Sheffield: Sheffield Academic Press; Pasadena: William Carey.

Swanson, Richard W. 1993. "They Said Nothing." *CurTM* 20:471-78.

Swete, Henry Barclay. 1927. *The Gospel according to St. Mark.* 3d ed. London: Macmillan.

Swift, C. E. Graham. 1970. "Mark." Pages 851-86 in *The New Bible Commentary.* Revised. Edited by D. Guthrie, et al. Grand Rapids: Eerdmans.

Synge, Francis C. 1975. "Exegesis: Mark 16.1-8." *JTSA* 11 (June): 71-73.

Talbert, Charles H. 1985. *What Is a Gospel? The Genre of the Canonical Gospels.* Macon, Ga.: Mercer University Press.

Tannehill, Robert C. 1979. "The Gospel of Mark as Narrative Christology." *Semeia* 16:57-95.

Tate, W. Randolph. 1994. *Reading Mark from the Outside: Eco and Iser Leave Their Marks.* San Francisco: International Scholars Publications.

Taylor, C. 1893. "Some Early Evidence for the Twelve Verses St. Mark XVI. 9-20." *Expositor,* 4th series, 8:71-80.

Taylor, Vincent. 1953. *The Names of Jesus.* New York: St. Martin's.

————. 1954. *The Gospels: A Short Introduction.* London: Epworth.

————. 1961. *The Text of the New Testament.* London: Macmillan.

————. 1966. *The Gospel according to St. Mark.* 2nd ed. New York: St. Martin's.

Telford, William R., ed. 1995a. *The Interpretation of Mark: Studies in New Testament Interpretation.* Edinburgh: T. & T. Clark.

————. 1995b. *Mark.* NTG. Sheffield: Sheffield Academic Press.

Tenney, Merrill C. 1963. *The Reality of the Resurrection.* New York: Harper & Row.

Theissen, Gerd, and Annette Merz. 1998. *The Historical Jesus: A Comprehensive Guide.* Minneapolis: Fortress.

Thomas, John Christopher. 1983. "A Reconsideration of the Ending of Mark." *JETS* 26/4:407-19.

Thompson, Mary R. 1989. *The Role of Disbelief in Mark.* New York: Paulist.

Thorpe, James. 1972. *Principles of Textual Criticism.* San Marino, Calif.: Huntington Library.

Thrall, Margaret E. 1962. *Greek Particles in the New Testament.* Grand Rapids: Eerdmans.

Throckmorton, Burton H., Jr. 1992. *Gospel Parallels: A Comparison of the Synoptic Gospels.* Nashville: Thomas Nelson.

Thurston, Bonnie Bowman. 2002. *Preaching Mark*. Minneapolis: Fortress.

Tindall, Christian. 1961. *Contributions to the Statistical Study of the Codex Sinaiticus*. Edinburgh and London: Oliver & Boyd.

Tischendorf, Constantine von. 1869–1884. *Novum Testamentum Graece*. 8th ed. 3 vols. Vols. 1-2, Leipzig: Giesecke & Devrient, 1869–1872; vol. 3, Leipzig: J. C. Hinrichs, 1884.

Tolbert, Mary Ann. 1989. *Sowing the Gospel: Mark's World in Literary-Historical Perspective*. Minneapolis: Fortress.

———. 1992. "Mark." Pages 263-74 in *The Women's Bible Commentary*. Edited by Carol H. Newsom and Sharon H. Ringe. London: SPCK; Louisville: Westminster John Knox.

Torgovnick, Marianna. 1981. *Closure in the Novel*. Princeton: Princeton University Press.

Torris, Jean. 1966. "Les fins de l'évangile selon Marc." *Cahiers du Cercle Ernest-Renan* 50 (April): 67-74.

Trainor, Michael. 1996. "The Women, the Empty Tomb, and *That* Final Verse." *TBT* 34:177-82.

Trebolle Barrera, Julio. 1998. *The Jewish Bible and the Christian Bible*. Grand Rapids: Eerdmans; Leiden, Netherlands: Brill.

Tregelles, S. P. 1854. *An Account of the Printed Text of the Greek New Testament*. London: Samuel Bagster & Sons.

Trevijano Etcheverría, Ramon. 1971. *Comienzo del Evangelio: Estudio sobre el Prólogo de San Marcos*. Burgos, Spain: Aldecoa.

Trobisch, David. 2000. *The First Edition of the New Testament*. New York: Oxford University Press.

Trocmé, Etienne. 1975. *The Formation of the Gospel According to Mark*. Translated by Pamela Gaughan. Philadelphia: Westminster.

Trompf, G. W. 1971–1972. "The First Resurrection Appearance and the Ending of Mark's Gospel." *NTS* 18:308-30.

———. 1973. "The Markusschluss in Recent Research." *ABR* 21:15-26.

Tuckett, C. M. 1992. "Messianic Secret." Pages 797-800 in vol. 4 of *ABD*.

Turner, C. H. 1913. "The Gospel of Peter." *JTS* 14:161-95.

———. 1925. "Markan Usage: Notes, Critical and Exegetical, on the Second Gospel." *JTS* 26:146.

———. 1927. "A Textual Commentary on Mark 1." *JTS* 28:145-58.

———. 1927–1928. "Did Codex Vercellensis (a) contain the Last Twelve Verses of St Mark?" *JTS* 29:16-18.

———. 1928. "The Gospel according to St. Mark." Pages 42-124 in *A New Commentary on Holy Scripture*. Edited by Charles Gore, et al. New York: Macmillan.

Turner, Eric G. 1968. *Greek Papyri: An Introduction*. Princeton: Princeton University Press.

———. 1974. "Some Questions about the Typology of the Codex." Pages 427-38 in *Akten des XIII: Internationalen Papyrologenkongresses.* Edited by E. Kiessling and H. A. Rupprecht. Munich: C. H. Beck.

———. 1977. *The Typology of the Early Codex.* Vol. 18 of the Haney Foundation Series. Philadelphia: University of Pennsylvania Press.

Turner, H. E. W. 1963. "The Life and Teaching of Jesus Christ." Pages 436-94 in *A Companion to the Bible.* 2d ed. Edited by T. W. Manson and H. H. Rowley. Edinburgh: T. & T. Clark.

Turner, Nigel. 1963. *A Grammar of New Testament Greek: Volume III, Syntax.* Edinburgh: T. & T. Clark.

———. 1965. *Grammatical Insights into the New Testament.* Edinburgh: T. & T. Clark.

Tyson, Joseph B. 1961. "The Blindness of the Disciples in Mark" *JBL* 80:261-68.

van Daalen, D. H. 1972. *The Real Resurrection.* London: Collins.

van der Horst, P. W. 1972. "Can a Book end with ΓΑΡ? A Note on Mark XVI.8." *JTS* n.s. 23:121-24.

van Haelst, Joseph. 1970. "Les Sources Papyrologiques Concernant l'Eglise en Egypte a l'Epoque de Constantin." Pages 497-503 in *Proceedings of the Twelfth International Congress of Papyrology.* Edited by Deborah H. Samuel. Vol. 7 of American Studies in Papyrology. Toronto: Hakkert.

———. 1976. *Catalogue des Papyrus Littéraires Juifs et Chrétiens.* Paris: Publications de la Sorbonne.

———. 1989. "Les Origines du Codex." Pages 13-35 in *Les Débuts du Codex.* Edited by Alain Blanchard. Turnhout: Brepols.

van Iersel, Bastiaan Martinus Franciscus. 1971. "Theology and Detailed Exegesis." Pages 80-89 in *Theology, Exegesis, and Proclamation.* Edited by Roland Murphy. New York: Herder & Herder.

———. 1982. " 'To Galilee' or 'In Galilee' in Mark 14,28 and 16,7?" *ETl* 58:365-70.

———. 1988a. "He will Baptize you with Holy Spirit (Mark 1,8)." Pages 132-41 in *Text and Testimony: Essays on New Testament and Apocryphal Literature in Honour of A. F. J. Klijn.* Kampen: J. H. Kok.

———. 1988b. *Reading Mark.* Translated by W. H. Bisscheroux. Collegeville, Minn.: Liturgical Press.

———. 1998. *Mark: A Reader-Response Commentary.* JSNTSup 164. Sheffield: Sheffield Academic Press.

Van Linden, Philip. 1983. *The Gospel according to Mark.* Vol. 2 of the Collegeville Bible Commentary. Collegeville, Minn.: Liturgical.

van Veldhuizen, A. 1919. "De Aanhef van Mk en Nog Wat Vooraf." *Nieuwe Theologische Studiën* 2:171-75.

Vawter, Bruce. 1967. *The Four Gospels: An Introduction.* Garden City, N.Y.: Doubleday.

Vermes, Geza. 1999. *An Introduction to the Complete Dead Sea Scrolls.* Minneapolis: Fortress.

Via, Dan O. 1985. *The Ethics of Mark's Gospel—In the Middle of Time*. Philadelphia: Fortress.

―――. 1988. "Irony as Hope in Mark's Gospel: A Reply to Werner Kelber." *Semeia* 43:21-27.

Victorino, Maria Gemma. 1999. "Mark's Open Ending and Following Jesus on the Way." Pages 53-64 in *The Personal Voice in Biblical Interpretation*. Edited by Ingrid R. Kitzberger. London and New York: Routledge.

Vielhauer, Philipp. 1975. *Geschichte der urchristlichen Literatur: Einleitung in das Neue Testament, die Apokryphen und die apostolischen Väter*. Berlin: Walter de Gruyter.

Vignolo, Roberto. 1990. "Una finale Reticente: Interpretazione narrativa di Mc 16,8." *RivB* 38:129-89.

Waetjen, Herman. 1965. "The Ending of Mark and Gospel's Shift in Eschatology." Pages 114-31 in vol. 4 of the *Annual of the Swedish Theological Institute*. Edited by Hans Kosmala. Leiden, Netherlands: Brill.

Wagner, Günter, ed. 1983. *An Exegetical Bibliography of the New Testament: Matthew and Mark*. Macon, Ga.: Mercer University Press.

Walker, William O. 1969. "Postcrucifixion Appearances and Christian Origins." *JBL* 88:157-65.

―――. 1972. "Christian Origins and Resurrection Faith." *JR* 52:41-55.

Walter, Nikolaus. 1973. "Eine Vormatthäische Schilderung der Auferstehung Jesu." *NTS* 19:415-29.

―――. 1992. "Mk 1,1-8 und die 'Agreements' von Mt 3 und Lk 3. Stand Die Predigt Johannes des Taüfers in Q?" Pages 457-78 in *The Four Gospels, 1992: Festschrift Frans Neirynck*. BETL 100. Edited by F. Van Segbroeck, et al. Leuven, Belgium: Leuven University Press.

Warfield, Benjamin Breckinridge. 1886. *An Introduction to the Textual Criticism of the New Testament*. New York: Thomas Whittaker.

Warmers, Erich. 1970. *Markus-evangelium*. Stuttgart: Ehrenfried Klotz Verlag.

Watson, George. 1978. "The Sense of a Beginning." *STRev* 86:539-48.

Way-Rider, R. 1982. "The Lost Beginning of St. Mark's Gospel." Pages 553-56 in *Studia Evangelica VII*. TU 126. Edited by Elizabeth A. Livingstone. Berlin: Akademie-Verlag.

Wedderburn, A. J. M. 1999. *Beyond Resurrection*. Peabody, Mass.: Hendrickson by arrangement with SCM, London.

Weder, Hans. 1983. " 'Evangelium Jesu Christi' (Mk 1,1) und 'Evangelium Gottes' (Mk 1,14)." Pages 399-411 in *Die Mitte des Neuen Testaments: Einheit und Vielfalt neutestamentlicher Theologie*. Edited by Ulrich Luz and Hans Weder. Göttingen: Vandenhoeck & Ruprecht.

Weeden, Theodore J. 1971. *Mark—Traditions in Conflict*. Philadelphia: Fortress.

Weiss, Bernhard. 1889. *A Manual of Introduction to the New Testament*. 2 vols. Translated by A. J. K. Davidson. New York: Funk & Wagnalls.

———. 1892. *Die Evangelien des Markus und Lukas*. Göttingen: Vandenhoeck & Ruprecht.

Weiss, Johannes. 1903. *Das älteste Evangelium*. Göttingen: Vandenhoeck & Ruprecht.

Welles, C. Bradford. 1964. "The Yale Genesis Fragment." *The Yale University Library Gazette* 39.1 (July):1-8.

Wellhausen, J. 1909. *Das Evangelium Marci*. 2d ed. Berlin: Georg Reimer.

Wells, Samuel. 2000. "He is risen!" *ChrCent* 117 (April 12): 421.

Wernle, Paul. 1899. *Die Synoptische Frage*. Leipzig and Tübingen: J. C. B. Mohr.

Wessel, Walter W. 1984. *Mark*. Expositor's Bible Commentary. Grand Rapids: Zondervan.

———. 1994. "Mark" in the *Zondervan NIV Bible Commentary*. Grand Rapids: Zondervan.

Westcott, Brooke Foss, and Fenton John Anthony Hort. 1882. *The New Testament in the Original Greek*. Vol. 2, Introduction and Appendix. New York: Harper & Brothers.

Whitney, S. W. 1892. *The Revisers' Greek Text*. Boston: Silver, Burdett & Company.

Wikenhauser, Alfred. 1958. *New Testament Introduction*. New York: Herder & Herder.

Wikgren, Allen. 1942. "ΑΡΧΗ ΤΟΥ ΕΥΑΓΓΕΛΙΟΥ" *JBL* 61:11-20.

Wilamowitz-Moellendorf, Ulrich von. 1926. "Die Verklärung Christi." Pages 280-93 in vol. 2 of *Reden und Vorträge*. 5th ed. Dublin and Zurich: Weidmann.

Wilckens, Ulrich. 1970. *Auferstehung: Das Biblische Auferstehungszeugnis Historisch Untersucht und Erklärt*. Stuttgart: Kreuz-Verlag. (ET, *Resurrection: Biblical Testimony to the Resurrection: An Historical Examination and Explanation*. Atlanta: John Knox, 1978.)

Wilder, Amos N. 1943. "Variant Traditions of the Resurrection in Acts." *JBL* 62:307-18.

Williams, C. S. C. 1951. *Alterations to the Text of the Synoptic Gospels and Acts*. Oxford: Basil Blackwell.

Williams, Clarence Russell. 1915. "The Appendices to the Gospel according to Mark. A Study in Textual Transmission." *Transactions of the Connecticut Academy of Arts and Sciences*. 18:347-447.

Williams, Joel F. 1994. *Other Followers of Jesus: Minor Characters as Major Figures in Mark's Gospel*. JSNTSup 102. Sheffield: JSOT Press.

———. 1999. "Literary Approaches to the End of Mark's Gospel." *JETS* 42 (March): 21-35.

Williamson, Lamar, Jr. 1983. *Mark*. Interpretation commentary. Atlanta: John Knox.

Willson, Patrick J. 1994. "Ending without end." *ChrCent* 111 (March 16): 277.

Wilson, Robert McL. 1963. "Mark." Pages 799-819 in *Peake's Commentary on the Bible*. Edited by Matthew Black and H. H. Rowley. London: Thomas Nelson.

Wimsatt, W. K., Jr. 1954. *The Verbal Icon: Studies in the Meaning of Poetry.* Lexington: University of Kentucky Press.

Wink, Walter. 1973. *The Bible in Human Transformation: Toward a New Paradigm for Biblical Study.* Philadelphia: Fortress.

Witherington, Ben, III. 1988. *Women in the Earliest Churches.* Cambridge: Cambridge University Press.

———. 1998. *The Acts of the Apostles: A Socio-Rhetorical Commentary.* Grand Rapids: Eerdmans.

———. 2001. *The Gospel of Mark: A Socio-Rhetorical Commentary.* Grand Rapids: Eerdmans.

Wohlenberg, D. Gustav. 1910. *Das Evangelium des Markus.* Leipzig: Deichert.

Wrede, William. 1971. *The Messianic Secret.* Cambridge: James Clarke.

Wright, N. T. 1992a. *The New Testament and the People of God.* Christian Origins and the Question of God 1. Minneapolis: Fortress.

———. 1992b. *Who Was Jesus?* Grand Rapids: Eerdmans.

———. 1998. "The Resurrection of the Messiah." *STRev* 41.2:107-56.

Wright, Tom [N. T.]. 2001. *Mark for Everyone.* London: SPCK.

Zahn, Theodor. 1975. *Geschichte des neutestamentlichen Kanons.* Hildesheim, New York: Georg Olms. [Orig., Erlangen and Leipzig: Deichert, 1890.]

———. 1977. *Introduction to the New Testament.* 3 vols. Minneapolis: Klock & Klock. [German orig. 1897–1899.]

Zahn, Theodor, and A. Resch. 1894. "The Authorship of the Last Verses of Mark." *Expositor,* 4th series, 10:219-32.

Zerwick, Max. 1937. *Untersuchungen zum Markus-Stil.* Rome: Pontifical Biblical Institute.

Zuntz, Günther. 1984. "Wann wurde das Evangelium Marci geschrieben?" Pages 47-71 in *Markus-Philologie.* WUNT 33. Edited by Hubert Cancik. Tübingen: J. C. B. Mohr.

Zwemer, S. M. 1945. "The Last Twelve Verses of the Gospel of Mark." *EQ* 17:13-23.